In honor of

Patricia Horner

2007 Spanish Immersion Students

MEXICO

WHITE STAR PUBLISHERS

MEXICO

EL TAJÍN

TULA

TEOTIHUACAN

TENOCHTITLAN

CACAXTLA

XOCHICALCO

CHOLULA

UUIJAZOO

YAGUL

MONTE ALBÁN

DAINZU

MITLA

LAMBYTECO

PACIFIC OCEAN

TEXT

DAVIDE DOMENICI

GRAPHIC DESIGN

PATRIZIA BALOCCO LOVISETTI

CONTENTS

MESOAMERICA AND ITS PEOPLES — PAGE 6
SUMMARY OF THE HISTORY AND CULTURE OF MESOAMERICA — PAGE 8
SOCIETY — PAGE 14
WAR — PAGE 18
RELIGION — PAGE 20
THE CALENDAR — PAGE 24
INDIGENOUS LITERATURE AND THE POPOL VUH — PAGE 24
THE IMPACT WITH THE OLD WORLD — PAGE 26

ITINERARY I :
• THE EMPIRES OF CENTRAL MEXICO — PAGE 28
• TEOTIHUACAN — PAGE 30
• TULA — PAGE 40
• THE HISTORY AND MYTH OF QUETZALCÓATL AND TOLLAN — PAGE 44
• MÉXICO-TENOCHTITLAN — PAGE 46

• THE TEMPLO MAYOR — PAGE 50
• THE MUSEO NACIONAL DE ANTROPOLOGÍA — PAGE 54

ITINERARY 2 :
• MORELOS, PUEBLA, TLAXCALA AND VERACRUZ: THE SACRED CITY OF CHOLULA AND THE SPLENDOUR OF THE EPICLASSIC CENTRES — PAGE 56
• XOCHICALCO — PAGE 58
• CHOLULA — PAGE 62
• CACAXTLA — PAGE 64
• EL TAJÍN — PAGE 68
• THE BALL GAME — PAGE 72

ITINERARY III :
• THE PEOPLES OF THE CLOUDS — PAGE 74
• MONTE ALBÁN — PAGE 76
• DAINZÚ, LAMBYTECO AND YAGUL — PAGE 82

• MITLA — PAGE 84
• HUIJAZÓO — PAGE 86

ITINERARY IV :
• THE CIVILISATIONS OF THE FOREST — PAGE 90
• LA VENTA: THE ARCHAEOLOGICAL SITE AND THE PARK — PAGE 92
• PALENQUE — PAGE 94
• WRITING — PAGE 102
• YAXCHILÁN — PAGE 104
• BONAMPAK — PAGE 110
• TIKAL — PAGE 114
• UAXACTÚN — PAGE 122
• COPÁN — PAGE 124
• QUIRIGUÁ — PAGE 134

ITINERARY V :
• THE MAYA IN THE YUCATÁN — PAGE 136
• THE RIO BEC AND CHENES STYLES — PAGE 140

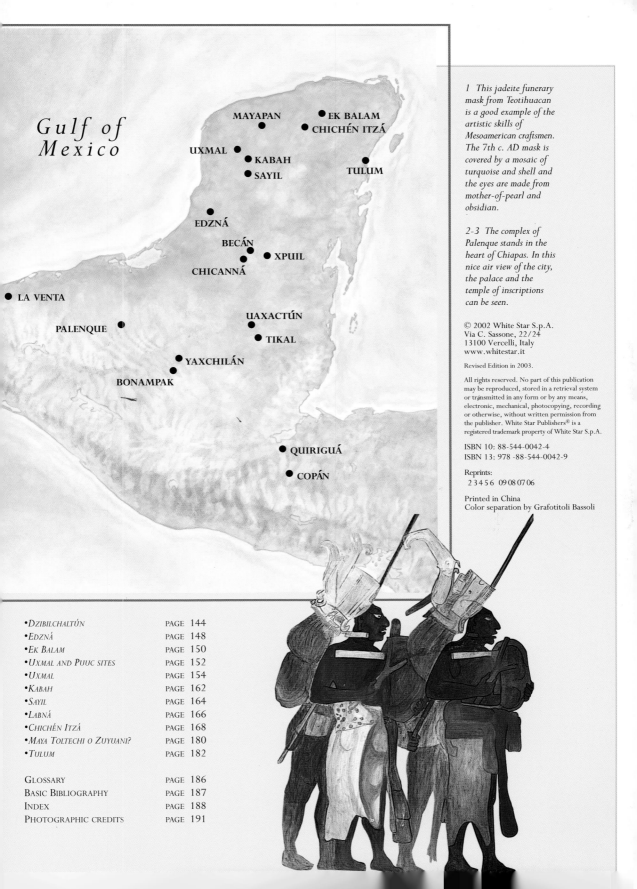

Gulf of Mexico

MAYAPAN
EK BALAM
CHICHÉN ITZÁ
UXMAL
KABAH
SAYIL
TULUM
EDZNÁ
BECÁN
XPUIL
CHICANNÁ
LA VENTA
UAXACTÚN
PALENQUE
TIKAL
YAXCHILÁN
BONAMPAK
QUIRIGUÁ
COPÁN

1 This jadeite funerary
mask from Teotihuacan
is a good example of the
artistic skills of
Mesoamerican craftsmen.
The 7th c. AD mask is
covered by a mosaic of
turquoise and shell and
the eyes are made from
mother-of-pearl and
obsidian.

2-3 The complex of
Palenque stands in the
heart of Chiapas. In this
nice air view of the city,
the palace and the
temple of inscriptions
can be seen.

© 2002 White Star S.p.A.
Via C. Sassone, 22/24
13100 Vercelli, Italy
www.whitestar.it

Revised Edition in 2003.

ISBN 10: 88-544-0042-4
ISBN 13: 978-88-544-0042-9

Reprints:
2 3 4 5 6   09 08 07 06

Printed in China
Color separation by Grafotitoli Bassoli

•*Dzibilchaltún*   PAGE 144
•*Edzná*   PAGE 148
•*Ek Balam*   PAGE 150
•*Uxmal and Puuc sites*   PAGE 152
•*Uxmal*   PAGE 154
•*Kabah*   PAGE 162
•*Sayil*   PAGE 164
•*Labná*   PAGE 166
•*Chichén Itzá*   PAGE 168
•*Maya Toltechi o Zuyuani?*   PAGE 180
•*Tulum*   PAGE 182

GLOSSARY   PAGE 186
BASIC BIBLIOGRAPHY   PAGE 187
INDEX   PAGE 188
PHOTOGRAPHIC CREDITS   PAGE 191

MESOAMERICA AND ITS PEOPLES

The history of Mesoamerica is the history of a large number of peoples who, over a period of four thousand years, gave rise to a cultural tradition with a common character that we can still recognize in different Mesoamerican forms of art. Although Mesoamerican archaeological sites contain a great variety of architectural, sculptural and pictorial styles, it is possible to distinguish the origins of a "common language" formed during millennia of trade, wars and alliances.

Teotihuacan, Toltecs, Zapotecs, Mixtecs, Totonacs, Mixe-Zoque, Maya and Aztecs are only some of the peoples that "built" Mesoamerica. They were organized in simple farming communities as part of local seignories, states and empires whose vestiges can still be seen in the large monumental centers discussed in this book.

needs. The pre-Hispanic past of Mesoamerica to be seen therefore enjoins examination of the most magnificent and "official" aspects of the cultures and ignores the life of the peasant masses who were the real basis of these cultures' histories.

However, that does not mean that the ruins should only be admired for their grandeur and splendor, because analysis of the monuments and their complex symbolic allusions is the key to understanding the ideology on which their power was founded and the cosmological concepts the ruins claimed to reflect. Although they were elaborated by the religious and cultural elite, these concepts had to be shared with the levels of the community who have left the most ephemeral archaeological traces. Our trip

qualities like everyone else, devoted to mathematics and astronomy as much as they were to war and political propaganda.

The Old World since the era of the Spanish conquistadors has always seemed to have difficulty in completely accepting the common humanity that binds it to the indigenous American world; ancient Americans have been viewed over the centuries as heartless animals, noble savages, pacific astronomers and the custodians of ancient secrets from Atlantis or outer space. Perhaps the difficulty experienced in accepting their humanity and their radical diversity from ourselves is also linked to the guilt felt by Europe that marked its entry to the modern epoch with the slaughter of the indigenous American peoples. The "conquests" of Mexico and Peru were no more than the greatest deeds of genocide in recorded humanity and events that brought a speedy end to the evolution of Mesoamerican culture.

Nor should you let yourself be drawn into another deceit: it is true that the pre-Columbian monuments are part of a past world and that it is very rare to find any continuity from that world to the present day, but it is also true that the indigenous world was not completely erased and that its remains are not purely to be seen in archaeological sites or museums. In Mexico alone over fifty indigenous languages are spoken: Maya, Nahua, Mixtec, Zapotec and many other ethnic groups descended from the pre-Columbian peoples still occupy their native lands. Their foods, manner of dress and beliefs are the most obvious legacy of ancient Mesoamerica.

What is described here is a journey comprising five itineraries that take in some of the most important archaeological sites in Mexico, Guatemala and Honduras on a trip through ancient Mesoamerican civilization. The selection of sites has obviously necessitated the leaving out of others that are also important, and even of entire cultural areas like northern and western Mexico; however, it is our opinion that the itineraries chosen will form a solid basis for getting to know Mesoamerica.

Before beginning the journey, some words of advice should be given. A trip to the ruins of ancient Mexico means visiting temples, palaces, tombs and the residences of kings and nobles, in other words, the buildings raised by the ancient ruling classes to meet their commemorative and political

therefore becomes a journey through the indigenous mentality and each monument represents a stopping point in its history.

It is best not to let oneself be carried away by the precision of their astronomic calculations, the complexity of their calendars and writing, or by the brutality of their rituals and sacrifices. These are certainly very real and interesting aspects of the Mesoamerican civilization, but to concentrate on them would be to fall into the trap of their ancient propaganda and to gaze upon an idealized image of their world. Likewise, the common view of Mesoamerica populated by peaceful astronomers and mathematicians is also the result of the same error, and careful observation of the monuments will teach you that the ancient peoples were simply humans, with good and bad

6 *This is a gold Mixtec lip ornament in the form of an eagle. Objects such as these, large round earrings and other jewels made from precious stones were worn exclusively by the nobility and were often indicators of rank.*

7 *Stucco model probably of Pacal, the ruler of Palenque. Contrary to what was believed some decades ago, many of the Mesoamerican works of art refer to historical figures and events.*

SUMMARY OF THE HISTORY AND CULTURE OF MESOAMERICA

At its largest, the cultural area referred to by the term Mesoamerica included parts of modern Mexico, Belize, Guatemala, Honduras, El Salvador, Costa Rica and Nicaragua. For over four thousand years, dozens of individual cultures developed within it in very different climatic and environmental conditions that nurtured relations and trade between the various peoples.

The historical and artistic development, therefore, of any single people lies within a continuum of Mesoamerican history as a whole that specialists conventionally divide into periods and sub-periods characterized by social and political traits.

THE EARLY PRE-CLASSIC PERIOD: THE BIRTH OF AGRICULTURE AND THE FIRST VILLAGE COMMUNITIES
(2500 BC-1200 BC)

The birth of Mesoamerica coincided with the spread of agriculture and the appearance of the first pottery objects. The process of domestication of wild plants had been started around 7000 BC by semi-nomadic groups of hunter-gatherers in dry and mountainous areas. This led progressively to domestication of all the plants that were to become the basis of the Mesoamerican diet: squashes, maize, beans, amaranthus and chili peppers.

These were the same hunter-gatherers who tamed the turkey and the dog, the only creatures to be domesticated until new animals were imported by Europeans. From around 2500 BC, the first sedentary farming villages appeared in the Valley of Mexico, Tehuacán valley, Oaxaca valley, the Tamaulipas Sierra and on the Pacific coast of what are now Chiapas and Guatemala. These Early Pre-Classic villages rarely comprised more than twenty huts made of wood, leaves and mud, but they formed the cultural and economic basis of all subsequent indigenous Mesoamerican society.

THE MIDDLE PRE-CLASSIC PERIOD: OLMEC CULTURE AND THE FORMATION OF SOCIAL HIERARCHIES (1200-400 BC)

The Middle Pre-Classic period saw great technological and cultural development with the improvement of farming technologies bringing a sharp increase in agricultural production. Social differentiation within the communities became clearer and formed the basis for the first dramatic examples of Mesoamerican art and architecture. In the south of the Gulf Coast, a large Olmec culture flourished between 1200-400 BC that was to leave an indelible mark on much of Mesoamerican peoples. The monumental centers of San Lorenzo, Laguna de los Cerros, La Venta and Tres Zapotes (to mention only the main ones) were embellished by earthen buildings and large basalt sculptures of Olmec governors and their guardian deities.

Olmec sculpture and architecture show how the ruling class managed to mobilize large quantities of manual labor, probably as a result of their control through a complex ideological system that was reflected in an artistic style that was to spread throughout all Mesoamerica. During the Middle Pre-Classic period, Olmec style objects spread throughout the Valley of Mexico, in Guerrero, Oaxaca, Chiapas and as far south as El Salvador and Costa Rica.

Scholars long thought there had been a sort of "proselytism" carried out by Olmec priests or that colonies had been established far from the cultural center on the Gulf. But today, although it is clear that Olmec influence was not evenly spread in all regions, it seems rather that Olmec objects (pottery, green stones, etc.) were considered luxury goods by the emerging political and religious elites in the various Mesoamerican zones who were anxious to confirm and justify their power through material goods that attested their contact with the prestigious Olmec society.

THE LATE PRE-CLASSIC PERIOD: REGIONAL DIFFERENTIATION (400 BC-300 AD)

The formation of social hierarchies rapidly developed from the Middle Pre-Classic period to create societies based on hereditary seigniories. During the Late Pre-Classic period, the new elite classes stimulated an intellectual and artistic development that was often linked to the need to exalt political power. This was the era when the first signs of calendar-making and writing appeared, and when the tradition of low relief carvings became established which almost completely replaced the full relief sculptures that had been typical of the Olmecs for centuries. With the waning of influence of the Olmec style came the growth of regional styles that were to reach their peaks during the Classic period that followed.

The Olmec legacy was developed at the site of Tres Zapotes on the Gulf coast (formerly inhabited during the Olmec era and then a main center of the "terminal Olmec" culture) where a distinctive sculptural style developed. Since the Middle Pre-Classic period, the settlement at San José Mogote in the Oaxaca valley had cast its influence over nearby centers, so bringing into being the thousand year artistic tradition of the Zapotecs that was to evolve from 400 BC in the large center of Monte Albán.

The various regional centers in the Valley of Mexico during the Middle Pre-Classic were progressively attracted into the orbit of the sites of Cuicuilco – with its large circular pyramid – and of Teotihuacan where construction of the Pyramids of the Sun and the Moon had begun. The eruption of the Xitle volcano just before the Christian era buried Cuicuilco, leaving the field clear for Teotihuacan to become the largest city ever in pre-Columbian Mexico.

In southern Mesoamerica, the Late Pre-Classic period marked the start of even more radical changes. The Pacific coast of Chiapas and Guatemala had been occupied by Mixe-Zoque groups who were in close contact with the Maya of the Guatemalan highlands from where colonization of the great tropical forests that stretch from Petén to the Yucatán had begun. Interaction between the Pacific coast and the highlands stimulated an extraordinary artistic and cultural development in sites such as Izapa (Mixe-Zoque) and Kaminaljuyú (Maya) where one of the most important sculptural styles of Mesoamerica was developed. In the meantime, important power centers like El Mirador began to establish themselves in the lowlands; El Mirador was a large Maya center that formed the prototype of the city-state during the Classic period.

8 The colossal head no.6 from San Lorenzo dating from the Middle Pre-Classic period. The basalt colossal heads produced by the Olmecs were probably portraits of their sovereigns and are one of the earliest examples of the close link between monumental art and Mesoamerican political propaganda.

9 The green stone Olmec sculpture is known as the "Lord of Las Limas" (Veracruz) after the place where it was found. It dates from the Middle Pre-Classic period and represents a very common theme in Olmec art: an adult holding a baby with the features of a jaguar that probably represented a rain god.

THE EARLY CLASSIC PERIOD: THE DEVELOPMENT
OF MESOAMERICAN CULTURES
(300-600 AD)

Mesoamerica attained the height of its splendor during the Classic period; the first part – called the Early Classic period – marked the advance of regional traditions, above all among the Teotihuacan, the Zapotecs and the Maya. Contemporaneously, agricultural techniques reached their peak, large cities grew and a vast trading network spread, thanks most of all to Teotihuacan, the influence of which was felt even in the most distant regions of Mesoamerica.

Teotihuacan was a massive city with hundreds of residential areas that spread as far as the eye could see around a monumental center. The extraordinary wealth of the city – which had close relationships with Monte Albán (Oaxaca), Cholula (Puebla), Matacapan (Veracruz) and Kaminaljuyú (Guatemala) – was principally due to control of the commercial routes and to a sort of monopoly of the obsidian market. Teotihuacan was also the first

10 Teotihuacan funerary mask, Early Classic period. The workmanship of precious stones was one of the most highly developed arts in the ancient city of central Mexico and specific districts have been discovered where this craft was carried out.

great multi-ethnic city of central Mexico with districts inhabited by Zapotecs from Oaxaca and by peoples from the Gulf, probably as traders and ambassadors.

The power of the Zapotecan capital, Monte Albán, which lay in the Oaxaca valley, grew as a result of military expansion and continued relations with Teotihuacan; it became a powerful centralized state that dominated the Zapotec world for centuries. The mountain valleys of the Mixteca Alta, on the other hand, developed small capitals in the Mixtec kingdoms that were later to become important to later Oaxacan history.

In the Maya lowlands, the Early Classic era was marked by the expansion of many city-states dominated by powerful royal dynasties and, above all, by Teotihuacan influence in cities like Copán and Tikal. The latter soon became the most important city in Petén following large military campaigns led against nearby cities. It is probable that the influence of Teotihuacan in the Maya world was mediated by Kaminaljuyú, the ancient Maya city in the highlands that turned into a main center of Teotihuacan culture. These were centuries during which the fundamentals of Maya art took form: the sculptural stele-altar, low relief carvings, polychrome pottery, wall painting and the use of the corbel vault in architecture.

The end of the Early Classic period came around 600 AD when two basic and probably associated events took place: the total disappearance of Teotihuacan influence in Maya art and the temporary interruption to the construction of monuments in Tikal caused by a devastating military defeat suffered in the war against the city of Caracol.

10 bottom Zapotec "urn" made from terracotta representing a noble lady, Classic period. The production of urns of this nature – which were in fact funerary offerings – was typical of Zapotec art.

11 Terracotta censer from the region of Palenque in Chiapas. The elaborate representation is typical of Maya art and represents a sovereign seated above the mask of a god from the underworld; he wears a headdress showing the image of a heavenly god. Late Classic period.

THE LATE CLASSIC AND TERMINAL CLASSIC PERIODS: PEAK AND COLLAPSE
(600-900 TO 1000 AD)

The Late Classic period was certainly the era that regional Mesoamerican traditions achieved their height artistically, culturally and demographically. Artists produced their greatest works of art and political structures reached their maximum complexity. It is calculated that during the first half of this period, Teotihuacan had 200,000 inhabitants, Monte Albán 30,000 and Tikal 40,000. But the Late Classic era was also Mesoamerica's swansong as, for reasons still partially not understood, the entire economic and political system rapidly collapsed throughout Mesoamerica between 750-1000 AD which led to a period of ethnic and cultural reorganization.

Once again the "motor" of many of these events was Teotihuacan. After reaching its economic and cultural peak between 400-650 AD, the great city of central Mexico began to show signs of crisis and marks of its influence in other areas of Mesoamerica disappeared. It is not known if this crisis was caused purely by internal socio-economic factors or whether the growing pressure caused by peoples moving south from northern regions was also responsible. It is known, however, that around 750 AD many buildings in the monumental center were burned down, that much of the population emigrated to other regions, and that the city was occupied by the northern "barbarians" known as Chicimecs who were to take the leading role in the centuries to come.

The collapse at the center of the Classic system was soon felt throughout all of central Mexico between 750-900 and 1000 AD (referred to as the Terminal Classic period). Many centers were abandoned while others flourished, and large migrations of people changed the ethnic picture of Mesoamerica. Settlements like Tula Chico (Hidalgo), Xochicalco (Morelos), Teotenango (Toluca) and Cacaxtla (Tlaxcala) managed to take advantage of the economic and political reorganization of the region and gave rise to splendid though ephemeral artistic styles distinguished by eclecticism and the appearance of Maya styles in regions where their influence had never previously been felt.

The city of El Tajín on the Gulf coast had flourished during the Classic period but now bloomed with an innovative artistic and architectural style. In the Oaxaca valley, Monte Albán – though not completely abandoned – experienced a deep crisis between 800-900 AD which encouraged the growth of what had previously been small centers in the valley.

The crisis, however, did not affect the Maya so quickly. Between 600-900 AD, the ruling dynasties reached their peak of splendor in cities like Tikal, Copán, Palenque and Yaxchilán and inspired distinctive and refined regional artistic styles. But around 900 AD, the crisis hit hard: no more monuments were built and almost all the great cities of the central lowlands were abandoned on a permanent basis. Aggressive Maya trader-warriors known as Putún or Chontal began to appear in many settlements. They were originally from the southern section of the Gulf coast and were the bearers of a strongly "Mexicanized" culture, i.e., marked by traits typical of central Mexico.

Not all the Maya world was affected by the collapse in the same way. Regions in the Yucatán were able to flourish from the events taking place and acted as links between the Classic world and the new ethnic and political universe of the Post-Classic era.

THE LATE POST-CLASSIC PERIOD: THE TOLTECS AND THE NEW MAYA WORLD (900-1000 TO 1250 AD)

The Classic and Post-Classic periods were thought for many years to have been in net contrast, with the former having been a peaceful period of artistic and cultural development, and the latter characterized by violent militarism and practices like human sacrifice. Today, this distinction is much less clear; we know that wars and sacrifices were also held during the Classic age and now the intellectual achievements of the Post-Classic period are also being reconsidered. The distinguishing characteristics of the second period seem to lie in the frequent migrations of peoples and the growth of large multi-ethnic political entities that overlay regional and ethnic customs.

The new players in the political scene in central Mexico were those peoples that came down in successive waves from the northern regions of the country and their process of "Mesoamericanization" and acculturation. Around 700 AD, one of these groups founded the city of Tula Chico to the north of modern Mexico City, and later the city of Tula Grande that was to become the capital of the new Toltec empire. Between 900-1150 AD,

Tula was the force behind a new political ideology and the capital of a vast commercial multi-ethnic empire whose influence was felt in much of Mesoamerica. However, Tula was abandoned around 1150 AD for unknown reasons, though probably related to new migrations from the north.

In the Oaxaca valley, the Early Post-Classic period was marked by the growth of many small political entities, the best known being those of Mixteca Alta. Splendid items of Mixtec jewellery and pottery found in tombs in Monte Albán and Zaachila are evidence that the warlike Mixtec kingdoms extended their influence into regions that were traditionally Zapotec; little is known, however, of what happened to the Zapotec kingdoms once

Monte Albán fell.

The presence of cultural characteristics from central Mexico in the world of the Maya, particularly in the highlands of Guatemala and the peninsula of the Yucatán, became stronger in this period and the city of Chichén Itzá in the Yucatán became the new capital of the great kingdom of the Itzá, a dynamic group of Mexicanized Maya. The city was like the "twin" of Tula and also became the main center of worship of Kukulkan, the Feathered Serpent, that dominated the Toltec pantheon.

But Chichén Itzá was unable to survive the fate of other Mesoamerican capitals and a century after the fall of Tula itself, the city was abandoned in 1250 AD.

12 top
This gold Mixtec
ornament from the
Post-Classic period
was part of the
valuable Mixtec
funerary goods found
in Tomb 7 at Monte
Albán (Oaxaca).

Tlaxcala managed to retain their
independence.

The power of the Mexica, who had
military command within the alliance,
was increasingly imposed on their
confederates by the political astuteness of
rulers like Itzcóatl (1426-1440 AD),
Motecuhzoma Ilhuicamina (1440-1468
AD) and Ahuitzotl (1486-1502 AD).
They succeeded in developing a political
and religious ideology founded on war
and sacrifice that became the catalyst of
the military and economic expansion of
the empire supported by the power of the
Triple Alliance armies.

Beyond its frontiers, however, new
political arrangements were taking shape:
to the northwest there was the powerful
Tarasco state, to the southwest the
Mixtec kingdoms, and in the areas of the
Maya new centers were taking the place
of Chichén Itzá at the top of the regional
hierarchy. The most visible was Mayapán,
the "true" capital of the Yucatán until
1450 AD, and Tulum, a small but rich
city that faced onto the Caribbean. It was
at coastal Maya centers like Tulum that
the ships were first seen which brought
the Spanish forces that would soon put an
end to over four thousand years of
independent, indigenous cultural
development.

THE LATE POST-CLASSIC PERIOD:
THE AZTEC EMPIRE
(1250-1521 AD)

At the same time as Tula fell, new
groups of Chicimecs moved down from
northern Mexico. Although Aztec
sources painted them as miserable
nomads, many of them were probably
farmers and the heirs of the
Mesoamerican groups that had gone
north in search of new lands to
colonize. Groups known collectively as
Nahua settled in the Valley of Mexico
where they founded cities like
Acolhuacan, Tenayuca, Azcapotzalco and
Texcoco, and their ruling dynasties
gradually filled the power vacuum
created with the fall of Tula.

At the start of the 14th century, a
new Nahua group arrived following a
long migration that had started from the
mythical locality of Aztlan. They entered
the Valley of Mexico and received

permission from the Tepanec lords of
Azcapotzalco to settle on the islands in
the center of Lake Texcoco where, in
1325 AD, they founded the city of
México-Tenochtitlan. The Mexica
people, better known by the improper
name "Aztecs," allied themselves with
the Acolhua of Texcoco in 1430 AD
after a century of subjection to the city
of Azcapotzalco and defeated their
Tepanec overlords. This led to the
foundation of the *Excan Tlatoloyan* (the
"Tribunal with Three Seats" or Triple
Alliance) that united the Mexica of
México-Tenochtitlan, the Acolhua of
Texcoco and the Tepanecs of Tlacopan.
The military expansion of this alliance
until 1502 AD was extraordinary and
occupied almost all the lands in central
Mexico, the Oaxaca valley, Veracruz
and, further south, the rich province of
Soconusco which is famous for its cacao
plantations. Only a few territories like

12 bottom
Toltec sculpture from
the Early Post-Classic
period. It shows a
human face with the
fangs of a
jaguar-serpent and
a nose decorated with
an ornament. Below
the face it is possible
to make out the forked
tongue.

13 top
Terracotta censer from
Mayapán (Yucatán).
The censer is from the
Late Post-Classic
period and represents
the rain god Chac who
can be recognized by
the long nose and
protruding teeth. He
holds two balls of
incense in his hand.

13 bottom Aztec
sculpture from the
Late Post-Classic
period. The fist
originally held
a standard or
a flag. The eyes
and teeth of
the man have
been created using
shell.

Society

The formation into hierarchical classes of Mesoamerican society reflected certain characteristics right from the Pre-Classic period: they were the division of the population into groups of extended family, the separation of two distinct classes (nobles and commoners), and the institution of hereditary political power. Much of Mesoamerican society was dominated by semi-divine rulers that belonged to the most important of the noble family groups who justified their power on descendancy from a mythical ancestor.

14 Carved panel from the Temple of the Sun in Palenque (Chiapas). The low relief shows the sovereign Chan Bahlum wearing the elaborate dress costume used during the celebrations of his ascent to the throne.

14-15 Drawing from the Historia de las Indias de Nueva España e Islas de Tierra Firme *by Diego Durán (1579). Note the tlatoani who, seated on the throne on the right and wearing a cloak and diadem, receives three nobles whose names are shown in the glyphs over their heads. Scenes of the founding of Tenochtitlan are shown in the background.*

The dynastic political system reached its peak in the Classic world of the Maya in which an enormous number of rulers of equal status (at least from a formal point of view) called *ahau* ("lord") or *ahpo* ("lord of the mat") reigned over individual city-states. Although the political relationships between the various Maya city-states were inconstant and never achieved organization on an imperial basis, the lords of the major cities could govern smaller cities through a *batab* ("governor") or through family relationships with local lords. Political relationships between the city-states were based on a complex network of alliances often endorsed by marriage between members of different dynasties and maintained by means of the continuous exchange of gifts and ambassadors.

A different political system seems to have been used in the great states of central Mexico. At Teotihuacan –

where no evidence exists of political power held by an individual or a dynasty – power was probably shared by groups of nobles-priests who based their right to govern on a sort of divine patronage offered by the Feathered Serpent or the Jaguar which were manifestations of the most important gods in the indigenous pantheon.

This system of government seems to have developed to suit a society of large multi-ethnic groups for which an ethnically defined lineage was not considered sufficient justification to govern. The origins of this system can be traced at Teotihuacan where it spread out during the Post-Classic period.

The two types of political power described should not however be considered as mutually exclusive, and it is probable that the second was superimposed on the more traditional model of dynastic power in various Mesoamerican regions.

15 bottom
Maya pottery
statuette, perhaps a
priest, wearing a
conical hat, earrings
and a feathered cloak.

16 top This is
another drawing from
the Florentine
Codex in which a
tlatoani (ruler) is
seated inside a palace.
He wears an elaborate
garment and a diadem
as an indication of his
rank. The two small
commas in front of his
mouth are ideographic
signs that he is
speaking.

basis that recognized their descendancy from a common ancestor. The Post-Classic period cities were divided into districts that corresponded to different *calputlin* whose members often performed specific technical or crafts-related activities. Each *calpulli* had its own school and a temple dedicated to its *calpultéotl* (patron deity). The administration of affairs in the *calpulli* was the responsibility of an adult man called the "great relative" belonging to the principal family. He was helped by a group of elders in the distribution of land (owned communally by the *calpulli*), the running of community

Thanks to historical sources from the colonial era, we have a fairly accurate idea of the organization of Aztec society. It was divided into the groups of commoners and nobles (called respectively *macehualtin* and *pipiltin*) whose social status was displayed in personal dress and ornamentation.

The former were mostly agricultural workers, artisans, tradesmen and soldiers while the nobles were governors, priests, artists and army officers. Both classes were trained to perform particular duties in special schools: the *telpochcalli* was the school for the common people which taught the art of war, whereas the *calmecac* was the strictly authoritarian school in which young nobles were instructed in art, religion, administration and military command.

The two social classes were not entirely closed as a noble might lose his privileges if he were guilty of a crime or did not pay his debts, but a commoner could only raise his social status by distinguishing himself on the battlefield. A third status was *tlatlacoliztli*, which was somewhat comparable to slavery, in which one could become *tlacotli* for non-payment of debts. In this case, one was obliged to serve one's creditor until

the debt was paid off which meant that the condition was temporary and non-hereditary. True slavery never played a major role in the Aztec world and this was probably true for all the other Mesoamerican societies.

At all social levels, individuals fell within large groups of extended families called *calpultin*. Each *calpulli* comprised families linked on a blood or territorial

work, training and worship in the *calpulli*. Any affairs between the *calpulli* and the state were the responsibility of the *tecuhtli* (a functionary appointed by the emperor) whose duties were the exaction of taxes, military organization, the administration of justice and the participation of members of the *calpulli* at religious ceremonies.

The tip of the Aztec social hierarchy

was the king himself, known as the *tlatoani* ("orator"); his status was considered semi-divine as he was the earthly representative of Tezcatlipoca – one of the most important Aztec gods – as well as being the descendant of the founder of the dynasty. He inherited his power from his father or an uncle (the brothers of the sovereign had priority over sons as heirs to the throne). The *tlatoani* was the military commander, priest and supreme judge and was aided by the *cihuacóatl* ("woman serpent") who ran the administration and judiciary as well as substituting the sovereign when he was absent. The government was run by a number of councils of nobles who were expert in specific fields of administration.

Each Mesoamerican political system was a reflection of the cosmology of the society it ruled over. The capital cities each claimed to be the "center of the world," the kings were the earthly representatives of their divine ancestors or of the major cosmic forces, and the duality of the most important government posts reflected the basic duality of the cosmos.

This microcosm of the universe legitimized the various forms of power and painted them as inevitable and unchanging. As will be shown, the purpose of much of Mesoamerican art was to confirm and exalt this close correspondence between earthly and cosmic order.

16 bottom This scene is taken from the Florentine Codex *and shows an Aztec family eating together inside a house. The various figures are seated on matting and seem to be eating maize tortillas.*

17 Aztec parents accompany their children to the telpochcalli (school for commoners). From the Florentine Codex.

WAR

It is an established fact that war was a common event in Mesoamerica from as early as the Pre-Classic period. One of the earliest pieces of evidence of war is Monument 3 in the Zapotec site of San José Mogote that dates from 500 BC: the stone threshold of a public building is decorated with images of a prisoner of war whose chest spurts with blood following the removal of his heart. The positioning of the carving meant that whoever entered the building stepped on it, thereby humiliating the memory of the prisoner and glorifying the local lord who was responsible for his capture.

A series of similar monuments with images of prisoners whose hearts or genitals have been removed (known as *danzantes* as they were mistakenly interpreted as being dancers)

embellished the oldest building in Monte Albán where the defeat of enemies was a favorite subject of monumental decoration for centuries.

The forests that covered so much of Maya territory were also the theater of ceaseless clashes between the nobles of the warring city-states. Tikal seems to have begun its rise to power following victory over nearby Uaxactún and was for centuries involved in a gruelling war against Calakmul and its allies that ended in ruinous defeat for itself. Many of the superb Maya low reliefs record military episodes and show the rulers grasping bound prisoners by the hair or mistreating them.

Many Maya wars were not aimed at conquest but were brought to an end by the capture of the king or most important nobles of the opposing

forces who were then sacrificed in the ceremonial center of the winning city. An extraordinary instance of the complex ceremony that surrounded sacrifices of this kind in the Maya world is given in the Maya Quiché text known as *Rabinal Achí*. The famous war between Tikal and Uaxactún seems to have started a new type of encounter that scholars refer to as the Tláloc-Venus Wars or "Star Wars" as their start was marked by the appearance of Venus as the Evening Star. On this occasion, the kings dressed in a special costume decorated with symbolic signs from central Mexico like circular ornaments around the eyes (symbols of the rain god Tláloc) and the sign of the year on the headdress. This has suggested that the Tláloc-Venus Wars originated in Teotihuacan where

19 top Drawing taken from the work of Diego Durán in which a scene from the War of the Flowers is shown. The War of the Flowers was the ritual war fought so that captured prisoners of war could be used for sacrifice; the Aztecs fought against the inhabitants of the nearby city of Tlaxcala. A warrior-eagle with a feathered costume and "sword" made from wood and obsidian can be seen.

19 bottom A Classic period Maya statuette from the island of Jaina (Campeche). It shows a warrior dressed in a long feathered garment.

warriors sacrificed below the Temple of the Feathered Serpent clearly demonstrate the association between warring and the planet Venus. The wars would have been spread through the world of the Maya by way of the cities that most felt the influence of the large metropolises of central Mexico such as Tikal and Copán.

Various wall paintings in Teotihuacan show soldiers-eagles and soldiers-jaguars which herald similar but more famous Aztec military orders like the two groups of warriors in the paintings at Cacaxtla in which the connection between war and the planet Venus is very clear.

With the introduction of new forms of political power and the increase in number of large multi-ethnic states during the Post-Classic period, wars of conquest became the norm. Toltec, Maya, Mixtec and Aztec armies conquered huge areas which were then obliged to pay tribute, and sacrifice and war (referred to in Nahuatl respectively as "water" and "fire") became the cornerstone of Aztec imperial ideology. The need for men to sacrifice became so pressing that traditionally rival cities like México-Tenochtitlan and Tlaxcala periodically organized "Wars of the Flowers" with the aim of the reciprocal exchange of prisoners.

18 Battle scene from wall paintings at Bonampak. The sovereign Chan Muan II holds a defeated enemy by the hair. Another warrior behind the king belongs to the highest ranks of the nobility. He may be an allied king.

RELIGION

To describe Mesoamerican religion is a very difficult task for two reasons: one, many regional religious traditions co-existed within the great cultural area, and two, because each of them had within it a range of gods with multiple manifestations that constantly doubled, quadrupled, changed aspect or were superimposed on one another.

All one can hope to achieve is a profile of the elements that the individual regional religions had in common and which formed their basis, limiting as much as possible lists of deities with complicated names whose individual characteristics are only identified with difficulty.

20 top The jaguar is one of the oldest and most important deities in Mesoamerican religions. The animal was associated with the cosmic forces of the underworld and darkness. Ritual sacrifices were also made to the jaguar and in this low relief from Chichén Itzá the animal is shown eating a human heart.

One of the unifying concepts of Mesoamerican religious tradition related to the form of the universe. The indigenous universe was perceived as though it were formed by two pyramids or cosmic mountains united at their horizontal and four-sided bases. The meeting point of the bases constituted the earth and was often represented in the form of a monstrous alligator called *Cipactli* by the Aztecs and *Itzam Cab Ain* by the Maya.

The heavenly mountain rose above the earth in thirteen layers that formed the abodes of particular gods. On the top of the mountain lived the dual creator god that the Aztecs called *Ometéotl* ("Dual God") and the Maya *Hunab Ku.*

The celestial world made the world fertile and dispensed assets. It was associated with warmth, light, dry weather and the male element of the universe. It contrasted with the underworld below which was damp, dark, female and organized on nine levels that were the dwelling places of divinities like the god of the dead

*20 bottom
This modern
reconstruction based
on original drawings*

*represents the
complex model of the
universe as the Maya
imagined it.*

(Náhuatl: *Mictlantecuhtli*, Maya: *Ah Puch*) and the god of water (Náhuatl: *Tláloc*, Maya: *Chaac*). Celestial gods usually manifested themselves as birds or feathered creatures, whereas the gods of the underworld were distinguished by the spotted coat of a jaguar and protruding fangs. Communication between the three cosmic levels was provided by five large trees that grew at the center of the world and in the four cardinal points. Life depended on the alternation of the forces of the universe that travelled inside their trunks and was modelled on the basis of duality in day/night, male/female, dry season/rainy season, etc.

The trunks of the cosmic trees were also the channels through which time was manifested; time was a divine essence that came down to earth and moved counter-clockwise around the trunks of the cosmic trees. Time and space were therefore inextricably bound up in the concept of the universe that underlay every manifestation of the sacred.

The gods and cosmic forces were composed of a "light" substance imperceptible to the senses. It was also common to worldly entities but these were more made up of a variable, "heavy" substance that was subject to deterioration. This heavy substance had appeared on earth when the sun "crystallized" living beings into their current form, but all animate and inanimate beings still conserved their "light" substance which represented the divine presence in every human, animal or object. The concept of "diffused divinity" helps to explain the reasons for the complexity of the Mesoamerican pantheon in which divine substances were a varying element in an unending weave of relations that made up the essence of the universe.

Revelations or manifestations of the sacred occurred in specific places or in living beings such as caves, springs, lakes, mountains, stars, trees, animals and human beings. Monumental city centers were often constructed as "cosmic models" where the sacred might be revealed thanks to their symbolic position at the "center of the world" where "flows" of sacred energy passed. By residing in these places, the city governors were able to become receptacles of sacredness and consequently influence fertility cycles.

21 This terracotta crenellation — called almena *— was produced in Teotihuacan during the Classic period. It shows water gushing from the beak of a bird decorated with volutes and signs in the form of an eye. The image probably referred to fertility cults that were at the base of political power in Teotihuacan.*

20-21 The page comes from a Mixtec codex; it shows several temples, each of which is distinguished by a specific roof decoration.

One of the most important Mesoamerican divinities was unquestionably the pair Sun-Venus which moved constantly through the heaven and underworld. The sun god was called *Tonatiuh* by the Aztecs and *Kinich Ahau* by the Maya. The maize plant was the manifestation of *Cintéotl* in Náhuatl or *Yum Kaax* in the language of the Maya and it was often depicted in the form of a young man. The supreme god of the Maya world was *Itzamná*, the heavenly dragon and son of *Hunab Ku* as well as being the manifestation of the celestial cosmic forces.

Another deity of great importance was *K'awil* (also known as *Bolon D'zacab* or god K) who was associated with the concepts of blood and fertility and believed to be a sort of patron of the royal Maya dynasties; he was often represented on the royal sceptre held by the king. Association of the king with the god of maize, the Sun-Venus dyad and other astral divinities was one of the most common aspects of Mesoamerican religious traditions.

The Aztec pantheon was also distinguished by the contrast between *Tezcatlipoca* ("Smoking Mirror"), who was associated with the underworld and the magical forces of darkness and was often represented as a jaguar, and *Quetzalcóatl* ("Feathered Serpent"), a celestial god and cultural hero who was variously represented as a priest, the creator of men, the provider of corn or the originator of time. One of his principal manifestations was *Ehécatl*, the god of the wind who wore a beaked mask. The constant opposition of Tezcatlipoca and Quetzalcóatl or, rather, the two cosmic principles that they represented, was the

dynamic that regulated the continuous cycle of creation and destruction of the world which had led to the creation of the Fifth Sun, i.e., our current world. The contrast between the two opposing forces was also reflected in the ideological references on which political power was centered: for example, the main factions of Teotihuacan and Toltec power and the most important Aztec military orders were probably all based on the principle of opposition.

The main innovation contributed by the Aztecs to the Mesoamerican pantheon was the placement of *Huitzilopochtli* ("Hummingbird of the South") at its peak. He was originally a tribal god who eventually developed into a powerful celestial divinity with strong solar attributes. His cult corresponded to that of Tláloc, the most important god of the underworld.

The complexity of Mesoamerican cosmology was matched by an equally complex public and private ceremonial. The huge number of rituals based on the Ritual Calendar (see Box: *The calendar*) were practiced with great pomp and usually accompanied by ceremonial dancing, music and offerings of food, incense and blood. Human sacrifice was practiced during all epochs and by all Mesoamerican peoples but the Aztecs made sacrifice of prisoners of war the cornerstone of a warring ideology that formed the basis of the military and economic expansion of their huge

empire. Another important form of blood offering was self-sacrifice during which spines of the agave plant or fish, if not blades of obsidian, were used to perforate the genitals, tongue, earlobes or other parts of the body. As low reliefs show, priests and kings did it to see visions or to make contact with the worlds of the gods or their ancestors that formed the source and justification of their power.

THE CALENDAR

The Mesoamerican concept of time was that it was a divine substance manifested in the world that deeply influenced human life. Interpretation of time was therefore a task of extreme importance that was entrusted to specialists who made use of complex calendars. The calendars employed in the various regions differed slightly but all shared certain fundamental characteristics; the examples described here are Maya and Aztec calendars.

One of the features that distinguished Mesoamerica from everywhere else in the world was their use of a sacred calendar based on a cycle of 260 days. Called the *Tonalpohualli* by the Aztecs (we do not know the Maya name), it was based on the association of thirteen numbers and twenty days (13x20 = 260). The calendar covered the entire cycle of religious rituals and was recorded on prophetic almanacs (Náhuatl: *tonalámatl*) used by priests to decree whether a particular day was favorable for the performance of certain activities, for example, which calendar name to attribute to a child in addition to his individual name.

Another calendar of 360+5 days (Náhuatl *Xiuhpohualli*, Maya: *Haab*) was based on eighteen "months" of twenty days each (18x20 = 360) to which five "sleeping" days were added to coincide with the approximate length of the solar cycle.

The combination of the two calendars, known as the Short Count, meant that each day had a name consisting of four elements (number + name of day + number + month). This signified that 52 years could pass before the same combination of numbers and names turned up again (52 years = 18,980 days = 73 cycles of the ritual calendar = 52 cycles of the solar calendar) The cycle of 52 years was therefore to the Mesoamericans what a century is to us and was symbolically represented by the Aztecs by a bundle of 52 canes (*xiuhmolpilli*) which was burned during the ceremonies that marked the end of the cycle. The ceremonies culminated in the lighting of the New Fire in which all the fires in the city were put out and a new fire lit in the chest of a sacrificed prisoner from which flames were taken to relight all the fires in the city and the empire. However, as the complete name of a day was repeated every 52 years, modern scholars cannot be sure to which "century" a certain date belonged.

The Mixe-Zoque and Maya, on the other hand, used a different method to record time which is referred to as the Long Count. This records the days from a mythical starting date (August 13, 3114 BC) which allows us to correlate Maya dates with our own calendar. Dates in the Long Count were described by a mathematical or positional system to base 20 (in fact a combination of base 20 and base 18 systems) that made use of three signs: a dot (equal to 1), a bar (equal to 5), and a shell (equal to 0).

These cycles were supplemented by a lunar cycle, a Venusian cycle and other, less important ones; one example is the cycle of the nine "Ladies of the Night" who corresponded to the nine layers of the underworld and whose influences alternated day by day. All these calendars were used for ceremonial and prophetic purposes as well for dating monuments that commemorated the achievements of the sovereigns, often using laborious astronomic and mathematical calculations to correlate the human and mythical events. This was the fundamental function of calendars, to record the close relationship between the world of men and the world of the gods.

24-25 This is a page from the Cospi Codex kept in the library at Bologna university. It is a calendar-cum-divination codex from the Pueblo-Mixtec region consisting of a strip of deer leather folded like a concertina, covered with lime and painted. This page shows a section of the tonalpohualli, the ritual calendar of 260 days.

INDIGENOUS LITERATURE AND THE POPOL VUH

Although few pre-Columbian books known to us deal with topics relating to the calendar, religion, history or genealogy (see the box *The Exploits of Eight Deer*), a great deal of information on ancient literary practices has reached the modern day from the descriptions of

written in Maya Quiché using Latin characters which he transcribed at the start of the 18th century. The first part of the text is a long account of successive creations following an initial state described as follows:

"This is the story of how everything was suspended in calm, in silence; the expanse of heaven was still, quiet and empty. [...]

"There was only stillness and silence in the dark, in the night. Only the Creator, the Shaper, Tepeu, Gucumatz, the Forefathers were in the water surrounded by radiance. They were surrounded by green and blue feathers [...]"

The creations of the gods are described from the origins of the main lines of the Maya Quiché. The most famous section of the *Popol Vuh* recounts the adventures of the twins Hunapu and Xbalanque which take place alternately on Earth and in Xibalba (the World of the Dead, literally "The Place of Fear") and alludes to the continual journeys in heaven and the underworld of Venus and the Sun whom the twins personify. On Earth, the twins defeat the evil Seven

the twins trick the gods by cutting off their own heads and coming back to life until the gods, One Death and Seven Death, want to try it too.

Naturally, the twins cut off the heads of the deities so that they die and thus triumph over the gods of the underworld. The story ends with their transformation into the Sun and the Moon (the reference to the Moon is probably European in origin as the older twin was the personification of the planet Venus).

The version we have dates from the colonial era but it is known that the *Popul Vuh* originated during the ancient past of Mesoamerica since some of the episodes of the twins are depicted on Pre-Classic stelae in Izapa and on many works of Classic Maya art. The two twins – whose Classic names were Hun Ahau ("One Lord," Venus) and Yax Balam ("Green Jaguar," Sun) – were considered the prototype of Maya royalty and many of the rituals performed by the kings alluded to their mythical feats.

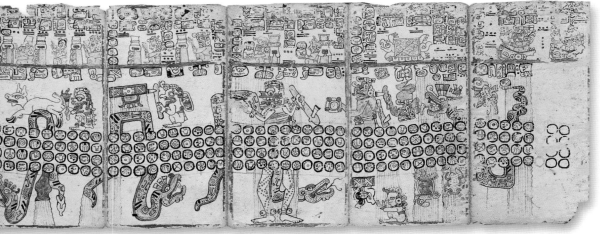

the first Spanish chroniclers. We know, for example, that poetry was a common art among the Aztecs and that two of their best known poets were Nezahualcóyotl and Nezahualpilli, who were kings of the Acolhua city of Texcoco, the capital of Nahua art.

The most extraordinary example of indigenous literature is the *Popol Vuh (The Book of the Council)*, a great mythological epic poem that Friar Francisco Jiménez found in the Guatemalan highlands

Parrot and his sons Zipacná and Earthquake; the adventures in the underworld begin with the challenge of the underworld gods who, disturbed by the spreading of Hunapu's and Xbanaque's fear, invite them to play in Xibalba as their ancestors had done though they were later sacrificed. The games that take place between the gods and the twins each night turn into terrifying trials in which Hunapu and Xbalanque prevail brilliantly. In the end,

24-25 bottom Section of the Madrid Codex, *one of the four Maya codices that have survived to the modern day. As with the other three – the* Paris, Dresden *and* Grolier *codices – it is a calendrical and divinatory codex.*

THE IMPACT WITH THE OLD WORLD

The "golden isolation" that Mesoamerica enjoyed for four thousand years was broken in 1517 when the first Spanish expedition under the command of Franciso Hernández de Cordoba reached the coast of Yucatán. Neither this, nor the one that was led a year later by Juan de Grijalva, made much impression apart from bringing strange stories to the ears of the Aztec emperor Motecuhzoma II (Montezuma) of mountains that sailed on the sea and of white men who exchanged strange glass beads for precious gifts.

The consequences of the arrival off the coast of the Yucatán in 1519 of a third expedition with 508 soldiers, 16 horses and 100 or so sailors under Hernán Cortés were, however, tragic. The Spaniards learned of two fellow-countrymen who had lived among the Maya for eight years following their shipwreck in the Caribbean. One of them, Jerónimo de Aguilar, promptly jointed Cortés' expedition as an interpreter while the other, Gonzalo Guerrero – who had married a Maya woman, been tattooed and wore large ear ornaments – preferred to stay where he was, thus becoming one of the symbols of the meeting of the two worlds.

Cortés soon realized that Yucatán was not the treasure-filled land he had dreamed of and continued his voyage northwest where he met with the occasional skirmish with the natives. In what is now the state of Tabasco, Cortés was presented with a priceless gift by several chiefs: an indigenous noble lady, Doña Marina, known as "La Malinche," who had been taken into slavery. Knowing both the Maya language of the coast and the Náhuatl language of the interior, she made a strong interpreting team with Aguilar. She did not need much time to learn Spanish and became Cortés' personal interpreter and the key figure in the conquest of Mexico. She also bore Cortés a son and converted to Christianity, whereupon she changed her name to Marina.

During the months that followed, Cortés expedition stopped at Veracruz and began to head inland towards the marvellous capital spoken of by the natives from where representatives continued to arrive bearing valuable gifts. The Spaniards alternated friendly overtures with force as they passed through Cempoala, Tlaxcala and Cholula, inciting rebellion against the Aztec overlords as they went and feeding the belief that they and their horses were divine beings.

The Spanish column followed by six thousand Tlaxcalctec soldiers was received by the court of Motecuhzoma II on the road that crossed Lake Texcoco to reach the capital México-Tenochtitlan. The emperor was brought forward on a gold litter covered by a canopy of feathers and preceded by three dignitaries who carried gold sceptres. When Motecuhzoma stepped down from his litter, a cotton rug was unrolled at his feet. He advanced with

the kings of Texcoco, Tacuba, Coyoacan and Iztapalapan to welcome Cortés. The meeting was very friendly and the only moment of trepidation occurred when the Spaniard tried to embrace the emperor whereupon he was immediately stopped by the Aztec dignitaries.

The Spaniards were taken into the city and lodged in the majestic palace that had belonged to Axayácatl. Soon the tension between the Aztecs and the Spaniards rose and the palace was turned into a sort of prison for Motecuhzoma who became increasingly uncertain of how to treat the newcomers. Events accelerated when Cortés was required to return to the Gulf of Mexico to deal with a Spanish army that had been sent against him by the governor of Cuba. During his absence, Pedro de Alvarado massacred a number of Aztec nobles, thereby triggering an armed revolt that forced the Spaniards to flee during the famous noche triste. This was the night that Motecuhzoma was killed by his own men while he tried to halt an attack on his palace; he was replaced by Cuitláhuac but the new leader died of smallpox only four months later. On Cortés' return, the city was besieged for several months until Aztec resistance under the last independent emperor, Cuauhtémoc, was routed in the battle at Tlatelolco. Today, a stone commemorates the events of that day with the words: "On August 13, 1521, Tlatelolco, heroically defended by Cuauhtémoc, fell into the hands of Hernán Cortés. It was neither a triumph nor a defeat, but the painful birth of the mestizo country that is modern Mexico."

marina

marques

thlascala

26 Scene taken from the Historia de las Indias de Nueva España e Islas de Tierra Firme by Diego Durán showing a battle between the Spanish and the Aztecs. The Spaniards were captained by the hidalgo Pedro de Alvarado; of the Aztecs we see a warrior-eagle and a warrior-jaguar.

26-27 This drawing from the work of Diego Durán illustrates the meeting of Hernán Cortés and doña Marina (Malinche) who, as the lover and interpreter of the Spanish captain, was to become one of the most important figures in the Spanish conquest of Mexico.

Much debate has centered on the reasons that allowed a handful of Spaniards to conquer the enormous Aztec empire whose armies had dominated all of Mesoamerica. There are many causes: firearms, horses, the fear that the Spaniards were divine, Cortés' ability to find allies among the indigenous peoples subjected by the Aztecs and, above all, disease. Disease was the main cause of the appalling proportions of the genocide that took place; although the demographic estimates are disputable, it is thought that between 1521 AD and 1600 AD the indigenous population of Mexico fell from twenty five million to just one million!

From the point of view of the native population, the entire colonial era was a period of tragedy marked by the decimation of the population and the constant social and cultural disruption caused by the new political and economic system imposed by Spain. This resulted in institutions called *encomienda* which enforced a system of land ownership that implied a form of slavery for the natives. Little or nothing changed even with the attainment of Mexican independence (1821 AD) when political and economic power was transferred to the hands of the Creoles (whites born on Mexican territory) as they represented a class still distant from the needs of the indigenous peoples.

A fresh wave of attention regarding the "native problem" followed the 1910 AD revolution when Mexico posed itself

the problem of finding a new identity, a mestizo identity whose spirit was well expressed in the commemorative stone in Tlatelolco. Anthropological and indigenist institutions were set up, but their work has often smacked of paternalism and contributed to portraying the indigenous world as "backward" and almost "reactionary" compared to the modernistic requirements of the new Mexico. In parallel, the archaeological discoveries of ancient Mexico tended to feed nationalistic and patriotic sentiments rather than rediscover the identity of the country rooted in its indigenous past.

Today things are not very different and the millions of natives in the modern republic of Mexico form the poorest social class of a country that seems blinded by the mirage of

the consumer world. Their faces are seen in travel agency advertisements beside images of ancient ruins as lures to bring in the foreign dollars that have ousted even the old feelings of nationalism.

27 bottom Drawing from Durán's work depicting the massacre of indigenous nobles by the Spanish at Tenochtitlan. This event sparked the indigenous revolt that culminated in the famous noche triste.

THE EMPIRES OF CENTRAL MEXICO

The Valley of Mexico and its surrounding regions have always been an important cultural zone in Mesoamerica. Groups of hunters exploited the natural resources of the lake area as early as the Stone Age and for all of the pre-Hispanic era occupied much of the valley. The long epoch during which agriculture became established is revealed by the millenary occupation of Zohapilco from around 5500 BC, while the spread of an "Olmecoid" culture and the parallel process of the creation of social hierarchies began in the important settlements of Tlapacoya and Tlatilco from the beginning of the first millennium BC. Around 400 BC, construction of the large round pyramid at Cuicuilco was begun. This was the new power center of the central highlands but its development was abruptly halted by the eruption of the volcano Xitle around 50 BC when the monumental center was buried by lava. The end of Cuicuilco contributed to the rise of Teotihuacan that had been occupied since 150 BC and which probably took in much of the population of the ruined city. The first construction at Teotihuacan was the Pyramid of the Moon around 100 AD. This marked the start of an epoch of extraordinary development of the city that was destined to influence much of subsequent Mesoamerican history. It was to become the largest and most important city in the Americas, the capital of an enormous commercial empire and, for nearly seven hundred years, the true "heart" of the large economic and cultural system that formed Mesoamerica during the Classic period.

Around 750 AD, after about a century of unexpected decline, the monumental center of Teotihuacan was burned down and the city occupied by peoples known as Coyotlatelco from the north who succeeded in maintaining the city as the principal urban center in central Mexico until the year 1000 AD. The Coyotlatelco people were also responsible for the foundation of Tula

Chico around 750 AD and, 150 years later, of Tula Grande, 40 miles northwest of Teotihuacan in the modern state of Hidalgo. Tula Grande became the new dominant center of central Mexico and a splendid city that for nearly three centuries controlled the fate of the Toltec empire, spread the cult of the Feathered Serpent throughout Mesoamerica and established an enormous trading network.

Around 1150 AD, Tula was abandoned, perhaps following continued pressure from northern peoples. When one of these groups – known as the Mixtecs or Aztecs – arrived in central Mexico in the 14th century, Tula had already been semi-abandoned for more than a century but this did not discourage the Aztecs from occupying its ruins on their migration south. Once they entered the Valley of Mexico, the Aztecs adopted the practice of making aristocratic marriages with the royal blood of the Toltecs in order to inherit the power of Tula lawfully. After nearly a century of establishing their own power through wars and alliances with other centers in the valley, during the 15th century the Aztec capital of México-Tenochtitlan became the power behind an expansionistic empire that conquered large swathes of Mesoamerica until 1521 AD when the city was besieged by the Spanish. Even these new conquerors made Tenochtitlan the capital of their New Spain and the city is still there today with the name Mexico City controlling the whole of the country.

Teotihuacan, Tula and México-Tenochtitlan were the three most important capitals in the whole of Mesoamerica and it is in their histories that it is possible to trace the origins and evolution of what was perhaps the most widespread myth in all of Post-Classic Mesoamerica: that of the city of Tollan. Historical and archaeological sources have shown that throughout nearly all of Mesoamerica a myth existed that recognized the city of Tollan as a cosmic city, a model on which many of its

terrestrial equivalents based themselves, and ruled by a sovereign, Quetzalcóatl, who became the prototype for every earthly lord. As we shall see, the myth of Tollan developed from the legacy of Teotihuacan and became established during the rule of Tula. Its memory was still fresh at the time of the Spanish conquest when the association of Hernán Cortés with Quetzalcóatl seems to have contributed to the sudden collapse of the Aztec empire.

28-29 Detail of one of the sculptures on the facade of the Early Classic period Temple of the Feathered Serpent at Teotihuacan. The sculpture shows the head of the Feathered Serpent, one of the most important gods in central America.

TEOTIHUACAN

history

Teotihuacan was probably founded around 150 BC as no more than a small village of farmers but, in the space of just a few decades, it grew to rival Cuicuilco as the central power in the Valley of Mexico. During the Tzacualli phase (1-150 AD), construction of the two main structures in the city was begun; these were the Pyramid of the Moon and, a little later, the Pyramid of the Sun. During the Miccaotli phase (150-200 AD), the urban structure of Teotihuacan began to take on its current form: a central axis known as the Avenue of the Dead, over 2 miles long, was laid down which formed the basis of all future planning of the city. Several of the monumental complexes were built along the sides of the avenue such as the Temple of the Feathered Serpent, the Temple of Agriculture and the Viking Group.

The largest architectural development at Teotihuacan took place during the Tlamimilolpa phase (200-400 AD) when most of the structures visible today were built. This included the residential complexes as well as monumental structures like the Temple of the Feathered Shells, the plaza of the Pyramid of the Moon and the Great Compound. During this phase, Teotihuacan became one of the largest political and commercial centers in Mesoamerica, extending its cultural and economic influence throughout the cultural area.

During the Xolalpan phase (400-650 AD), the city enjoyed its period of greatest splendor. It is calculated that the city had two hundred thousand inhabitants, which would have made it the sixth largest city in the world at the time. Works during this period were Quetzalpapálotl Palace and most of the wall paintings visible today.

A clear crisis was suffered during the hundred years of the Metepec phase (650-750 AD) in which the number of inhabitants was reduced to eighty five thousand. It is probable that the interruption of several trading routes had created a crisis in the city's economy which was to a great extent dependent on long distance commerce. The increase in iconographic elements of a military nature suggests that the Teotihuacan elite attempted to maintain power through force in the face of social tension. Around 750 AD (though more recent research tends to move this date forward), many of the buildings in the monumental center were burned down and Teotihuacan lost forever its role as the pre-eminent city in Mesoamerican politics. Nevertheless, for at least two hundred years it continued to be the largest settlement in the Valley of Mexico and was occupied by peoples that had moved down from the north. After 1000 AD, the city was finally abandoned and began, instead, to become an important part of Mesoamerican mythology.

The almost total absence of individual representations of the city's rulers, of inscriptions or calendar dates indicates that Teotihuacan was not governed by a political power based on dynastic rule typical of other Mesoamerican regions. The city's social and economic life was instead run by a solid, centralized state administration overseen by groups of nobles who legitimized their power through links with divine "patrons" that represented basic cosmic forces. The enormous population of the city lived in residential complexes that were probably divided into family and corporative groups similar to the *calpultin* in the Aztec era.

The lack of historical and epigraphic sources means we do not know the original name of Teotihuacan and by which ethnic group the site was founded (those proposed are the Otomí, the Totonachi and the Nahua) but it is very probable that Teotihuacan was the center of the first great multi-ethnic empire in Mesoamerica and the

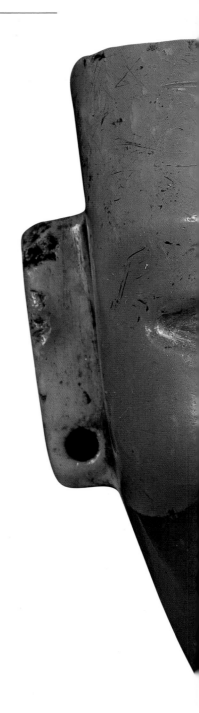

"prototype" of the later Post-Classic empires. Even after its fall, Teotihuacan was never forgotten and the Aztecs – who continued to visit its ruins – gave it the name by which it is known today: "The Place where the Gods Live." Aztec tradition believed that it was at Teotihuacan that the gods met to create the Fifth Sun.

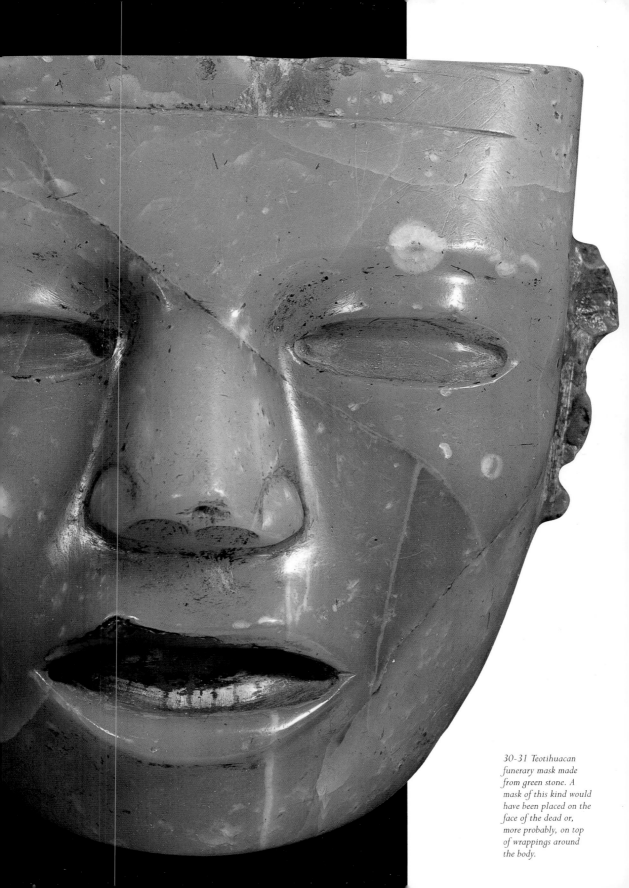

30-31 Teotihuacan funerary mask made from green stone. A mask of this kind would have been placed on the face of the dead or, more probably, on top of wrappings around the body.

the site

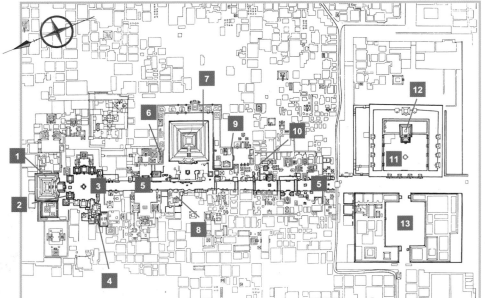

T E O T I H U A C A N	
1 PYRAMID OF THE MOON	8 PATIO OF THE FOUR TEMPLES
2 BUILDING OF THE ALTARS	9 PALACE OF THE PRIEST
3 SQUARE OF THE MOON	10 VIKING GROUP
4 QUETZALPAPALOTL PALACE	11 THE CITADEL
5 AVENUE OF THE DEAD	12 TEMPLE OF THE FEATHERED
6 PALACE OF THE SUN	SERPENT
7 PYRAMID OF THE SUN	13 THE GREAT COMPOUND

The city of Teotihuacan extends well beyond the boundaries of the actual archaeological site which is limited to the monumental center where the two main pyramids dominate. The ancient residential quarters which have mostly not yet been excavated stretch as far as the feet of the surrounding mountains.

The Avenue of the Dead is the main city road and is intersected perpendicularly by the river San Juan; the course of the river was deviated in order to divide the city area into four large sections that were probably endowed with symbolic significance.

The southeast quadrant contains the most awe-inspiring structure in Teotihuacan: the Citadel. This four-sided platform topped by small pyramidal bases is the location of the Temple of the Feathered Serpent, the stepped body of which is decorated with polychrome sculptures of feathered serpents whose heads project

from the walls. Surrounded by aquatic symbols, the bodies of the serpents are covered with headdresses (at one time mistakenly thought to be faces of Tláloc) that probably depict *Cipactli*, the earth monster in the form of an alligator. A series of tombs was found below and around the temple that contained men and women buried in groups of 4, 8, 9, 18 and 20 (for a total of 260) who had had their hands tied behind their shoulders and been sacrificed.

The number buried below the Temple of the Feathered Serpent corresponds to the number of days in the ritual calendar and it is probable that the headdresses in the form of *Cipactli* on the temple also have a calendaric significance as, for most Mesoamerican peoples, *cipactli* was the name of the first day of the cycle of 260 days.

The temple's symbolism referred to the ritual calendar and, in particular, to

the myth of the creation of time and the role that the Feathered Serpent played in that event.

If, as seems to be the case, the nearby residential complexes were the seat of Teotihuacan political power, it is probable (at least for a certain period) that the Feathered Serpent was the "patron" of the governors who ruled the city "where time began."

Perhaps less than a century after the construction of the Temple of the Feathered Serpent, a second pyramid (seen facing the temple) was built to hide the view of the older building. It is likely that this event was the result of important political changes at the apex of the Teotihuacan state as, in other places in the city, the images of feathered serpents were covered over or replaced by jaguars, and this new image appears to have remained the "patron" of the new governing class until the city's final decline.

32 top left
Steps of the Temple of
the Feathered Serpent.
Various sculptures of the
god's head can be seen
on the alfardas
(balustrades). On either
side of the steps,
headdresses in the form
of Cipactli (the
alligator, symbol of the
earth and first day of
the ritual calendar) rest
on the bodies of serpents.

32-33 Panoramic 2 miles
view of the Avenue of
the Dead from the top
of the Pyramid of the
Moon. In the
foreground we see the
Square of the Moon
and, on the left, the
mass of the Pyramid
of the Sun.

2 miles long!

33 bottom right
Pyramidal bases in
Teotihuacan showing
the typical
alternation of talud
(sloping batter) and
tablero
(quadrangular panel
with inset) which was
practically a
trademark of the
architecture of the
city.

33 bottom left
Annex to the Temple
of the Feathered
Serpent. This building
was constructed in the
lee of the Temple of the
Feathered Serpent a few
decades after the temple
was built. The apparent
attempt to cover the

reliefs on the facade
(see right) suggests that
the construction of the
annex was linked to a
political change in
which the ancient
dominant class
"protected" by the
Feathered Serpent was
replaced.

34 top One of the buildings in the Complex of the Sun. It is possible to see how the squared, plastered and painted stones covered a central body of tezontle (porous volcanic rock) used to construct all the city's buildings.

34-35 Measuring 207 feet high and 722 on each side, the Pyramid of the Sun was one of the largest buildings in the New World. Its original form was built during the first stages of the city's development.

34 bottom View of the Avenue of the Dead. In the background the Pyramid of the Moon can be seen framed by the outline of the Cerro Gordo, the sacred mountain that was probably used as a model for the pyramid.

The Great Compound stands in front of the Citadel. It is an enormous rectangular platform that encloses a large plaza and, according to some scholars, may have been the site of the city market.

Proceeding north along the Avenue of the Dead, the visitor crosses the San Juan river that may have symbolized the threshold of the "ultramundane" section of the monumental center. The avenue is lined by large political and administrative complexes and temples, like the Overlaid Buildings complex, where it is possible to admire a platform painted with volutes and images of nasal ornaments made from green stone. Next come the East and West Complexes of the Avenue of the Dead which were religious or perhaps administrative in nature. The West Complex contains wall paintings and two overlapping stairways: the lower of the two is decorated at the sides with sculptures of serpents and the upper stairway (built at a later date) is adorned with the heads of wild cats.

The Pyramid of the Sun dominates the eastern end of the avenue. It stands 207 feet tall and has a four-sided base measuring approximately 722 feet on each side. It was built over a large cave-

35 top View of an administrative complex located on a side of the Avenue of the Dead. The four-sided pillars of the porticoes that surrounded the open terraces can be seen. It is thought that the complexes were used by priests responsible for the main religious celebrations in the city. In the background there is a large archaeological monticulo that has as yet not been excavated.

35 center Aerial view of the Pyramid of the Sun which was, in fact, probably dedicated to the rain god. The pyramid rises above a partially remodelled cave-sanctuary around which the pyramid was probably constructed.

sanctuary (probably a natural feature that was remodelled) which must have been one of the original reasons for construction of the original settlement. We do not know with certainty to which god the temple on top of the pyramid was dedicated and it is as well to recall that all the names of the buildings at Teotihuacan are late Aztec in origin and consequently may have nothing to do with the buildings' original functions. Some experts believe that the Pyramid of the Sun was dedicated to the god of water and thunder that the Aztecs called Tláloc as his temples were often found in caves that had the symbolic role of being the entrance to his underworld abode. The fact that the final room in the cave-sanctuary below the pyramid was divided into smaller rooms brings to mind the myth of Chicomóztoc ("The Cave of the Seven Rooms") which was the "original hollow" for many Mesoamerican peoples.

The stepped sections of the Pyramid of the Sun, like those of the Pyramid of the Moon, are the only ones that do not feature the *talud* (sloping batter) and *tablero* (vertical panel with projecting cornice) architecture seen everywhere else in the city and which was to become a sort of trademark of the Teotihuacan presence in Mesoamerica. In all probability, this style had not been developed at the time the two pyramids were built and the various remodellings practiced upon them in later centuries retained their "archaic" character.

35 bottom Pyramidal base along the Avenue of the Dead. The name of the avenue (from the Náhuatl word Miccaotli) — like many of the names of the buildings in the city — is of Aztec origin; it was derived from the fact that the Aztecs believed the side monticulos to contain tombs but modern research has shown this not to be the case.

pyramid) is the place where most of the city's water sources were sited. The smaller structure in front of the pyramid is a later addition that was built at the same time as the other bases that surround the plaza. Recent excavation inside the Pyramid of the Moon has unearthed tombs of sacrificed prisoners who were buried with jaguars, birds and offerings made from obsidian, green stone and shell.

The southwest corner of the Plaza of the Moon is occupied by two buildings, one on top of the other: the Palace of the Quetzalpapálotl ("Feathered Butterfly") and the Temple of the Feathered Shells. The central patio of the Quetzalpapálotl Palace (Xolalpan phase, 400-650 AD) has been substantially restored and is surrounded by a portico with pillars decorated with low reliefs of birds; the top of the portico is embellished with paintings and a series of *almenas* (merlons) in the form of the symbol of the year. Paintings on the side walls of Greek key patterns symbolize sectioned shells which were emblems of the planet Venus. From the patio one enters the Court of the Jaguars, the walls of which are painted with figures of the animal, some wearing a feathered headdress and playing a musical instrument in the shape of feathered shells. A sort of "comma" comes from the instruments to indicate that music is being played. The aquatic symbolism of these pictures is revealed by the drops that fall from the instruments and shells that surround the bodies of the jaguars.

Below the Palace lies the more ancient temple of the Feathered Shells (Tlamimilolpa phase, 200-400 AD). This name is given by the low reliefs that decorate the facade. On the low part of the outer base of the temple, pictures of birds can be seen from whose beaks water spurts out.

The site museum stands to the northeast of the Pyramid of the Sun where it is possible to see many masterpieces of Teotihuacan art and the reconstruction of some of the sacrificial tombs from the Temple of the Feathered Serpent.

36 top left Portico of the central terrace of Quetzalpapálotl Palace. The heavily restored portico has carved pillars that support a painted roof decorated with crenellations in the shape of symbols of the year.

36 bottom left Carved pillars in Quetzalpapálotl Palace. The low reliefs show birds of prey from the front and the side. The lower and upper frames of the reliefs contain symbols for water such as eyes and volutes.

36 top right Small altar inside an administrative complex that faces the Pyramid of the Sun. The rows of small stones in the walls show that the structure was built in a more modern era.

Heading north once more, the visitor passes a large wall painting of a puma; on the west side of the Avenue of the Dead it is possible to see the masses of one of the largest architectural complexes yet to be excavated, the "Plaza of the Columns." Passing by the Temple of Agriculture whose frescoes no longer exist, one enters the Plaza of the Moon surrounded by minor structures; the pyramid that dominates the plaza is in turn overshadowed by the profile of Cerro Gordo, the sacred mountain that forms the backdrop to the entire city. The original function of the Pyramid of the Moon is also unknown to us but it seems likely that it was dedicated to the goddess of terrestrial waters whose name in Náhuatl is Chalchiutlicue ("She with the Jewelled Dress.") The goddess was depicted in a large statue found in the Plaza of the Moon that has since been moved to the Museo Nacional de Antropología in Mexico City. The link between the pyramid and terrestrial waters is supported by the fact that Cerro Gordo (the "model" for the

36-37 The Pyramid of the Moon dominates the square of the same name. Important offerings have recently been found inside the pyramid. The base, decorated with talud *and* tablero *on the facade like the Temple of the Feathered Serpent and the Pyramid of the Sun, was later built against the original construction.*

37 top Pyramidal bases in the Pyramid of the Moon. All bases in Teotihuacan supported temples at one time but they have now disappeared.

37 bottom left Stairway that leads to the entrance portico of Quetzalpapálotl Palace in the southwest corner of the Square of the Moon. The sculpture of a jaguar with open jaws can be seen to the extreme right of the stairway.

37 Wall paintings in the Court of the Jaguars. The jaguars wear feathered headdresses on which feathered shells tinkle, hence the "commas" that indicate sound is being made.

THE RESIDENTIAL COMPLEXES

The residential complexes stretched out of view around the buildings in the monumental center. The complexes were proper blocks defended by walls inside which it is probable that groups of extended families lived that specialized in particular trades. The walls of these "quarters" were covered with splendid wall paintings which can still be seen in some complexes located outside the enclosure that marks the archaeological site.

TEPANTITLA

The residential complex of Tepantitla lies northeast of the Pyramid of the Sun. It contains famous wall paintings in Portico 2 of dozens of people dancing, singing and playing ball in a rural setting in which a stream emerges from a cave-spring inside a mountain. The entire scene is dominated by the figure of a god and surrounded by mouldings formed by intertwined serpents and the faces of Tláloc. It was long thought that the paintings in Tepantitla portrayed Tlalocan, the aquatic paradise under the rule of Tláloc that, according to Aztec tradition, was the destination of souls of those whose death was related to water (drowning, struck by lightning, dropsy, etc.). However, more detailed studies have shown that the main divinity seems to be the Great Goddess, a Teotihuacan deity that may have been identified with

the Aztec Chalchiutlicue. Although the precise meaning of the paintings is unknown, it is clear how it refers to the symbolic conjunction of goddess-mountain-water that can be seen in the monuments in the Plaza of the Moon.
The paintings on the walls of Room 2

38-39 Detail of the wall painting on the residential complex of Tepantitla known as Tlálocan. We see figures dancing, playing and

singing in a rural setting. Note the various butterflies and the large flowered "commas" that indicate the singing.

38 bottom Two priests presiding over the sowing ritual are shown in this wall painting in the Tepantitla quarter.

39 left Detail of the large fresco in Tepantitla known as the "Tlalocan" in which a figure is shown swimming.

39 top right One of the Great Goddesses that adorn Portico 2 at Tetitla; note the large plumed headdress and rich ornaments

39 bottom right This jaguar with the threatening appearance is part of the rich wall decoration in the White Patio at Atetelco.

Portico 1 still has traces of the original painting of a procession of coyotes and diagonal bands in the upper section delimit a series of panels containing the fragmentary images of warriors-coyotes. Portico 2 has a parade of coyotes and jaguars, the latter differentiated by their "grid-like" patterned coats. The upper section is divided into panels by a grid similar to the coats of the jaguars; the panels contain figures with large shell-like trumpets that blast out the "commas" that represent music. The lower part of Portico 3 is filled with dancing and singing warriors carrying arrows and slings and the upper part shows figures of warriors-birds of prey surrounded by intersecting bands below shields with the heads of birds of prey.

The representations in the White Patio in Atetelco demonstrate how the military was present at Teotihuacan in the form of orders of soldiers that were similar to the eagle and jaguar warriors of the Aztec era.

LA VENTILLA

La Ventilla is the name for various residential complexes to the southwest of the monumental center. The one known as Sector 1 was probably a political and administrative complex that contains the Temple of the Red Borders and the Plaza of the Chalchihuites. The temple is decorated with sectioned shells and polychrome volutes that resemble the iconography of the Gulf coast, and the Plaza with the figures of chalchihuites

in Tepantitla depict a procession of priests scattering seeds from which emerge "commas" representing music and singing. This was a typical impersonal representation of the Teotihuacan elite laying claim to their power by associating themselves with concepts linked to fertility.

ATETELCO

The large complex of Atetelco to the west of the city is where restoration work has provided us with a better understanding of the internal structure of residential complexes. They were organized around one or more patios in which the altar dedicated to the group's guardian deity stood. The altar in the form of a temple rebuilt in the center of the Painted Patio is an example.

The White Patio is the most famous in Atetelco. Three arcades on its sides are decorated with wall paintings from the Xolalpan phase (400-650 AD);

TETITLA

Tetitla residential complex lies close to Atetelco; it is the one that has the greatest variety of wall paintings and is perhaps that one that best gives the idea of how these multicolored complexes used to be.

Some of Tetitla's most famous paintings are of the individual collecting shells underwater (Portico 26), the spread eagles (Portico 25), the jaguars eating human hearts (Portico 13), the man-jaguar kneeling in front of a temple (Room 12) and, above all, the series of Great Goddesses on Portico 11.

These figures face the viewer head on, wearing enormous plumed headdresses and jade necklaces, earrings and nose ornaments.

Streams of water come from their hands containing various symbolic images.

(jade circles that were symbols of great value) and human hearts stuck through with sacrificial knives.

Sector 2 includes the Complex of the Jaguars, decorated with the silhouettes of mountains containing stars and orange jaguars crowned by human figures, and the Plaza of the Glyphs, in which the pavement is decorated with a series of elegant glyphs whose meaning is obscure. Also in Sector 2, a pavement beside a drainage channel shows an ithyphallic figure from whose organ a stream of water flows to the channel's drainage point.

Other paintings can be seen in Sector 4 whereas Sector 3, less interesting architecturally, contains a large number of tombs in which rich sets of stone grave goods were found, some of which are displayed in the Site Museum. It is probable that this was the residence of a family group that specialized in stoneworking.

TULA

history

The city of Tula was the capital of the Toltec empire and, although it only flourished for three centuries, it became a truly legendary city, the *Tollan* par excellence, from which the Aztecs claimed their power was derived.

Founded around 700 AD by groups of Nahua from the north (the modern states of Guanajuato, Querétaro, Zacatecas and Jalisco), Tula developed for about two hundred years as one of the many Epiclassic centers that enjoyed the vacuum of power left by the fall of Teotihuacan. During the first phase of construction, the settlement was limited to the area known today as Tula Chico that lies 1 miles north of the monumental center.

Around 900 AD, Tula Chico was abandoned and the new Tula Grande built on the top of the hill known as El Tesoro, partially in the image of the older settlement. Around a century later (1000-1050 AD), the monumental centre was rebuilt in its current form; in this phase Tula eventually covered 6 square miles and must have been home to several tens of thousands of inhabitants.

Toltec art has not provided us with individual portraits of governors and it is probable that Tula, like Teotihuacan, was governed by groups of nobles under the aegis of "divine patrons" such as the feathered serpent and the jaguar. The elite lived near the monumental center whereas most of the population – probably divided into family groups similar to the Aztec *calpultin* – lived in the many districts that excavation has shown to have been based on craft skills.

As had happened for Teotihuacan, Tula also became one of the most important centers in a large pan-Mesoamerican trading network that stretched as far as Nicaragua and the southern United States.

The means by which the Toltecs expanded their influence are unknown but it is possible that it involved military conquest (and consequently the creation of tribute paying provinces) and specifically commercial missions. It is also possible that the area directly dominated by Tula reached the valley of Puebla.

We do not know the causes of the unexpected crisis that led to the final abandonment of Tula around 1200 AD when many of the buildings were plundered and burned, perhaps by the citizens of Tula itself.

We can hypothesize internal class tensions or perhaps the collapse of the trading system that formed the primary source of the city's wealth, maybe as a result of the immigration of new groups into the area.

But Tula was not forgotten: the Aztecs visited the city and dug among the ruins of what they believed was *Tollan*, the source and justification of their power.

40 The famous Atlases of Tula that supported the roof of Temple B. They are typical images of Toltec warriors with small feathered caps, butterfly pectorals and a spear sling held in the right hand.

41 left Polychrome basalt sculpture of an Atlas. These sculptures supported stone slabs used as altars. Note the pectoral which was probably made from plaques of shell.

41 right Carved vase featuring a warrior with a helmet in the form of a coyote head, found at Tula. The mother-of-pearl shells it is lined with come from the Gulf of California whereas the central body of the article is made from plumbate pottery produced in Guatemala.

the site

The monumental center of Tula is laid out around a central square onto which the most important buildings face.

On the north side there stands Temple B, also known as the Temple of Tlahuizcalpantecuhtli or Venus as the Morning Star, i.e., one of the manifestations of Quetzalcóatl. The temple is a terraced pyramid with sides

at one time entirely lined with sculptural panels depicting jaguars, pumas and eagles eating human hearts in the lower part of the masonry. There are also images of warriors and Tlahuizcalpantecuhtli himself with a face that appears from the jaws of a jaguar.

The roof of the temple on top of the pyramid is supported by three rows of pillars.

The central row is formed by what are referred to as Atlases, i.e., four colossal stone figures in full relief of warriors each wearing a plumed headdress, a butterfly shaped pectoral, decorative discs on their backs and holding weapons in their hands. The row at the back consists of four-sided pillars with low reliefs of warriors, while the front row, unfortunately in very poor condition, was formed by cylindrical columns of feathered serpents that were probably very similar to those in the Temple of the Warriors at Chichén Itzá.

The rear of the pyramid is the location of a section of the Coatepantli ("Wall of Serpents") that marked the boundary of the sacred enclosure and formed the prototype of similar walls in Aztec cities.

The *coatepantli* at Tula is decorated with low reliefs of serpents devouring skeletal figures, Greek key patterns and a row of "merlons" in the form of sectioned shells.

To the west of Temple B stands the building known as the Burned Palace that was probably the seat of the Toltec government. It is formed by three large

42 top View of the Burned Palace. This type of structure with wide colonnaded rooms originated in northern Mesoamerica and, during the Post-Classic period, spread across Mesoamerica as far as Chichén Itzá. It is thought that the function of these rooms was linked to the large assemblies of warriors that must have been one of the most important ceremonies in the Post-Classic military states.

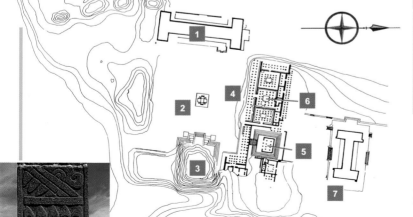

	T U L A
1	BALL COURT
2	CENTRAL ALTAR
3	TEMPLE OF THE SUN
4	GREAT COLONNADE
5	TEMPLE OF TLAHUIZCALPANTECUHTLI
6	BURNED PALACE
7	BALL COURT

42 bottom Detail of one of the pillars in Temple B. Note the sheaf of arrows tied with a complex knot.

42-43 View from Tula's tallest pyramid, Temple C. We can see Temple B, the Burned Palace and the colonnade in front of the two structures.

colonnaded rooms and a series of smaller rooms. The entire perimeter of the palace is surrounded by large colonnaded halls lined with white plaster like the front of Temple B. Inside there are several stone benches decorated with polychrome low reliefs of processions of warriors.

In the center of the main room of the palace, important offerings have been found including a wooden disc with 3000 turquoise tiles depicting four "serpents of fire," and a pectoral made

43 top Three rows of columns stood on the top of Temple B. The first row comprised cylindrical columns in the form of feathered serpents, the second Atlases, and the third four-sided pillars with low reliefs of warriors.

43 center right Pectoral consisting of shell pendants, and more than 1600 small plaques made of mother-of-pearl and the highly prized red shell, Spondylus. This pectoral was found as part of an offering in the center of the Burned Palace.

43 bottom Toltec stele with the figure of a warrior adorned with a headdress, earrings, a pectoral, and ornaments on his legs and sandals.

from 1600 plaques of red *Spondylus* shell. Both the disc and pectoral can be seen in the warrior's dress worn by the Atlases.

A very similar building to the Burned Palace but in worse condition marks the edge of the south side of the square. It is probable that this too was used for official functions.

As neither of these buildings seems to have been used for residential purposes, it is thought that the elite of the Tula population lived in the large platforms to the east of the plaza on whose surfaces many luxury objects imported from distant regions have been found.

The east side of the square is dominated by Pyramid C, the largest religious structure in the city. It is, sadly, in very poor condition, but it is thought to have been dedicated to Tezcatlipoca, Quetzalcóatl's "cosmic antagonist," or to the evening aspect of the planet Venus.

One of the city's ball courts lies behind Temple B; its I-shaped plan is similar to the one that bounds the west side of the plaza. Near to one of the ball courts, archaeologists have found a platform containing thousands of fragments of human skulls.

These were the remains of a *tzompantli*, the frame used to display the skulls of individuals sacrificed in the main square and probably also in the ball court.

Like the polychrome benches, the colonnaded rooms, the sculptures known as chac mool and the coatepantli, the *tzompantli* was also an architectural feature from the north; all were to become prototypes of similar objects used by the Aztecs. The presence of these features establishes Tula as the model that the Aztec artists and politicians were to study centuries later.

THE HISTORY AND MYTH OF QUETZALCÓATL AND TOLLAN

Quetzalcóatl, the lord of Tollan, was the central figure in a complex series of mythological events in which cosmology, mythology and history were inextricably entwined. The Nahua people used the name Quetzalcóatl ("Feathered Serpent") to signify both the ancient god of the Feathered Serpent and a "hero" – legendary or real is not known – who was the main character in a sort of epic cycle.

The god was one of the oldest in Mesoamerica. He participated in a cycle of creation and destruction with his antagonist Tezcatlipoca ("Smoking Mirror"), and he played a fundamental role in the creation of men, maize, the calendar and many other aspect of Mesoamerican culture. Some of his most important manifestations were Tlahuizcalpantecuhtli (Venus as the Morning Star) and Ehécatl, the god of the wind.

The human figure usually stands out from that of the god simply because he was referred to by his full name, *Topiltzin Quetzalcóatl*, preceded by his calendaric name *Ce Acatl* ("One Reed"). He was evidently a man who was considered divine which resulted in him becoming the spokesman and representative of the gods and him being conferred with the power to lead his people. Given the intimate relationship between the two figures, it is not surprising that is almost impossible to distinguish one from the other.

According to many documents from the Aztec and colonial era, Ce Acatl Topiltzin Quetzalcóatl was born in miraculous circumstances and, after retrieving the bones of his dead father, he became king of the city of Tollan ("The Place of the Reeds") where he built four temples and distinguished himself by the intensity of his ceremonial acts and his penitence. Under his leadership, Tollan enjoyed a time of splendor and the Toltecs, extraordinarily skillful craftsmen, transformed Tollan into a marvellous city.

The splendid reign of Quetzalcóatl ended when his adversary, Tezcatlipoca, persuaded him to get drunk which resulted in Quetzalcóatl committing an infringement of a ritual which led to his having to leave the city. Ce Acatl Topiltzin Quetzalcóatl then led a group of

followers east towards a place called Tlapallan where he was transformed into the Morning Star.

The Tollan of Quetzalcóatl became a sort of ideal city for many Mesoamerican peoples; the Aztecs, for example, claimed that the royal blood of their governors was derived directly from the reigning lineage of Tollan which they had acquired through marriage of Aztec lords with noble women from the city of Culhuacan where the Toltecs had taken refuge after Tula fell.

A clear division has been created among scholars who concentrate on identifying the historical substrate of this legend: some see Teotihuacan as being the only possible historical Tollan while others believe that it is to be found among the many other archaeological sites with names related to Tollan. The controversy was in some manner brought to a close when precise documentary evidence showed that the Tollan referred to in Aztec documents could be no other than the archaeological Tula in the state of Hidalgo. The migration of Quetzalcóatl east was confirmed by the extraordinary resemblance between the monuments at Tula and those at Chichén Itzá in the Yucatán where, from the 10th century, magnificent buildings in Toltec style were constructed. The Maya city would therefore have been the Tlapallan where Ce Acatl Topiltzin Quetzalcóatl arrived bringing with him the Toltec cult of the Feathered Serpent.

Despite this thesis being largely accepted today, particularly regarding the identification of the Aztecs' Tollan with the archaeological Tula, some experts have begun to doubt certain aspects of the event. First of all, Chichén Itzá seems very strongly to be a much more grandiose "sister" city to Tula rather than its copy but, more importantly, many of the ideological and political elements recognisable in the story of Quetzalcóatl appear to have originated at Teotihuacan: the cult of the Feathered Serpent as the god that created the calendar, his close links with the governors of a splendid city that was the location of superb craftsmen, the conflict between the Feathered Serpent and the jaguar, etc.

What is increasingly clear is that the combination of myth and historical

reality that we find in the documents must have been characteristic of a political and religious ideology that existed in much of Mesoamerica for centuries. If it is true that the Aztecs identified the ruins of Tula with ancient Tollan, it is also true that the place where the political and religious ideology linked to it took form was Teotihuacan, the city that in Aztec mythology had by then developed into the place of creation. Later in the book (see the box "Toltecs or Zuyuani"), we will see how these new analyses have made a strong contribution to our understanding of the history of the many "earthly Tollans" that arose in Post-Classic Mesoamerica.

44 Toltec sculpture of a figure whose face emerges from the jaws of a feathered serpent. It is probably a representation of Ce Acatl Topiltizin Quetzalcóatl, the mythical king of the city of Tollan.

45 Aztec sculpture of the Feathered Serpent, one of the most important deities in Mesoamerica, known to the Aztecs as Quetzalcóatl. One of the god's many attributes was his "patronage" of ruling lineages.

MÉXICO-TENOCHTITLAN

The capital of the Aztec empire was the most impressive city that the Spaniards saw on their arrival. México-Tenochtitlan stood on islands in the middle of Lake Texcoco and was, like Venice, an aquatic city; its islets were divided by canals but joined to the mainland by four large earthen causeways. The description by Bernal Díaz del Castillo of the Spaniards' advance along one of these roads is famous: "… when we saw so many populated cities and villages in the water and other great cities on the mainland, and that straight road that led to México, we stood there in admiration and said that they seemed to be the things and charms described in the book of Amadigi because of the large towers and temples and buildings that had water inside and were made from lime and stone; some of

our soldiers wondered if what they saw was not a dream."

Tradition has it that the city was founded in 1325 AD when the sight of an eagle perched on a prickly pear cactus plant brought an end to the long migration during which the Mexica people, who had left from the mythical Aztlan, had been led by their tribal god, Huitzilopochtli. In actual fact, we know that the Mexica were forced to settle on these rather undesirable islands by the Tepanecs, the strongest people in the region at the start of the 14th century Twelve years later, a group of dissident Mexica founded México-Tlatelolco, the twin city that soon rivalled Tenochtitlan until it was conquered by the Tenochca people (inhabitants of Tenochtitlan) in 1473 AD.

Although Tenochtitlan was certainly

the indigenous city best known by the Spaniards, we know very little of it from an archaeological point of view. After the conquest in 1521 AD, Cortés decided that Tenochtitlan should be transformed into the capital of New Spain and the frightening growth of colonial and modern Mexico City – which dried up the lake as one of its side effects – covered the remains of the ancient city, hiding the sacred enclosure that, according to the description by Bernardino de Sahagún, contained seventy eight monumental buildings, including some that stood higher than the Templo Mayor, the

empire's most important temple.

Although important Aztec ruins can be seen today in the Plaza of Three Cultures (in the center of ancient Tlatelolco), the best place for an appreciation of the majesty of ancient Tenochtitlan is the Templo Mayor, the religious and political heart of the empire which is today flanked by buildings of equal symbolic value such as the cathedral of Mexico City and the National Palace, in which the frescoes by Diego Rivera constitute a "temple" of the ideology of revolutionary and modern Mexico.

Before continuing to a description of

the ruins of the Templo Mayor, a short summary of what the colonial sources and archaeological excavation have revealed of the temple's symbolism is in order. The temple was in fact a model of the cosmos, the symbolic and real center of a city that, like a new Tollan, stood at the center of the universe.

The platform on which the temple stood was a representation of the earth that lay over the underworld; on this there stood two twin pyramids that represented the celestial levels of the cosmos. The pyramid to the north was crowned by the temple of the rain god

46 Sculpture of the head of a warrior-eagle with a helmet in the form of a bird of prey. Identification of orders of warriors with certain sacred animals (and therefore with the cosmic forces they represented) was well known during the Aztec epoch and had a long tradition in the continent, dating back at least to the Classic period.

46-47 Reconstruction of the sacred enclosed area of Tenochtitlan. It is dominated by the Templo Mayor with its two temples dedicated to Tláloc and Huitzilopochtli. The round temple opposite was dedicated to Ehécatl, the God of the Wind. The other buildings in the area include several temples, a tzompantli, a ball court, a school for sons of the nobility, and buildings where meetings of orders of warriors were held.

48 Large Aztec sculpture of Coatlicue, "She with the Skirt of Serpents," terrestrial goddess and mother of the Sun, the Moon and the Stars. Note the two-headed serpentine head, the necklace of human hearts and hands, the skull as a pendant and the skirt of snakes. The sculpture was found in 1790 and was considered so ghastly that it was buried again and left for several decades.

49 top left This Aztec sculpture was found in the Templo Mayor. Known as a cuauhxicalli, it has a hollow on the back that was supposed to hold the heart of a sacrificed prisoner. Human sacrifice and the wars fought just to win prisoners for human sacrifice played a fundamental role in the Aztec imperial ideology.

49 bottom left The low relief on the famous Stone of the Sun features symbolic elements and the Fifth Sun or "Sun Movement" surrounded by symbols of the four preceding suns and the names of the days of the calendar. The stone was a sacrificial slab on which prisoners of war were stretched out and killed.

Tláloc and symbolized Tonacatépetl, the "Mountain of Sustenance," a sort of "fertility store" from which maize was supposed to have come. The pyramid to the south was crowned by the temple of the warrior god Huitzilopochtli and represented Coatepec (the "Mountain of the Serpent") that was the setting of the gods' "astral activities;" these were clearly metaphors for the conflict between the Sun and the stars in the night sky. Local tradition told that Huitzilopochtli was born on this mountain to Coatlicue ("She with the Skirt of Snakes") and immediately had to face the hostility of his brother Centzon Huitznahua ("The Four Hundred of the South"), i.e., the stars, and his sister Coyolxauhqui ("Rattles on her Cheeks"), the moon. Huitzilopochtli defeated them with his magic weapon Xiuhcóatl ("Serpent of Fire") and threw their dismembered bodies down the sides of the hill.

49 top center Aztec terracotta sculpture from central Mexico. The figure shown is probably a priest wearing typical attributes of the god of death.

49 bottom right Aztec basalt sculpture of Teteoínnan, the "Mother of the Gods" and universal mother goddess of the Aztec pantheon.

THE TEMPLO MAYOR

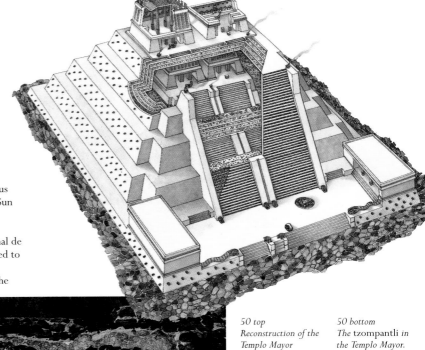

The correlation between the ancient ceremonial enclosure and the current central square in Mexico city has always been known, but knowledge of the exact locations of the ancient buildings and monuments were lost over the centuries until they began to be discovered by chance.

In 1790, two of the most famous Aztec sculptures were found, the Sun Stone and the colossal statue of Coatlicue, that today stand in the Mexica room in the Museo Nacional de Antropología. Although this find led to excavation, another chance find provided the spark that launched the

50 top
Reconstruction of the Templo Mayor showing how the double temple was remodelled seven times, each one encapsulating the one before, like Chinese boxes. The only one of the structures to have remained whole and completely visible today is the second. Note how the round sculpture of Coyolxauhqui stands directly below the temple of Huitzilopochtli.

50 bottom
The tzompantli in the Templo Mayor. What you see is the sculptural base adorned with images of skulls. The wooden rack that held the skulls of sacrificed prisoners rose above this base.

discovery of the Templo Mayor: in 1978, some workers found a large round sculpture of the dismembered Coyolxauhqui. Knowing that this had stood at the foot of the steps of the Temple of Huitzilopochtli – and therefore in the position where his brother had thrown the body – it was possible to locate the various structures that made up the Templo Mayor with certainty.

The large research project stimulated by the finding of the statue led to identification of the remains of the seven reconstructions (Epochs I-VII) that the Templo Mayor underwent

between 1325-1521. Today the ruins of many of these phases can be seen like layers of an onion cut horizontally with the best preserved, from Epoch II, in the center.

Very little remains of the later versions of the temple and the first version (Epoch I, ca. 1325 AD) cannot be seen because it is covered by the second version and submerged by the water table below the temple.

On entering the archaeological area, one immediately comes across the base platform (Epoch IVb, ca. 1470 AD) which is decorated with the bodies of undulating serpents, large braziers and

an altar topped by two frogs. Passing between the remains of a series of overlaid stairways, one reaches the temple area. In front of the temple of Huitzilopochtli there is a copy of the statue of Coyolxauhqui (Epoch IVb, ca. 1470 AD) below which a previous version of the sculpture can be seen that is made in stucco (Epoch IV, ca. 1454 AD).

Heading towards the older structures, the visitor passes a series of standard-holders resting on the Epoch III stairway of the temple (ca. 1431). The standard-holders may represent the Centzon Huitznahua defeated by the god.

51 top left
Polychrome Chac
Mool in front of
Tláloc sanctuary on
the Templo Mayor; it
dates from the second

phase of building of
the temple. The
purpose of the image
was to receive
offerings in the
hollow on its stomach.

It originated in
northern
Mesoamerica but
spread throughout the
cultural area during
the Toltec age.

51 top right Some of
the offerings buried in
the platform of the
Templo Mayor
contained masks of
Mictlantecuhtli, the
God of Death. This
example was made by
cutting a human skull
(probably of a
sacrificial victim) and
decorating it with
false eyes made from

shell and hematite,
and the nose and
tongue made from
flint sacrificial
knives.

51 center
Polychrome basalt
sculpture of a
serpent's head. This
sculpture can be seen
on the platform of
the Templo Mayor.

51 bottom Large
stone sculpture of
Coyolxauhqui. The
chance discovery of
this sculpture —
associated with the
fourth remodelling of
the temple — gave rise
to the Templo Mayor
Project and
excavation of the
entire temple
complex.

52 top View of the Templo Mayor at Tlatelolco with its large stairways that, like at Tenochtitlàn, lead to the temples dedicated to Tlaloc and Huitzilpochotli.

52-53 The monumental center of Tlatelolco, the twin city of Tenochtitlan. This was where the definitive battle between the Spanish troops and Aztec soldiers under Cuauhtémoc took place. The presence of the Aztec ruins, the colonial church of Santiago Tlatelolco and surrounding modern buildings has resulted in the city's central square being named the Square of the Three Cultures.

The two temples from Epoch II (ca. 1390 AD) have been almost completely preserved and give us a good idea of how the Templo Mayor must have looked in antiquity. To the south, to the right of the observer, Huitzilopochtli's temple is faced by a sacrificial stone on which prisoners were tied down for sacrifice before their bodies were thrown from the stairway during ceremonies that replayed part of the myth of Coatepec. To the north stands the Temple of Tláloc preceded by a polychrome Chac Mool, a sculpture on which offerings to the god were placed.

Immediately to the north of the Templo Mayor there are three other buildings from the sacred enclosure, all from Epoch VI (ca.1500 AD). Included is a *tzompantli* decorated by sculptures of skulls that was the support for the real wooden skull holder. Next to the *tzompantli* stands Temple C (known as the Red Temple) in Teotihuacan style decorated with red circles that symbolized water and great value; a similar temple stands on the south side of the Templo Mayor.

To the north of the three temples lies one of the loveliest architectural complexes in the enclosure, the House of the Eagles.

This complex (Epoch VI, ca. 1500 AD) comprises different sections with polychrome benches along the sides that are very similar to those at Tula. The benches are decorated with two rows of warriors that converge on the *zacatapayolli*, the straw ball in which the spines were placed that were used during ceremonies of self-sacrifice. Two life-size terracotta statues of eagle warriors were found in this complex.

Recent excavation of the north side of the enclosure (below the modern street

that runs alongside the archaeological area) has led to the discovery of two other large rooms with more than 98 feet of polychrome benches. Two large braziers representing the god Tláloc crying were found near the entrance and two terracotta statues of Mictlantecuhtli (the god of the dead) were found on the benches.

Mictlantecuhtli is shown as a skeleton with his liver hanging from his chest and with long finger and toe nails. His shoulders and head have holes dirtied with blood into which human hair was inserted.

Excavation of the Templo Mayor has turned up more than one hundred valuable offerings buried in the base platform and therefore, through

symbolism, in the underworld. These offerings contained exceptional items like stone statues (often representing Xiuhtecuhtli, the god of fire), objects made from jadeite, alabaster and obsidian, terracotta pots, the remains of sea and land creatures and, in one case, fabrics and painted paper ornaments. It is curious that some of the objects were found by Aztec excavations of Toltec, Teotihuacan and even Olmec materials that were already 1500 years old when they were used as offerings by the Aztecs.

Many of the offerings, such as the large terracotta sculptures, the original statue of Coyolxauhqui and many other treasures of Aztec art can be admired in the superb museum that lies behind the Templo Mayor.

53 top Detail of the ruins of Tlatelolco with an annex to Temple R in the foreground. The Temple of the Numerals or Calendar Temple can be seen at the top left; it is decorated with stone panels with low reliefs showing the names of the 260 days of the calendar.

53 bottom left Aztec sculpture found in the Templo Mayor representing Huehuetéotl, the Old God of Fire. This unusual Aztec version of the god is marked by distinctive elements of the rain god Tláloc (circles around the eyes and projecting canine teeth).

53 bottom right Life-size terracotta sculpture of a warrior-eagle. It was found with a "twin" sculpture in the House of the Eagles near the Templo Mayor. It dates from about 1480 AD.

THE MUSEO NACIONAL DE ANTROPOLOGÍA

The archaeological collection of the Museo Nacional de Antropología numbers 100,000 pieces if those not on display are included. Its twelve rooms are arranged around a large column fountain designed by the architect Pedro Vásquez Ramírez and classified by theme.

The visit begins in the rooms dedicated to anthropology, Mesoamerica and the origins of the Mexican people. The next room is devoted to the Pre-Classic period of the Highlands and contains the famous Olmec ceramics of Tlatilco and Tlapacoya. The Teotihuacan Room has masterpieces of the great Classic era city such as the mask with a turquoise mosaic, the scorer used in the ball game, the theater censers and the great sculpture of Chalchiuhtlicue, but the room is dominated by the life-size polychrome model of the facade of the Temple of the Feathered Serpent. The Toltec Room holds objects from Epiclassic sites like Xochicalco, Cacaxtla and Xochitécatl besides Toltec masterpieces such as the head of the warrior-coyote covered with shells, a chac mool and an Atlas from Temple B. In the monumental Mexican Room the visitor can admire an extraordinary range of Aztec sculptures including the Sun Stone, the Coatlicue, the Tizoc Stone and the sculpture of Xochipilli.

54 top This elegant Aztec stone shell is part of the collection in the Templo Mayor museum.

54 center Sculpture of a Chac Mool from Chichén Itzá. The name of the god ("Red Claw") is modern in origin and has nothing to do with the god himself.

54 bottom Teotihuacan stone mask with inserts of shell, obsidian and green stone earrings. This splendid example was found among Aztec offerings in the Templo Mayor and was probably obtained by the Aztecs when excavating in the ruins of Teotihuacan.

Moving on to the Oaxaca Room, there is a display of objects like the jade mask in the form of the Bat God, an exceptional set of Zapotec urns, some of the best examples of Mixtec jewellery and pottery, and two tombs with murals of Monte Albán which have been reproduced at actual size. The next room is the Gulf Room dominated by the colossal head no. 6 from San Lorenzo; there is also a fine collection of works from the Olmecs and other cultures that lived on the Gulf including a terracotta sculpture of the Fire God

55 left Terracotta polychrome censer from Mayapán. The censer dates from the Late Post-Classic period and shows the rain god Chac.

55 right Terracotta Zapotec vase representing a god wearing an extraordinarily complex costume.

from Cerro de las Mesas and some superb Huastec sculptures. The following room, the Maya Room, contains too many masterpieces to be listed but standing out among them all are architrave 26 from Yaxchilán and the reconstruction of Pacal's tomb with its splendid funerary goods.

The last two rooms are dedicated to northern Mexico (Casas Grandes, a non-Mesoamerican culture related to the Pueblos that lived in the United States) and western Mexico and contains a lovely range of terracotta sculptures.

THE MUSEO DEL TEMPLO MAYOR

The museum, remarkable also for its construction, stands just behind Templo Mayor and contains many of the objects found during excavation of the temple. In the entrance there is a large model of the ancient ceremonial enclosure at Tenochtitlan and an object that is not archaeological in nature but of great importance: the Nobel Peace prize awarded to the Mayan, Rigoberta Menchú.

The eight rooms in the museum are named Predecessors, War and Sacrifice, Tribute and Trade, Huitzilopochtli, Tlaloc, Fauna, Agriculture and Historical Archaeology. A further room holds temporary exhibitions.

Among the many masterpieces in the Museo del Templo Mayor are the original circular sculpture of Coyolxauhqui, the large face of the same goddess, the large terracotta statues of

two warrior-eagles and two Gods of Death, the sculpture of the Old God of Fire and, above all, the many objects found in the offerings buried in the temple platform: vases, sculptures, sacrificial knives, masks made from human skulls, animal skeletons and jewellery made from precious stones. Particularly worthy of note are the ancient and exotic objects that the Aztecs offered to the gods, such as Olmec jade items, masks from Teotihuacan and sculptures from the state of Guerrero.

Also important are the bases of columns from sacred buildings from the colonial period below which the indigenous artists engraved the images of the God of the Earth Tlaltecuhtli who was secretly worshipped even during the period of the subjection of the indigenous world to the European one.

ITINERARY II

MORELOS, PUEBLA, TLAXCALA AND VERACRUZ: THE SACRED CITY OF CHOLULA AND THE SPLENDOR OF THE EPICLASSIC CENTERS

The regions that stretch immediately to the south and east of the Valley of Mexico are the best areas to have an understanding some of the ethnic, political and economic events that led to the end of the Classic period. Traditionally zones of transit between the central highlands and the two coasts, the modern states of Morelos, Tlaxcala, Puebla and Veracruz boast spectacular archaeological sites that commemorate a sequence of complex historical and ethnical events.

All these regions during the Classic period were more or less directly part of the Teotihuacan sphere of influence and some of the city's primary means of expansion. Morelos valley was the main area through which the commercial route ran between the central highlands and the rich tropical depression of the river Balsas and the Pacific coast. The Puebla-Tlaxcala valley, on the other hand, was the obligatory place of passage of the communication routes that joined the highlands to the Gulf coast and the world of the Maya.

Cholula was a site in Puebla valley that has been continuously inhabited from the Pre-Classic period until today and was certainly the most important Classic city in the region. For centuries it dominated the southern part of the valley and was in constant contact with the settlements in the "Teotihuacan corridor" at the north end of the valley that joined the city to the Gulf coast from 600 AD onwards. El Tajín became the most important regional center in the north where the millenary

cultural tradition of the Huastecs flourished. In the southern part of the coastal region close to the Epi-Olmec site of Cerro de las Mesas, stood Matacapan, a Teotihuacan colony on the Gulf that was probably established to control the commercial route that brought the tropical goods from the Maya area and Gulf region to Teotihuacan.

When Teotihuacan was hit by the crisis at the end of the Classic period, all the regions that had lain within its political orbit became the theater of mass migrations of peoples and of the establishment of new sites that during the Epiclassic period threw the ethnic and political landscape of Mesoamerica into confusion.

Centers like Teotenango (Toluca), Xochicalco (Morelos), Cacaxtla (Tlaxcala), Cantona (Puebla) and El Tajín (Veracruz) are perhaps the best examples of those political centers that profited by the great crisis that occurred during the Classic period, and they stimulated an intense but brief artistic and cultural development. The art of the Epiclassic era was distinguished by an eclectic and sophisticated style that seems to have merged elements from various regional traditions and was a clear reflection of the ethnic melting pot that Mesoamerica had become in the period.

The warlike and dynamic political landscape of the Epiclassic period underwent profound reorganization between 900 and 1100 AD when new ethnic and political frameworks began to

take shape that were to dominate the Post-Classic period. The Tolteca-Chichimeca settled in the area of Puebla, the Otomì occupied the northern part of Tlaxcala valley and the Totonacs expanded their control over the Gulf coast. These developments made it possible for some of the most important Post-Classic settlements to be established like Cholula, Tlaxcala and the Totonac centers of Tuzapan and Cempoala; all these cities prospered until the arrival of the Spanish. Tlaxcala, which had remained unconquered even by the Aztecs, became the principal ally of the Spanish during the conquest of Mexico and contributed substantially to the defeat of the imperial armies.

56-57 Low relief decoration of the facade of the Temple of the Feathered Serpents at Xochicalco. The detail shows of the head and body, decorated by signs which represent sectioned shells. The association between the Feathered Serpent the shell and the planet Venus lasted until the Conquest period. In sites like Xochicalco during the Epiclassic, the political ideology that centered on the Feathered Serpent (Teotihuacan in origin) was redrawn to create the zuyuana ideology that was typical of many multi-ethnic regimes during the Post-Classic period.

XOCHICALCO

history

Construction of the monumental center of Xochicalco ("Place of the House of Flowers") began in 650 AD in the western part of the Morelos valley. It was the work of several different groups that joined together to create a power center that replaced the increasingly weak dominion of Teotihuacan over the valley. Like many other Epiclassic centers, the ruins of Xochicalco display a defensive architecture, evidence of the warring political situation of the era.

During the Classic period, the Morelos valley had been a trading area through which tropical products such as cocoa beans, plumes, cotton and green stone passed from the south and west towards Teotihuacan. During the Epiclassic period (650-900 AD), Xochicalco cut its relations with the central highlands but continued trading with regions like Guerrero, Mixteca, Michoacán, the Puebla-Tlaxcala valley and the Gulf coast. It is probable that the rise of settlements like Xochicalco

played a notable part in the crisis suffered by Teotihuacan during the Classic period by in some way diminishing trade with the city "at source" and investing their resultant new riches in their own development.

The end of Xochicalco was as rapid as its establishment had been and, around 900 AD, the city was destroyed and abandoned, probably caused by an internal revolt. The buildings were burned down and many of the sculptures were damaged. A short while later, the new center of Miacatlán replaced it at the apex of the regional hierarchy.

58-59 Altar in the Square of the Stele of the Two Glyphs topped by the stele of the same name at Xochicalco. Structure E, the main pyramid, can be seen in the background.

58 bottom left The main square at Xochicalco with the Temple of the Feathered Serpents.

58 bottom right Funerary mask and green stone necklaces found in tombs at Xochicalco. The style

of the funerary mask clearly shows how the art of the city was in many instances derived from that of Teotihuacan.

the site

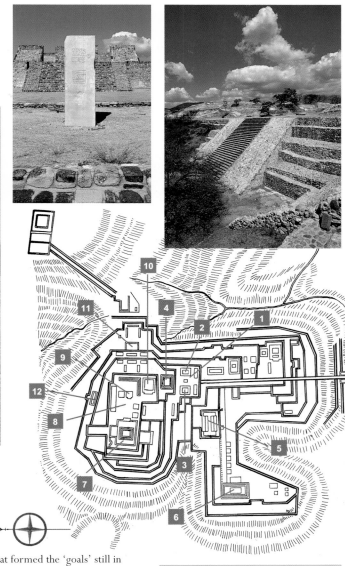

Xochicalco covers two square miles much of which crowns the tops of seven hills. The buildings are laid out on terraces defended by natural precipices and large vertical walls as well as by an elaborate system of ditches and trenches. The central section of the settlement lies on Cerro Xochicalco while the residential quarters cover the large manmade terraces on the sides of the hills.

The city is entered from the south across a ramp that led to the Square of the Stelae with Two Glyphs in the southern section of Cerro Xochicalco. A large pyramidal building (Structure E) overlooks the north side of the square and temples C and D to the east and west respectively. An altar topped by a large stele decorated with the glyphs '10 Reed' and '9 Reptile Eye' stands in the center of the square where the main collective ceremonies were held.

The architectural complex on the top of the hill named Cerro de la Malinche can be seen from the square; it comprises several buildings and the largest ball court in the city with the

rings that formed the 'goals' still in position on the sides. The court was found to contain a sculpture in the form of a parrot, a solar animal that referred to the astral significance of the game. On the other side of the ball court, "Malinche Avenue" leads to a religious building, a magnificent palace and the large Malinche Pyramid which takes its name from the stone female figure on the top.

---

59 top left
The Stele of the Two Glyphs. This is a copy of the original and shows the two glyphs: '10 Reed' and '9 Reptile Eye.' Structure C can be seen in the background.

59 top right One of the entrance stairways to the upper part of Xochicalco. The remains of the structures that shaped the acropolis of the Epiclassic city are visible behind.

X O C H I C A L C O
1 SQUARE OF THE STELE WITH TWO GLYPHS
2 TEMPLE C
3 TEMPLE D
4 PYRAMID E
5 SOUTH BALL COURT
6 MALINCHE PYRAMID
7 ACROPOLIS
8 CERIMONIAL PLAZA
9 TEMPLE OF THE FEATHERED SERPENTS
10 STRUCTURE A
11 EAST BALL COURT
12 NORTH BALL COURT

To the north of Pyramid E stands the highest complex in the city. The top of the hill is occupied by the Acropolis, a vast architectural complex where members of the Xochicalco elite would have lived. It is composed of two-story residential buildings arranged around patios and joined by ramps, stairways and structures of various function, for example, the storehouses and a *temazcal* (steam bath).

The Acropolis faces the Main Plaza, in the center of which stands Xochicalco's most famous building: the Temple of the Feathered Serpents. Its *talud* and *tablero* base stands over 13 feet high and supports the bottom of the walls of the temple that once stood there. Each *talud* of the base is decorated with low reliefs of the bodies of two feathered serpents and jaws wide open. The coils of the serpents' bodies contain six figures wearing large headdresses (probably governors of the city), two '9 Reptile Eye' glyphs and symbols that refer to the ceremony of the New Fire. Although many of the iconographic elements are clearly derived from Teotihuacan, others, like

the crossed legs of the figures, demonstrate a Mayan influence that probably arrived via the Gulf coast.

Thirty figures wearing headdresses are shown with the "speech comma" and an incense bag seated in front of an enigmatic sign on the vertical cornice of the *tablero*. The sign is composed of an open mouth that appears to be eating a circle containing a cross (probably a symbol meaning "precious"); in addition, a different glyph appears to the side of each individual.

Many suggestions have been made regarding the meaning of these figures but two in particular have found most consensus: the first identifies the reliefs of the *tablero* with the onomastic glyphs of the various cities conquered by Xochicalco; in this meaning, the complex "mouth that devours preciousness" signifies the act of conquest or collection of tribute. The second, and less convincing, hypothesis proposes that the figures are priests who have gathered on the occasion of the eclipse of the sun in the year 743 AD, a phenomenon symbolized by the jaws and circle.

60 top left View of the Temple of the Feathered Serpents. Note how the talud-tablero architecture originally Teotihuacan in origin has been developed by the architects of Xochicalco. The talud is much higher and the tablero has a projecting cornice.

60 center left Figures probably identified with the rulers of the city sit among the coils of the feathered serpents at Xochicalco. Note how the man is portrayed with many Mayan stylistic elements, a demonstration of the eclectic styles that distinguished the Epiclassic.

60 right Stele 2 at Xochicalco found with stelae 1 and 3 in the Temple of the Stelae. The main face of Stele 2 shows — from top to bottom — glyph 7 Rain, the face of Tláloc with a headdress in the sign of the year, and a pectoral with the jaws of Tláloc.

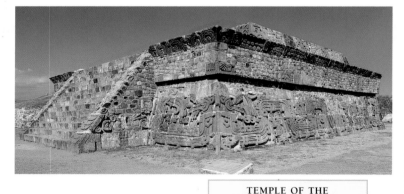

TEMPLE OF THE FEATHERED SERPENTS

1 SEASHELLS, SYMBOL OF THE WIND
   AND THE FEATHERED SERPENT
2 CALENDRIC SYMBOL
3 SCALES OF THE FEATHERED SERPENT
4 FEATHERED SERPENT
5 CALENDRIC SYMBOL

One of the most discussed reliefs at Xochicalco is the one that shows a hand emerging from a calendaric glyph and pulling a cord tied to another glyph which can be seen on the *talud* to the left of the stairway in the Temple of the Feathered Serpents. It was long believed that the image alluded to an alteration in the calendar decided upon by a group of priests-cum-astronomers depicted in the figures on the Temple of the Feathered Serpents who met in Xochicalco. This hypothesis no longer receives much credit but the true sense of the low relief still remains obscure to scholars.

Excavations in the temple of the Feathered Serpents have disclosed that it was built over three different periods though within a particularly short arc of time.

In one of the oldest structures the builders buried a rich set of offerings containing shells, small sculptures, terracotta bowls and a splendid alabaster pot painted using the fresco technique.

Structure A is a large platform to the south of the Temple of Feathered Serpents with an arcade on top that gives entrance to a patio surrounded by three buildings. The central building is known as the Temple of the Stelae because the very lovely Stelae 1, 2 and 3 were found inside; they had been ritually "killed" and buried in a trench. To the north a temple in the same shape as that of the Feathered Serpents was decorated with paintings rather than low reliefs.

On a lower level past two other buildings that surround the patios to the east of the Ceremonial Plaza lies the East Ball Court and the ramp composed of 252 stone slabs sculpted with the images of creatures like butterflies, birds and serpents. The North Ball Court lies on a lower level to the north of the plaza.

One of Xochicalco's most mysterious sectors is the one to the northwest known as "The Vaults" consisting of a series of manmade caves whose function other than being a source of building materials remains unknown.

It is certain that at least some of the caves had an astronomic function because in the one known as the "Observatory" the sun's rays penetrate a hole in the roof twice a year (May 14-15 and July 28-29) and project the hexagonal outline of the hole onto the pavement.

60-61 Head of one of the Feathered Serpents that decorate the facade of the temple of the same name.

61 bottom right View of the interior of the Temple of the Feathered Serpents. We see part of the tip of a previous version of the temple.

CHOLULA

history

Cholula was one of the longest lived religious centers in Mesoamerica; it has been inhabited uninterruptedly since the Pre-Classic period and made famous by the largest pyramid in the American continent. Following early occupation during the Pre-Classic era (500-200 BC) close to a lake that has since dried up, the settlement was slowly transformed into a vast monumental center of temples and sculptures over the early centuries AD. Throughout the Classic period, Cholula was the primary center of power in Pueblo valley and it is calculated that between 400-500 AD the city was home to thirty thousand inhabitants. It had close ties with the peoples on the Gulf and with Teotihuacan and, with the latter, divided dominion of the Pueblo-Tlaxcala region.

Around 650 AD, Cholula experienced the culminating moment of a serious crisis marked by the sudden arrival in the region of new ethnic groups, some of which may have originated from the declining Teotihuacan. The Olmeca-Xicalanca – a group with close cultural

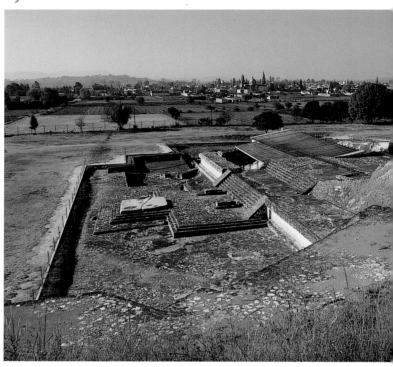

links with the peoples of the Gulf and the Maya of Campeche – dominated the area of Cholula during one of the darkest periods in its history when it was overshadowed by the importance of the new Olmeca-Xicalanca capital of Cacaxtla. We know that during this period, the city was governed by two lords: the Olmec lord *Tlachiyach Tizacozcue* who was associated with the land, and the Xicalanc lord *Aquiyach*

Amapane whose realm was water and who resided on the great pyramid.

At the end of the Epiclassic period, further social changes helped to consolidate two new ethnic and political spheres in the valley of Puebla-Tlaxcala. The northern part of the region was dominated by the development of an Otomì seigniory that held power until the 16th century, and the southern part was occupied by a group that had

emigrated from Tula, the Tolteca-Chichimeca. These new arrivals settled at Cholula and chased out the Olmeca-Xicalanca during the 12th century.

The *Historia Tolteca-Chichimeca*, a document in the Náhuatl language from the second half of the 16th century, tells the story of how the Tolteca-Chichimeca people emigrated from Tula under the leadership of their king-priest Couenan who went to do penance in the large religious center of Cholula where Quetzalcóatl, who was miraculously manifested there, convinced him to settle with his people. The Tolteca-Chichimeca lived in Cholula with the Olmeca-Xicalanca from 1168 AD until, inspired by the god Tezcatlipoca, they took over control of the city.

Under the control of the Tolteca-Chichimeca, Cholula flourished once more and became *Tollan Cholollan*, one of the many Tollans in Mesoamerica, and the site of a very important sanctuary dedicated to the cult of Quetzalcóatl. The name *Tollan Cholollan* ("The Place of Reeds of those who Fled") was added to with the suffix *Tlachihualtépetl*

62-63 The photograph shows the Great Pyramid surrounded by a series of satellite buildings, plazas and stairways.

62 bottom Restoration using the original materials has recreated a section of the immense stairway that rose to the top of the Great Pyramid. Its original volume of roughly 141 million cubic feet probably makes it the largest monumental structure built by man.

63 top The monolithic stele stands in front of one of the stairways that faces the Great Pyramid.

63 bottom Excavations around the Great Pyramid turned up this monolithic sculpture of the head of a man-jaguar.

the site

The monumental center of Cholula today consists essentially of the great pyramid and nearby structures. These belong to the Classic period since the monumental center built during the Post-Classic period was destroyed by the growth of the colonial and modern city; the famous Temple of Quetzalcóatl, for example, was covered by the Monastery of San Francesco.

At 203 feet tall and covering sixteen hectares of land, the Great Pyramid is the largest structure in the New World, though today it only appears like a hill topped by the 18th century Catholic church of Nuestra Señora de los Remedios. 5 miles of tunnels dug inside the structure have revealed its architectural history, showing that it was built over four phases between 200 BC and 800 AD. The first construction was in some ways similar to the Pyramid of the Sun in Teotihuacan, with large taludes separated by narrow horizontal surfaces. Additions of various buildings in Teotihuacan style with taludes and tableros painted with images of what

formed by a massive nucleus of adobes (sun-baked mud bricks).

In addition to the various construction phases that can be recognized inside the tunnels, excavation has revealed several other structures. A large base with taludes and tableros from the third construction phase was built on the front of the pyramid and other buildings and sculptures made from stone can be seen on the south side. This is the area of the famous "Drinkers" wall painting (unfortunately closed to the public) that shows various figures with birds' faces drinking pulque (fermented agave juice).

Sculptures decorated with elegant volutes on the Courtyard of Altars reveal the close contact between Cholula and the Gulf coast at the end of the Classic period.

The Great Pyramid should not be confused with the famous temple of Quetzalcóatl that made Post-Classic Cholula famous. It is probable that the pyramid was dedicated – like the Pyramid of the Sun at Teotihuacan – to the rain god Tláloc. This hypothesis is based on the resemblance of the two buildings and on several pictorial decorations of shells; confirmation seems to have been established by a description from the year 1581 of the pyramid being crowned by a temple containing an idol called chiconahuiquiáuitl, literally "New Rain." According to the Historia Tolteca-Chichimeca, a great block of jade in the form of a toad fell onto the top of the pyramid and toads were animals associated with the underworld and aquatic regions. It was probably from this legend that the two other names by which the pyramid is known were derived: Chalchiutepec ("Mountain of Jade") and Cholollan-Tamazol-Xamiltepec, in which the last two terms mean "toad" and "mountain of mud bricks."

It is interesting to note that the cult of the Virgen de los Remedios that now stands on top of the pyramid was principally centered on the propitiation of rain.

("Mountain made by Hand") which was a clear reference to the great Classic pyramid that still dominates the ancient monumental center. The city under the Tolteca-Chichimeca re-established contact with central Mexico and, during the Post-Classic period, Cholula became the main center of the refined Puebla-Mixteca artistic tradition known for its polychrome pottery and pictographic symbols. We know that many rulers of different Mesoamerican regions travelled to Cholula-Tollan to receive a sort of official investiture by the god Quetzalcóatl and his earthly representatives.

Cholula's renewed power lasted for centuries and the city was still prosperous when the Spaniards arrived; it was here that the Europeans perpetrated one of the most violent massacres in the history of the conquest of Mexico. Since then, the city's status as a religious center of great importance has been maintained by the large number of churches built which are traditionally numbered at 365, one for each day of the year.

seem to be the faces of insects or human skulls were added from around 200 AD, then, around the year 300 AD, a new great pyramid was built that incorporated the earlier structures and added new buildings. The final construction, the gigantic pyramid visible today, dates from 800 AD and is

CACAXTLA

history

The development enjoyed by cities in the Tlaxcala valley of the Pre-Classic period is revealed by the large structures in the monumental center of Xochitécatl but, during the subsequent Classic period, the peoples in the valley had to face the expansion of Cholula in the southern half of the valley and of Teotihuacan with the "Teotihuacan corridor" through the northern part.

Like many Epiclassic artistic expressions, their style fuses elements of Teotihuacan iconography with a dynamism and chromatic range that clearly demonstrate a Mayan influence and display that intricate interaction of ethnic and cultural values that was the distinctive mark of the Epiclassic period. The rule of the Olmeca-Xicalanca over Tlaxcala valley was

64 View of the ruins of Cacaxtla palace in the region of Puebla-Taxcala; the volcano Ixtlacihuatl looms in the background.

64-65 Detail of a frieze of red painted stucco showing a warrior wearing a headdress and earrings. The influence of Mayan art is clearly apparent in all of the decorations at Cacaxtla, and this is rather surprising considering that Cacaxtla lies only 70 miles from Mexico City. The conclusion must be that cultural exchanges between the various Mexican regions were very active during the Epiclassic period.

When these two large Classic centers entered a period of serious decline (ca. 650 AD), the arrival of new ethnic groups in the valley gave rise to a cultural renaissance.

Groups raised in the cultural sphere of El Tajìn on the Gulf coast settled in the "Teotihuacan corridor" area and groups of Otomí, Mixteca and Olmeca-Xicalanca occupied other areas of the valley.

It was the Olmeca-Xicalanca from Cholula who founded the capital of Cacaxtla around 600 AD close to the ancient center of Xochitécatl ("The Place of the Lineage of the Flowers") which was also reoccupied and enlarged. The monumental center of Cacaxtla ("The Place of the Merchant's Bundle") was located in a defensive position on the top of a low hill protected by walls and earthworks, and decorated with paintings that were some of the most splendid in Mesoamerica.

thrown into confusion by the arrival of new ethnic groups between 900 and 1100 AD that took possession of Cholula and by the rise of powerful and prosperous territories under the Otomì and Tlaxcalteca who dominated the valley until the arrival of the Spanish.

the site

Cacaxtla archaeological site essentially comprises a large fortified complex containing residential structures that divide the area into two squares surrounded by the main sacred buildings.

The important Pre-Classic site of Xochitécatl lies on the mountain that overlooks Cacaxtla and the two

probably formed a joint city following occupation of the latter.

Cacaxtla's North Plaza is surrounded by a large porticoed structure with a base decorated with the famous Battle Mural. It shows an armed clash in which jaguar warriors painted with animal skins defeat eagle warriors who wear large plumed headdresses. The Mayan derivation of the extremely crude and realistic representation is evident in the unusual dynamism of the scene and the widespread use of light blue.

The two main scenes are to the sides of the central stairway and depict the capture of two eagle warrior chiefs; the chief on the right is shown as he extracts a spear from his face, while the one on the left stands still with his arms crossed, wrapped in a sort of white cloak adorned with symbols of the planet Venus.

Innumerable interpretations have been offered of the scene which tend to

fall into two groups: those who think the battle a historical event, i.e., the victory of the Olmeca-Xicalanca over some other ethnic group, and those who consider it symbolic of a clash between cosmic forces or, more probably, between power groups identified with these forces.

Along the west side of the plaza, we reach the Red Temple in which the two walls to the sides of a stairway are decorated with paintings from an earlier period to the Battle Mural. An old man wearing a jaguar skin stands in front of the large bundle of a merchant (*cacaxtli* in Náhuatl, from which the site's name is derived). On the bundle we see a headdress in the form of an animal, a turtle shell, bunches of plumes and what may be blocks of *copal* (incense).

In front of the figure (whose calendaric name may be '4 Deer' as seen in a glyph) there stand a cocoa

plant with a bird and two maize plants whose ears of corn are made up of human heads.

A large toad (painted blue on one wall and spotted like a jaguar on the other) and a second animal stand on the ground between the plants where a stream of water is shown by a band of

65 bottom In order to protect the delicate wall paintings and polychrome stucco work from atmospheric damage, many of the structures have been covered with permanent roofing. Their brilliance of color and skill of execution make the Cacaxtla paintings the loveliest in all Mesoamerica.

aquatic symbols and the body of a large feathered serpent that frames the entire scene. The entire painting features aquatic and underworld symbols but its overall meaning is not understood: the figure of the merchant (perhaps a guardian deity) and the traditional name of the site seem to refer to the role that trade had in the development of Cacaxtla.

An older step in the Red Temple is decorated with paintings of the bodies of prisoners and glyphs that probably indicate the names of conquered cities.

The pillars of the Temple of Venus on

66 top left Detail of the famous Battle Scene in which two eagle warriors have been knocked down by jaguar warriors; note the crude descriptive realism of the painting.

66 bottom left and center Turtles, molluscs, deer and other creatures embellish the cycle of frescoes so far discovered at Cacaxtla. The two details shown are part of the paintings in Portico A.

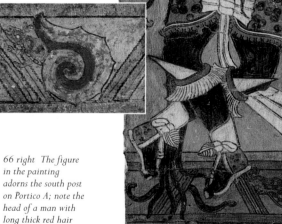

66 right The figure in the painting adorns the south post on Portico A; note the head of a man with long thick red hair emerging from a shell.

the southwest edge of the complex are decorated with two symmetrical human figures that appear to represent two aspects of the planet.

The more complete one is the man who wears a jaguar skirt with a large symbol of Venus, he has a large scorpion's tail and feathered scorpion's limbs that end in jaguar's claws. The man seems to float on a stream of water and is framed by a series of symbols of Venus similar to those on the "cloak" of the chief eagle warrior in the Battle Mural. The second figure in the Temple of Venus is a woman who is shown with one breast visible and dressed in similar clothes to the man but without the tail or limbs of the scorpion.

The paintings in the Temple of Venus

show how this planet – whose cult was often characterized with close associations of war and the underworld – was at the center of the ideology of the Olmeca-Xicalanca; it is seen in the Red Temple-Temple of Venus complex, in the Battle Mural and also in more recent paintings found in Portico A that date from around 800 AD.

Portico A stands on a corner of the North Plaza adjacent to the Battle Mural but it was painted at a date after the Mural had been carefully lined by a layer of sand and buried below new buildings. The later pictures are of two figures, probably sovereigns, who support two large "command bars."

On the north wall, the man is completely dressed in a jaguar skin while

drops of water fall from his "command bar" (in his case a bundle of spears). Behind him, a large glyph represents '9 Reptile Eye' while smaller glyphs in front of his face may represent his calendaric name.

The scene is framed by an aquatic band and a speckled serpent with a large feathered tail. The figure on the south wall is dressed as a bird with a large beaked headdress and the talons of a bird of prey; his "command bar" is in the more traditional form of a two-headed serpent. A bird and the glyph '13 Feather' are painted behind him.

The jambs next to the figures are also decorated with (more recent) low reliefs and the paintings of two human figures: the one on the north jamb is

dressed as a jaguar and pours water from a vase decorated with the effigy of the rain god, Tláloc; the figure on the south jamb wears an extraordinary headdress that falls to his feet and holds a large shell from which a small figure with red hair emerges. Both figures are flanked by the glyph '7 Reptile Eye' while the second is also shown with a large '3 Deer.'

Although the paintings in Cacaxtla belong to different periods, there is a constant reference to symbols of water and the planet Venus and to the clash between the jaguars and feathered beings.

As already seen in the myth of the dispute between Quetzalcóatl and Tezcatlipoca and in the organization of Aztec soldiers at Teotihuacan, these concepts are often associated with

political events and the presence of military orders involved in "cosmic battles" like the one at Cacaxtla. The dual conception of power that emerges from interpretation of the paintings at Cacaxtla matches the ethno-historic data relating to the two Olmeca-Xicalanca rulers that governed the city of Cholula during the same period.

El Tajín

history

The central area of the coast of the Gulf of Mexico where the modern state of Veracruz lies has always enjoyed prosperity owing to the extreme fertility of its soil and its position as an obligatory area of passage for the traders that headed towards the region of the Maya. During the Classic period, El Tajín dominated the political landscape of the region and had close links with Teotihuacan, Cholula and the Teotihuacan enclave of Matacapan.

After the collapse of Teotihuacan's power, El Tajín benefited from a period when it reached its cultural apex and generated a spectacular architectural and sculptural style. The city was home to about twenty thousand inhabitants; it controlled large deposits of obsidian and dominated the central region of the Gulf with the military power of its rulers, for example, 13 Rabbit who was the protagonist in many war scenes sculpted in low reliefs in the city.

Identification of the people that built El Tajín is a complex historiographic problem. It was long thought that the city had been constructed by the Totonaca, the ethnic group that ruled the central section of the Gulf coast at the time of the Spanish conquest, but today it is believed that the Totonacs only arrived in the zone during the 8th century. Some scholars claim the Totonacs settled in El Tajín when it was a multi-ethnic center and contributed to its late development, learning the artistic and architectural styles that they were to develop in their own Post-Classic cities.

68-69 View of Structure 16 which marks the north side of the Square of El Tajín Torrent.

68 bottom Terracotta sculpture from El Zapotal (Veracruz). It shows a figure wearing a curious headdress. The circles around the eyes seem to associate him with the rain god.

69 center Building C at Tajín Chico, decorated with the Greek key pattern typical of the art and architecture of El Tajín. It is thought that the symbols represent sectioned shells and that they are therefore linked to the cult of Venus and the Feathered Serpent.

Others think that the Totonacs were responsible for the destruction of the city and the subsequent reorganization of the politics and economy of the region.

What is certain is that around 1100 AD, El Tajín was destroyed and abandoned and that the Totonacs founded a series of prosperous independent cities like Tuzapan and Cempoala, the latter being the first large Mesoamerican city that the invading Spaniards came to know.

EL TAJÍN

A PLAZA OF THE TORRENT
    GROUP
B BUILDING 5
C BUILDING 2
D PYRAMID OF THE NICHES
E BUILDING 3
F BUILDING 4
G THE TAJIN CHICO GROUP
H BUILDING OF THE COLUMNS
I PYRAMID OF THE ACROPOLIS

1-10 BALL COURTS

69 bottom View of a section of the low part of El Tajín. The ball court formed by structures 24 and 25 is in the center of the photograph.

the site

The monumental city of El Tajín is divided into a low, flat section and the upper part located on a hill. The first architectural complex the visitor comes across in the lower section is the Torrent Group (*Grupo del Arroyo*) in which monumental buildings 16, 18, 19 and 20 face onto the city's main plaza where large ceremonial gatherings and commercial activities were held. The architectural style of the city is already evident in these buildings: large pyramidal bases decorated with niches and mouldings that "lighten" their bulk and endow them with an orientalizing aspect.

Several of the city's seventeen ball courts can be seen around the Torrent Group, some of which are decorated with corner sculptures of the Earth Monster.

The South Court (to the north of the plaza) is famous for its low reliefs. The four corner panels show two scenes that take place before the game and two scenes after in which the players are sacrificed; the two central panels depict other ritual acts, for example, self sacrifice in the form of perforation of the phallus.

Heading north one reaches the city's best known religious complex dominated by the Pyramid of Niches which was probably a mausoleum for the ruler 13 Rabbit.

The seven levels of the pyramid are adorned with 365 niches that have a clear calendarial reference. On the stairway of the nearby Building 5 there is a sculpture of Tajín, the god of rain and lightning.

Continuing to the northeast, there is another dramatic structure, the Xicalcoliuhqui, which is a wall 101 feet long in the form of a Greek key and that contains two ball courts and other cult buildings.

The Greek key pattern is very common in the city and alludes to the sectioned shell that is one of the most important symbols of Quetzalcóatl and often used to form pectorals. Several

buildings that probably formed the residences of the city elite. A tunnel in Building D joined the residential area to the monumental center below. The whole of Tajín Chico is dominated by the large Building of Columns on the top of the hill that is thought to have been the city governor's residence.

Its columns are in the form of monolithic drums sculpted with historical scenes including the capture

of prisoners, sacrifices and offerings that often include the image of 13 Rabbit whose reign occurred at the city's period of greatest glory.

The many wall paintings and the fragments of full relief polychrome stucco sculptures found during excavation are indicative of the ancient splendor of the elegant buildings of El Tajín.

70 top The Pyramid of the Niches is partially covered by the profile of Building 5. The projecting cornices at El Tajín and the "lightness" given to the buildings by the use of niches have resulted in the style of the city being compared to that of the Far East.

wall paintings at El Tajín show feathered serpents in confirmation of the importance of the cult in the Epiclassic city.

The monumental section on the hill is known as Tajín Chico. It comprises a series of richly decorated residential

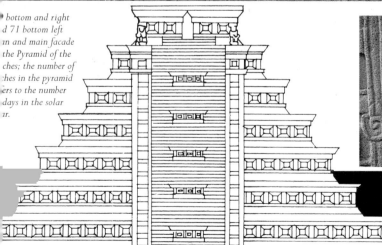

*bottom and right
d 71 bottom left
in and main facade
the Pyramid of the
ches; the number of
hes in the pyramid
rs to the number
days in the solar
ar.*

70 bottom left Low
relief from the south
Ball Court decorated
with a scene that
seems to show the
beginning of the

game. Two players in
the center seem to be
speaking; they are
equipped with belts,
"axes" and "palms."
Between them we see

the sign ollin
("movement") carved
above the ball that
lies close to their feet.
The other people at
the sides include a

god-coyote and the
God of Death on the
far right.
The scene is framed
by volutes typical of
El Tajín.

70-71 The famous
Structure 1 is known
as the Pyramid of the
Niches for the 365
that decorated its
facades in a clear
reference to the cycle
of the sun. Some
experts think this may
be the mausoleum of
the famous ruler,
13 Rabbit.

71 bottom right
Low relief of a god
with protruding
teeth handing a sort
of sceptre to a
dignitary. The
figure on the left
wears a star-shaped
symbol probably
associated with
Venus and
Quetzalcóatl.

THE BALL GAME

The ball game was one of the oldest and most widespread ritual game activities in Mesoamerica and seems to have been especially popular in the region of the Gulf of Mexico. There were seventeen ball courts at El Tajín (only exceeded by the twenty two in nearby Cantona) and this was the area where an extraordinary series of stone sculptures was found that shows the principal elements of the players' clothing: yokes, "axes" and "palms." The ball game was in fact played throughout Mesoamerica from the Pre-Classic period (the earliest courts have been found on the Pacific coast in Chiapas) to the time of the conquest when a large court occupied a place of importance in the sacred enclosure at Tenochtitlan.

The courts were normally in the shape of a capital "I" and often decorated by "scorers" of various types and low reliefs carved on the facings of the court. Some

of the most famous courts are those at Copán which have circular scorers with low reliefs placed horizontally on the ground and sculptures of parrot heads that bear a clear reference to the solar symbolism of the game (the parrot was the most common solar creature in Mesoamerican iconography). Strangely, the only large city that had no ball court was Teotihuacan but the games were played – as shown by paintings at Tepantitla – in open fields with the use of clubs and sculptural scorers fixed in the ground. One such scorer was found in the Teotihuacan complex called La Ventilla and another identical one at Tikal in an architectural complex built in Teotihuacan style.

The rules of the game and its symbolic associations are, unfortunately, not clear, nor do we know whether the rules of this thousand year old game remained the same geographically and temporally. We do know, however, that the players were protected by large leather belts, knee pads and gloves and were required to hit a heavy rubber ball; they could also use their shoulders and ankles with the aim of preventing the ball from bouncing on the ground. The end of the Classic period saw the introduction of stone circles placed vertically at the sides of the court something like the "baskets" in basketball. We also know that the side that managed to get the ball through the ring, a rare event, won immediately.

The most useful information on the symbolism of the game is to be found in the *Popol Vuh*, the Maya epic in which ball games between the twin heroes and the gods of the underworld are described. The astral allegory of the game is made clear from the "battle" held every night between the Sun and Venus during the twins' journey through the underworld.

The various episodes of decapitation referred to in the *Popol Vuh* highlight the analogy of the heads of the players to the ball which explains both the decapitation sacrifices illustrated at El Tajín and Chichén Itzá and the frequent images of balls containing human skulls. Despite the common rumor that it was the winner that was decapitated, there is no indication that this was the case and we can only imagine that sacrificial games were a sort of ritual staging in which it was clear from the beginning who was to

die, for example, when victorious kings, perhaps dressed like the twins in the *Popol Vuh*, played against kings defeated in battle. This is why the courts were thought of as gateways to the world of the dead, both symbolically and literally.

In addition to these ritual and symbolic aspects, there most certainly also existed a sporting factor that perhaps became more important with the passage of time. This is how Bernardino de Sahagún described the game at the time of the Aztec empire, *"The lord, perhaps as a pastime, played the ball game and for this reason they put by balls of Ulli; these balls were the size of large bowling balls and were*

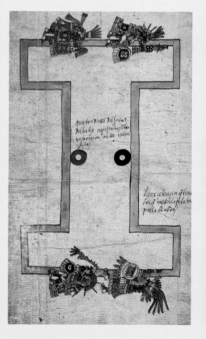

made solid of the resin or rubber known as
ulli, which is very light and bounces like a
ball filled with air; the lord captained a
group of good players who played in his
presence and other well known players on the
other side, and played for prizes of gold …
turquoise, slaves and rich coverings … and
fields of maize and houses and plumes and
cocoa beans and feathered vestments."

Sahagún and other Spaniards were
very struck by the rubber balls (uhle) – a
material previously unknown to
Europeans – and by the acrobatics of the
players, and a group of athletes were
sent to the court of Spain to perform
before King Charles V. In the Aztec
period although the ball game still had a
cosmological significance, the practice of
playing secular games spread out, during
which the audience could bet on the
match result. Even after the conquest,
the tradition was continued and several
versions of the game are still played in
some regions of northern Mexico.

*72 left Terracotta
figure from the Maya
regions of Guatemala.
The image of this
athletic player with a
belt at his waist as he
prepares to throw the
ball is unusually
realistic.*

*72 top right
Maya stele with the
image of a player
elaborately dressed in
the standard playing
costume and with a
complex head
covering. The players'
dress had reference to
the cosmological
symbolism of the
ritual ball game.*

*72 bottom right
Page of the Bourbon
Codex from the first
period of the colonial
era in which we see a
typical I-shaped ball
court with the two
rings at the side used
as "baskets" that were
common later in
Mesoamerica. The
figures at the sides are
supporters.*

*73 top Stone scorer
found at La Esperanza
near the Classic Maya
city of Chinkultic
(Chiapas). Note a
player in the central
section wearing a belt,
knee and elbow
coverings and a large
head covering as he
hits a large ball.*

*73 bottom Maya stone
scorer from the Classic
period showing the ruler in
the center and a Long
Count date in the outer
band. Generally, three
scorers of this kind were
arranged horizontally on
the ground along the
central line of the court.
Their exact function is
unknown.*

ITINERARY III

THE PEOPLES OF THE CLOUDS

The mountains of Oaxaca seem pressed down by the most majestic skies in Mexico and it is not difficult to understand why the principal peoples of the region had names meaning "The People of the Clouds." The region was home to many ethnic groups including the Zapotecs and Mixtecs whose millenary cultural traditions played an important part in the long formation of Mesoamerican culture.

During the Pre-Classic period, the urban centers in Oaxaca valley were leaders in the creation of social hierarchies and complex societies. As early as 1400 BC, the village site of San José Mogote (with 150 huts) had a public building and held sway over several satellite villages. Between 1150-500 BC, during the Middle Pre-Classic period, San José Mogote became the dominating center of the region: it had a population of 1400 and the threshold of one of its public buildings was a sculpture of a sacrificed prisoner.

The study of the relations between San José Mogote and the Olmec region is the one that has contributed the most to our understanding of the interactions between the Olmec culture and other regions of Mesoamerica. It was based predominantly on the trading of luxury goods and on mechanisms to legitimize its political power. The Zapotec elite imported green stone items, the spines of sea rays for purposes of self-sacrifice, shells, musical instruments and other prestigious articles that demonstrated their power. This also seems to have been the reason behind the early development of Zapotec writing which was one of the earliest ancient scripts in Mexico, perhaps the first.

From about 500 BC, the prestige of San José Mogote was eclipsed by the new city of Monte Albán which became the capital of the Zapotec state for all of the Classic period. The Zapotec elite ruled much of Oaxaca for centuries from its splendid monumental center and maintained strong relations with Teotihuacan by means of groups of emissaries that lived in the "Zapotec quarter" of the large capital of central Mexico. Zapotec architecture, sculpture and painting reached their peaks at Monte Albán and the city became one of the most important centers of cultural influence during the Classic period. Contemporary Zapotec cities were Lambyteco, Huijazoo and the smaller Mitla and Yagul. Like the other great capitals of the time, Monte Albán also suffered the crisis at the end of the Classic period and the subsequent Epiclassic period (750-1000 AD) in the Zapotec world was characterized by the development of sites like Zaachila, Jalieza, Mitla and Yagul; these centers were all destined to remain powerful and influential until the arrival of the Spanish and also to serve as a ground where the cultures of the Zapotecs and their neighbors, the Mixtecs, were able to meet.

The northwestern region of the state of Oaxaca, Mixteca was an area of passage towards the valley of Puebla-Tlaxcala and one of the few zones that of Oaxaca that remained independent of the Zapotec state.

This was the territory of the Mixtecs (in Náhuatl, "The People of the Clouds") who gave rise to a plethora of independent seigniories during the Pre-Classic and Classic periods and who extended their influence into the Puebla-Tlaxcala region after 650 AD.

The most important Mixtec Pre-Classic seigniory was Etlatongo in the Nochixtlán valley which developed at the same time as San José Mogote, but, during the Classic period, it was the small cities of Cerro de las Minas, Diquiyú, Huamelulpan, Monte Negro and Yucuita that dominated the Mixtec political landscape. The period of greatest development of these Mixtec seigniories coincided with the end of Monte Albán's Zapotec supremacy. Centers like Yucuñudahui and, later, Tilantongo, Chalcatongo and Yanhuitlán became the capitals of warring seigniories whose rulers became involved in a complicated set of political wars and wedding alliances that resulted in the extension of their power into the Oaxaca valley, where Cuilapan and Xocotlán were founded, and along the Pacific coast, where Tututepec may have lain. This was a period of intense interaction between the Mixtecs and Zapotecs: historical sources speak of mixed marriages between nobles while superb works of Mixtec art formed part of the grave goods of the dead buried in the Zapotec tombs of Zaachila, Mitla and Monte Albán.

For the whole of the Post-Classic period, Mixtec style was one of the most admired in Mesoamerica and contributed fundamentally to what is referred to as the Mixteca-Puebla artistic tradition which comprised a truly "international vocabulary" in Post-Classic Mesoamerica.

The political break-up of the Oaxaca region favoured the expansionistic aims of the Aztecs; for about sixty years after 1458 AD, the armies of the Triple Alliance carried out campaigns in Oaxaca where, with few exceptions, they succeeded in subjecting the local seigniories. It was much more difficult, however, for the Aztecs to keep control of these regions which, until the Spanish conquest, were one of the most uncontrollable and turbulent provinces of their empire.

75 Gold Mixtec pectoral found in Tomb 7 at Monte Albán. The figure has a skeletal face and has two calendrical signs on his chest with the names of the years, Wind and House. The high quality Mixtec funerary goods in this Zapotec tomb are evidence how the interethnic relations between the Zapotecs and Mixtecs increased substantially from the end of the Classic period with a resulting exchange of luxury items.

MONTE ALBÁN

Monte Albán stands on a hill at nearly 6562 feet of altitude where the three branches of the Oaxaca valley meet.

Defendable but a long way from the best farming land, this position was chosen around 500 BC by a confederation of Zapotec groups in the valley as the site of a new city that was to become one of the most splendid monumental centers in Mesoamerica and the powerful capital of the Zapotec state following the eclipse of power centers like San José Mogote.

During the phase Monte Albán I (500-200 BC), several important buildings were constructed such as the Temple of the Danzantes. During the phase Monte Albán II (200 BC-300

AD), the large central plaza was levelled and the permanent layout of the city laid down to allow elaborate architectural buildings like the North Platform and the famous Building J to be built. It has been calculated that Monte Albán was home to approximately sixteen thousand inhabitants during this phase who lived in residential quarters equipped with public and religious buildings.

The city reached its peak during the Classic period when most of the buildings that surround the large plaza were either built or rebuilt. Between 300-500 AD (Monte Albán IIIa), the city maintained close relations with Teotihuacan but the decline in contact with central Mexico from 500-750 AD (Monte Albán IIIb) marked the city's

cultural peak. Indicative of the height to which Monte Albán had risen are the hypogean tombs that contained magnificent grave goods and decorated with elaborate pictorial cycles that appear to reflect a political organization closely tied to the family and based on ancestor worship rather than cults of powerful cosmic and protective gods.

Despite the crisis that hit the city between 750-1000 AD (Monte Albán IV) at the time of the political turmoil of the Epiclassic period, Monte Albán was never abandoned and continued to be inhabited throughout the Post-Classic era. In 1400 AD one of the most extraordinary sets of grave goods to have been discovered was buried in a Classic tomb that was being reused (Tomb 7). It contained articles made from gold, turquoise mosaics, polychrome pottery, and bones engraved with other materials in pure Mixtec style that were placed with the bodies of nine individuals. The reason for the presence of these objects is not clear but, rather than a Mixtec occupation of the city, it is probable that the Zapotec elite of the Post-Classic period considered Mixtec workmanship of great prestige. The Mixtecs were at the time at the height of their development and were extending their cultural hegemony into the traditional heart of the Zapotec world.

76-77 The central square in Monte Albán seen from the top of the North Platform. The city was built around 500 BC and became the Zapotec capital (and one of the most important cities in all Mesoamerica) around the end of the Classic period.

77 Pendant made from green stone and shell found at Monte Albán inside a sacrificial tomb dated to between 100 BC – 200 AD. It depicts the bat god who was associated with caves and darkness and, consequently, with the underworld of the gods of water and death.

76 left This magnificent gold pendant comes from Tomb 7 in Monte Albàn where Adolfo Caso discovered a remarkable set of gold ornamental grave goods in 1932. The art of the Mixtec goldsmiths had clearly reached a remarkably high level.

78 top The famous
Danzantes Gallery.
The stone slabs are
decorated with
representations of
sacrificed prisoners
who are known as
danzantes because
their distorted
poses originally
suggested they were
dancers.

78 bottom View of
Monticulo M which,
together with
Monticulo O, form
System M. The
various steps of the
facade of Monticulo
M are decorated
with distinctive
mouldings that were
typical of Zapotec
architecture.

the site

The monumental center in Monte
Albán is organized around a large plaza
(886 x 410 ft) that is one of the most
beautiful of the archaeological sites in
Mexico. The remains of one of the
city's oldest buildings, the Temple of
the Danzantes, stand in the southwest
corner of the square. This platform was
built during the earliest of the city's
phases, Monte Albán I, and was
originally covered by about three
hundred stone slabs decorated with
images of sacrificed prisoners often
missing their hearts and genitals and
with short Zapotec inscriptions that
probably recorded their calendaric
names and dates of capture. Some of
these slabs were used in a later
alteration to the construction.

On either side of the Temple of the
Danzantes stand two similar
architectural complexes known as
System IV and Monticulo M. Each is
crowned by a temple and decorated
with the typical Zapotec "double
scapula" moulding that can be seen in
other buildings in the city, for example,
the South Platform and the
architectural complexes with large
stairways on the east side of the plaza.

MONTE ALBÁN

1 NORTH PLATFORM
2 BUILDING B
3 BALL COURT
4 SYSTEM IV
5 BUILDING U
6 BUILDING P
7 BUILDING G
8 BUILDING H
9 BUILDING I
10 TEMPLE OF THE DANZANTES
11 BUILDING S OR THE PALACE
12 BUILDING J OR THE OBSERVATORY
13 BUILDING Q
14 SYSTEM M
15 SOUTH PLATFORM

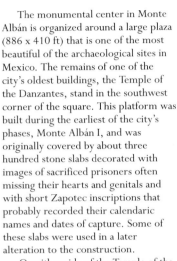

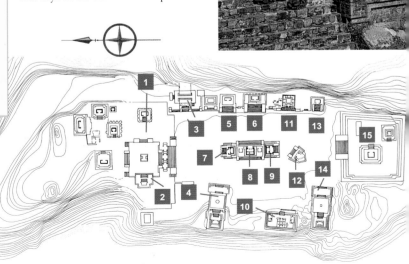

79 *top* View of Monticulo IV and the adjacent platform N. The small square bounded by two structures contains the remains of a small central altar. This complex — known as System IV — was initially built during the first phase of Monte Albán and remodelled up to phase IIIb (500-750 AD).

79 *bottom left* The presence of images of sacrificed prisoners in the Danzantes shows how war and its related symbolism were of great importance from ancient times in the development and establishment of emerging Zapotec political entities.

79 *bottom right* Detail of one of the stone slabs of the Danzantes. They date from the first phase of Monte Albán between 500-200 BC and are typical of the sculptural style seen in the Zapotec area during the Pre-Classic period.

78-79 *View of Monticulo L in the southwest corner of Monte Albán's central square. Note the series of stones at the extreme left known as danzantes. They originally came from an ancient building in this part of the city.*

Buildings G, H, I and J stand in the center of the public space; the last is an "arrow" structure from the Monte Albán II phase that probably had an astronomic function. Several of its walls were embellished with stone slabs carved with the names of conquered cities represented by an upturned human head.

80 top The North Platform seen from the top of Monticulo IV. It is thought that this large complex was the seat of the governing classes at Monte Albán whose elaborate tombs have been found in this zone.

80 bottom The half underground court in the center of the North Platform was probably a sort of square with access limited to the Zapotec elite of the city. The ruin of an altar can be seen in the center of the court.

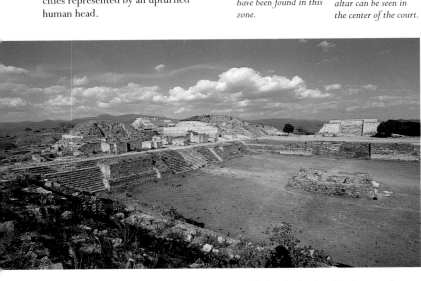

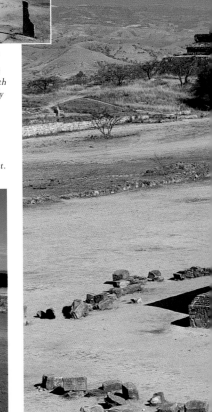

A large ball court lies in the northwest corner of the plaza with niches in its corners whose function is unknown. The adjacent North Platform has a large porticoed entrance, a semi-underground court, a central altar and minor buildings that were probably used by groups of ruling nobles. Close by the North Platform, a set of residential complexes of four chambers overlooking a central patio were found to have superb Zapotec tombs below them.

The burial chamber in Tomb 104 has a terracotta sculpture of the maize god Pitao Cozobi on the entrance and three painted walls. The central wall depicts a fantastic creature towards which two figures on the side walls approach; the figures wear large headdresses, carry *copal* bags and are preceded by large glyphic elements. The individuals buried in this tomb were undoubtedly from the

noble family that lived in the complex above.

The walls in Tomb 105 portray a sort of procession of eighteen richly dressed figures – nine men and nine women – indicated by their calendaric names. The picture is very probably a representation of the divinized ancestors of the noble family that buried its dead in the tomb. In this, as in the 175 other tombs so far discovered in the city, examples of the famous Zapotec "urns" have been found; these are pots with three dimensional decorations that are one of the masterpieces of Mesoamerican ceramic art. Regardless of their appellation "urns," these vases that were often decorated with the images of the most important Zapotec gods were actually funerary offerings and not used to hold the ashes of the dead.

80-81 Building J is one of the most mysterious and controversial Zapotec constructions. Its curious arrow-shaped form has stimulated innumerable hypotheses on its function. It is certain that this building had an astronomical meaning and the presence on its walls of many stone slabs bearing the names of conquered cities indicates that its function was probably linked to the chronological distribution of the sacred wars undertaken by the Zapotec nobility.

81 bottom left Low relief stele at the foot of the steps of the North Platform. Although the craftsmanship of the Zapotec artists was primarily expressed in painted tombs, the custom of raising commemorative stelae was constant throughout the Classic period.

81 bottom right The ball court at Monte Albán is located in the northeast corner of the square. The I-shaped court is unusual for its side but not particularly steep facings.

Dainzú, Lambyteco and Yagul

Dainzú

Dainzú was one of the most important Zapotec centers contemporary with the rise of Monte Albán. Its original name was probably *Quiebelagayo* ('5 Flower') which corresponds to *Macuilxóchitl*, the Náhuatl name for a modern local community as well as being one of the gods associated with the ball game. It is perhaps not by chance that Dainzú is famous for its archaic Zapotec-style low reliefs of ball players.

The site lies in the branch of the Oaxaca valley known as the valley of Tlacolula; it was first occupied around 700 BC at the time that San José Mogote dominated the northern branch known as Etla valley. During the first centuries after the birth of Christ, an elaborate drainage system and the first monumental structures (which included Buildings A and B) were built at Dainzú.

Building A is a large pyramidal base consisting of three terraces; the bottom one is decorated with a series of stone slabs with low reliefs of ball players in a style that bears similarities to that of the *Danzantes* at Monte Albán. The reliefs show the players with helmets in the shape of jaguar heads and knee-pads, belt ornaments and gloves to grasp the small balls they played with. Similar low reliefs showing helmets and the decapitated heads of players are seen on rocks on the top of Cerro Dainzú.

An indication of how important the ball game was at Dainzú is given by the

several ball courts in the city. One of them, excavated in 1967, is in the standard "I" shape of the Classic period and therefore much later than the game represented by the low reliefs.

Dainzú continued to be occupied during the Classic period as is shown by the many buildings from that era and by Tomb 7 in the center of Building B although, sadly, it was plundered in antiquity. The posts and architrave of the entrance to the tomb – which represented the entrance to the underworld – are decorated with a low relief of the head and front legs of a wild cat.

The city's period of glory ended with the crisis that afflicted Monte Albán though it was in all probability also occupied during the Post-Classic period. It may have been the Macuilxóchitl mentioned in several colonial documents which record that in 1580 the community was governed by a Mixtec lord named Oconaña.

Lambyteco

Lambyteco also lies in Tlacolula Valley and was also contemporaneous with the development of Monte Albán. It was a Zapotec center that was probably inhabited by groups whose economy was based on the production and export of salt.

Two palatial structures on the site stand out. Monticulo 195, decorated with Greek key patterns, was probably

the residence of the *coqui*, the lord of the city; the *tableros* of the altar in the center court feature stone and stucco low reliefs of two lords and their wives. One side of the altar shows the lord known as '4 Face' and the lady '10 Monkey' and the other shows '8 Owl' and his wife '3 Turquoise;' both men are shown gripping human femurs.

The entrance to Tomb 6 faces the altar, its facade embellished with stucco low reliefs portraying the lord '1 Earthquake' and his wife '10 Reed.'

Monticulo 190 is considered to have been the residence of the *bigaña*, or high priest. Its central altar is decorated with superb masks of Cocijo, the god of rain and thunder that was the Zapotec equivalent of the Teotihuacan and Aztec Tláloc, the Totonac Tajín, and the Mayan Chaac. Burial chambers have also been found inside Building 190, in particular

Tomb 2 with its architrave decorated with the typical Zapotec "double scapula" moulding.

Lambyteco was abandoned around the year 800 AD when the political landscape of the Zapotecs was shaken by the fallout of the collapse of the state of Monte Albán.

behind the Council Room is similar to those seen in the palaces at Mitla. The highest part of the site is occupied by a vast residential complex called the Palace of Six Courts that has rooms of different sizes that face onto its six porticoed courtyards.

The architecture of this complex –

83 top The large Monticulo 195 at Lambyteco would have been the residence of the local lord.

83 bottom Panorama of Yagul; the building for the ball game (the largest in all Oaxaca) can be seen on the left and the massive Palace of Six Courts stands in the center.

YAGUL

Yagul is located quite close to Lambyteco in Tlacolula valley. It is a good example of the sites that experienced growth at the time of the crisis that struck others like Monte Albán, Dainzú and Lambyteco. Occupied since the Pre-Classic period, Yagul began to take its current form around 800 AD when (perhaps following the arrival of the people of Lambyteco) a large, multi-level monumental complex was built on the slope of a hill.

On the lowest level, Patios 4 and 5 are surrounded by ancient monticules. On the next level up, there is the largest ball court in all of Oaxaca. Patio 1, a little higher up, is overlooked by the Council Room whose entrance is lined by two large pillars.

A long mosaic frieze in the passage

that was probably where the nobles of Yagul lived – has affinities with the oldest architectural complexes at Mitla that it would have been contemporary with.

Cross-shaped tombs with architraves decorated with stone friezes have been found in some of the structures in the city. Like many Post-Classic Zapotec

tombs, these contained luxury goods of Mixtec origin that were probably acquired through exchanges of gifts that celebrated alliances or aristocratic marriages.

A fort on the hill that overlooks the site of Yagul is evidence of the warlike nature of the politics of the Epiclassic period.

MITLA

history

Mitla, the most sophisticated and elegant monumental center in the Zapotec world, lies about 31 miles east of Monte Albán. It was inhabited from the Pre-Classic period but enjoyed its epoch of greatest splendor when Monte Albán began to decline around 750 AD. Like the other Epiclassic cities of Yagul and Zaachila, Mitla developed into a flourishing city-state whose wealth was probably founded on a thriving commercial economy that continued until and even after the Spanish conquest.

The Náhuatl name the city is known by (from *Mictlan*, "the World of the Dead") and its original Zapotec name (*Liubá*, "burial") are evidence that the fame of the city was linked to the memory of the nobles who were buried in its tombs.

Although it was founded by the Zapotecs, during the Post-Classic period Mitla was obliged to participate in the interethnic relations of the Zapotecs and Mixtecs to the extent that examples of its art are clearly in Mixtec style. A sign of the dynamic and turbulent politics of the Post-Classic period is the fort near the city that would have been the refuge of the social elite who governed Mitla until the arrival of the Spanish.

MITLA	
A SOUTH GROUP	**1** SOUTH COURT OF THE
B ARROYO GROUP	GROUP OF THE COLUMNS
C GROUP OF THE COLUMNS	**2** NORTH COURT OF THE
D ADOBE GROUP	GROUP OF THE COLUMNS
E CHURCH GROUP	**3** NORTH COURT OF THE
	CHURCH GROUP

the site

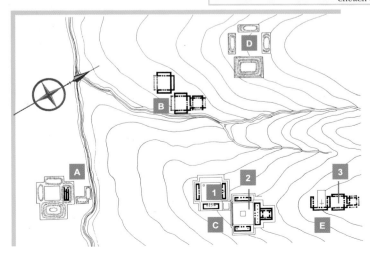

Mitla's monumental center has five architectural complexes around which the residential areas lie. The oldest section seems to include the Adobe (or Western) Group and the Southern Group; the latter contains an underground tomb from the Classic period that was contemporary with the phase Monte Albán III.

Both architectural complexes comprise four buildings arranged around a central open area with open corners.

84-85 The Columns Building is the main structure in the Columns Group at Mitla. The elegant Greek key pattern in mosaic form on the facade became a distinctive feature of Zapotec architecture in the Late Classic and Post-Classic periods.

85 top left The mosaic Greek key patterns on the Columns Building (like on other buildings at Mitla). Note a motif in the upper part of the photograph that seems to derive from the form of a sectioned shell.

A similar structure characterizes the Columns Group which probably dates from some time between 750 and 900 AD, i.e., during Mitla's era of greatest development. The Columns Group is the city's finest complex; it stands in a central position with two courts, each of which is surrounded by four large structures. The facades of the buildings in the group are decorated with extraordinary stone friezes that have made Mitla famous. Sometimes carved

arcade leads into what was once a large covered room with massive monolithic columns.

The two complexes known as the Arroyo Group and the Church Group were built during the Post-Classic period. The latter takes its name from the 17th century church of San Paolo that was built on top of it.

Both groups have three patios surrounded by buildings but, unlike the more ancient ones, these patios are

85 top right The north court of the Columns Group. The Greek key patterns are emphasized by the *contrast of light and shade within mouldings that are developments of the Zapotec "double scapula" design.*

on a single stone slab and sometimes formed by a technique similar to mosaic, the friezes consist of complex Greek key patterns and other geometrical designs laid out on several registers. The "flared" profile of the buildings increases the effect of the shadows created by the friezes which would have been even more striking when the original colors were still in existence.

closed at the corners and the structures that look onto them are decorated with single register friezes on the upper part of the walls.

Several architraves in these complexes still bear traces of the paintings that decorated them: the main topic in the Arroyo Group seems to be the birth of the Sun, and the paintings in the Church Group appear to refer to the

85 bottom left The entrance room to the Columns Building contains a series of large monolithic columns that supported the covering; the entire architectural complex was named after these columns. *85 bottom right Facade of the North Building in the South Patio of the Columns Group. The entrance to Tomb 1 – a typical cross-shaped Zapotec tomb – can be seen in the foreground.*

Below the two structures of the south patio in the Columns Group stand the entrances to two cross-shaped tombs similar to those in Monte Albán.

The north patio is the location of the superb building after which the group has been named in which an

underworld journey of Venus and the Sun which was one of the basic themes of Mesoamerican mythology. The paintings are clearly influenced by Mixtec style which is an indication of the strong interethnic relations that characterized the Post-Classic life of Mitla.

HUIJAZÓO

The archaeological site of Huijazóo is known as Suchilquitongo or Cerro de la Campana; it is a Zapotec site from the Classic period consisting of twenty or so structures, almost none of which have been studied scientifically. Nonetheless, the site is famous for Tomb 5 which is one of the most beautiful Zapotec funerary structures known to us. The tomb lies below a residential architectural complex and was built in the typical shape of a Zapotec noble's house.

The real entrance to the tomb is found below a stone cover weighing two and a half tons and down a stairway of nine steps (a reference to the nine levels of the Underworld). The inner entrance has a double scapula relief in the center of which the face of a bird emerges from the open jaws of a serpent-jaguar.

One then passes into Antechamber I which is adorned with four large pillars decorated with a series of hieroglyphic registers above low reliefs of individuals wearing headdresses and carrying a copal bag.

Passing through another entrance with painted architraves, one reaches Antechamber II which is the equivalent of the open patio in a house belonging to a noble family. The north architrave is decorated with polychrome paintings

and calendaric names of ancestors that would have been decorated at the time of the tomb's construction (i.e., 500-750 AD, the phase Monte Albán IIIb); the south architrave has somewhat coarser glyphs and was painted when the tomb was reopened for an additional burial, probably during the phase Monte Albán IV (750-1000 AD), when Mixtec grave goods were deposited.

The antechamber has portals on all sides, the entrance and three others, each crowned by white double scapula mouldings with a red square and flanked by pillars with low reliefs. The two side entrances lead into two niches decorated with images of noble men and women, processions of warriors and a scene that is reminiscent of the Aztec ceremony of the New Fire.

86 top left Above the architrave in the entrance to Tomb 5 a bird's head emerges from the menacing head of a serpent-jaguar. The complicated decoration was carved in the stone and lined with stucco.

86 bottom left This monolithic stele stands at the bottom of the burial chamber in Tomb 5. Completely painted bright red, it is divided into two registers with a woman and an old man in the lower scene and a young man and a middle aged man in the upper.

86 right The left post in the east niche in Antechamber II of Tomb 5 is adorned with the relief of a standing figure seen in profile. The man wears rich plumes, earrings, a copal bag and sandals and carries weapons and a shield. Glyphs, numeric symbols and the "jaws of the sky" (a typically Zapotec motif) are seen above the post.

87 The entrance to the burial chamber seen from Antechamber II. A stucco mask of a jaguar head with open jaws can be seen over the architrave with a bizarre figure emerging that has a bat's head and human arms. The door has four monolithic posts, two on each side, on which reliefs of a man-jaguar and a priestess are seen.

The door in front (which leads to the funeral chamber proper) is flanked by double pillars and topped by a relief of a man-bat emerging from the jaws of a jaguar on whose head a large headdress contains a symbol of the year. The burial chamber has paintings on two registers: the upper one shows elderly individuals wearing bird-shaped headdresses and the lower one a series of players wearing helmets and headdresses and holding a ball.

The back of the burial chamber has a stele painted red and decorated with low reliefs which probably was placed here during the second use of the tomb. The reliefs are divided into two panels and show a young man and a girl seated in front of two old men in a representation of a family tree.

Although the details of the pictorial cycle in Tomb 5 cannot be made out, the allusion to the world of the dead and the role of the ancestors is clear. The paintings related to the ball game also refer to the underworld in that the game was closely linked to "descents" into the world of the dead. The importance of this ritual game to symbolic meanings related to the tomb is also seen in the placement of a ceramic ball measuring about 12 inches in diameter in the entrance.

88 This is a famous and well preserved wall painting from Tomb 5. It shows an elaborately dressed priestess with a bag for copal. The painting is on the north wall of the west niche in Antechamber II.

89 left This figure is painted on the inside of the left door post of the burial chamber in Tomb 5.

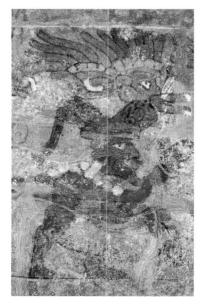

89 top right The west wall of the burial chamber in Tomb 5 has a wall painting with a procession of elderly people on the top register. The detail shows one with an elaborate and brightly colored headdress.

89 bottom right The painting on the back wall of the east niche in Antechamber II shows four figures spinning. This detail shows the two in the center; both wear a short cloak and a skirt and have their hair tied up.

ITINERARY IV

THE CIVILIZATIONS OF THE FOREST

The dense tropical landscape of southeast Mesoamerica was the setting for the rise and progress of peoples like the Olmecs and the Maya who produced some of the most dramatic cultural and artistic expressions to be seen in this area of the continent.

Olmec culture was developed on the coastal plain of the southern Gulf of Mexico between 1200-400 BC. It was the most influential culture of the Pre-Classic period and contributed substantially to the progress of the more undeveloped complex societies in Mesoamerica. Olmec art, particularly the products found in the sites of San Lorenzo and La Venta, became a sort of "cipher" for political and social communication in the Pre-Classic period when works of art in Olmec style spread to distant regions following the trade routes used by merchants who dealt in luxury goods.

Although the old definition of Olmec art as the "mother culture" of Mesoamerica is today called into question, it is unquestionably true that many of the fundamental concepts of the Mesoamerican religious tradition and its iconographic themes originated in the Olmec area. Even after the end of what is properly referred to as the Olmec culture, its heirs – known as the Epi-Olmecs – continued to play a major role until at least the beginning of the Classic period. It was in the world of these peoples (who spoke Mixe-Zoque languages like the Olmecs and the modern day Mixe, Zoque and Popoluca peoples) that the first forms of writing and the oldest calendaric documentation seem to have appeared.

It is undeniable that much of the Olmecs' cultural baggage lies at the foundation of the rise of the Maya in the lowlands during the Classic period, yet, contrary to what is often said, contact between the Olmec world and the lowland Maya was very limited or only indirect. The most intense and productive interaction between their two worlds seems to have occurred in the Pacific coastal area of Chiapas and Guatemala and in the adjacent highlands of Guatemala. At the end of the Pre-Classic period, it was here that an extremely innovative artistic style called "Izapeño" developed, the fruit of the interaction between the Mixe-Zoque centers like Izapa and the Maya centers like Kaminaljuyú. As peoples migrated from the Guatemalan highlands, following the river courses and colonizing the tropical forests of the lowlands, continual contact between the two regions ensured that the lowland Maya received elements of Olmec or Epi-Olmec origin that they developed to form the basis of the exceptional cultural and artistic expressions of their Classic period city-states.

Palenque, Tikal, Yachilán, Bonampak and Copán are certainly the monumental centers that best exemplify the variety and refinement of Mayan art. Much of Mayan art glorified dynastic power, heroic rulers and their divine ancestors, and these centers were a true reflection of the splendor and power of the royal dynasties of the Classic era. The constant fragmentation of political power in the lowlands fostered cultural diversification and gave rise to the development of a large number of artistic styles, all of which had in common a "cipher" that was the fruit of the constant and intricate political relations between the dynasties that dominated the dozens of Mayan cities during the Classic period in the central lowlands.

The extent of the supremacy of the larger city-states over the smaller ones, whether direct or indirect, is still not clear, and the uncertainty of scholars is mirrored in the variety of hypothetical reconstructions of the political landscape of the Mayan lowlands during the Late Classic period. For example, the number of individual political entities varies between sixty three and eight! The latter hypothesis is based on five large regional states in the central area under the leadership of Palenque, Yaxchilán, Tikal, Copán and Calakmul, and three states in the Yucatán, Cobá, Río Bec and Chenes-Puuc.

The world of the Maya felt the effects of the crisis that occurred during the Classic period, although slightly later than those cultures based in central Mexico. It was during the 7th-9th centuries AD that the Mayan cities reached the peak of their glory but were then unexpectedly abandoned around 900 AD. As in all of Mesoamerica, the Classic crisis was more a huge transformation than an inexplicable collapse and not all Mayan regions were affected in the same way. New "Mexicanized" groups of Maya occupied sites like Seibal along the river Usumacinta while new artistic styles in the Yucatán (that bring to mind the Epiclassic styles of central Mexico for their elegance and brevity) formed a link with the enormous progress of the Post-Classic era made by the dozens of Mayan groups of the highlands in Chiapas and Guatemala where some of the largest groups of modern Maya like the Tzotzil, Tzeltal and Quiché live today.

90 Terracotta sculpture of the Old God found in the tomb of a noble at Tikal. The loveliest Maya ceramics were made as funerary offerings for the tombs of nobles and sovereigns.

91 Detail of Stele F at Copán in which we see the features of the ruler 18 Rabbit. Many Maya works of art were produced for reasons of propaganda, generally to commemorate the feats of the divine sovereigns that governed individual city states.

LA VENTA: THE ARCHAEOLOGICAL SITE AND THE PARK

history

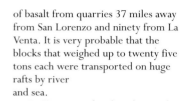

The large Olmec settlements of San Lorenzo in Veracruz and La Venta in Tabasco were the two principal ceremonial centers in Pre-Classic Mesoamerica; their large architectural constructions made from earth and adorned with sculptures are one of the high points of American art. Although the fame of Olmec art is widespread, we know very little of the civilization that produced it. Settlements of prime importance like Laguna de los Cerros remain unexplored archaeologically and even the history of the two largest sites – where excavations are currently being carried out – is only known to us very approximately.

of basalt from quarries 37 miles away from San Lorenzo and ninety from La Venta. It is very probable that the blocks that weighed up to twenty five tons each were transported on huge rafts by river and sea.

La Venta was abandoned around 400 BC when twenty of its twenty four monuments were defaced as had happened at San Lorenzo hundreds of years earlier. The reason for the damage is not yet known and for a long time it was thought that a sort of revolt had taken place against the ruling powers, but now the possibility is being debated that the mutilation was ritual in nature or that they were an attempt to make use of the stone for other purposes.

the site

La Venta was founded around 900 BC but it was not until the 6th-5th centuries BC that its monumental center appeared in the form seen today. It is roughly laid out on a northsouth axis and is formed by a series of open spaces bounded by buildings. The largest architectural group is Complex C where the large earthen pyramid referred to as C1 – more than 98 feet high – dominates the plaza onto which the Stirling Acropolis faces. To the north of the pyramid stands Complex A, La Venta's principal ceremonial group. The central open space is dominated by the pyramid, lined by long parallel monticulos and divided into two patios. The north patio is surrounded by a "stockade" made of monolithic basalt columns and was the location of some of the most extraordinary Olmec offerings: buried at a depth of 26 feet below layers of different colored sand were two huge "masks" measuring about 66 feet across

composed of thousands of blocks of serpentine stone. The same procedure was used to bury two "pavements" also made from tons of serpentine. The "masks" are often thought to represent the faces of jaguars but today that interpretation is being questioned. More than twenty smaller offerings found in Complex A contained Olmec works of art: pottery, green stone axes and the famous group of anthropomorphic statuettes (now in the Anthropology Museum in Mexico City) that seem to be involved in a sort of meeting near the stone "stockade." Overlooking the area where these offerings were found there used to be earthen monticulos and monuments such as a burial chamber made from basalt columns, a large stone sarcophagus and colossal heads that stood at the north tip of the complex.

If the large Olmec sculptures surprise us with their stylistic vigor, no less startling was the effort required by the Olmecs to transport the huge blocks

THE PARK

In recent times the site of La Venta has been partially destroyed following installation of oil facilities and its monumental sculptures have been taken to the La Venta Park in Villahermosa in the state of Tabasco. Although it is more of an open air museum than an archaeological site, the park is the best place to admire a wide range of Olmec sculpture and it is an obligatory stop in southeast Mexico. The thick vegetation is the setting for dozens of sculptures like the colossal heads, the large altar-thrones, statues and stelae, basalt tombs and one of the huge serpentine masks.

The colossal heads are the works that best represent Olmec art and are the symbol of this culture, but no less impressive are the large altar-thrones. Altar 4 is adorned with the figure of a lord emerging from the jaws of the Earth Monster holding a cord in his hand that joins him to figures carved in low relief on the sides who may be either prisoners or relatives. On Altar 5 we see the sovereign appearing from the jaws of a monster with a baby jaguar in his arms and the sides of the monument are similarly decorated with

babies jaguars held by other dignitaries.

Stele 2 depicts the sovereign with a sceptre and a large headdress surrounded by small flying creatures like the attendants known as Tlaloques of the Aztec rain god. Similar figures are seen on Stele 3 above a scene that seems to portray the meeting between two dignitaries; the profile of the figure on the right (known as "Uncle Sam") has stimulated speculation on his origin. The magnificent Monument 19 shows a ruler seated on the body of a large rattlesnake holding a *copal* bag in his hand.

The stelae represent a transition from the large three dimensional sculptures of the Olmecs to the refined art of low reliefs and it seems possible to see in them the origin of the formal and stylistic characteristics that were to dominate the great art of Classic Mesoamerica.

93 left
Colossal head no.4 in the grounds of La Venta Museum in Villahermosa. These portraits of ancient Olmec sovereigns are evidence of the rulers' capacity to mobilize huge quantities of manpower to transport the blocks of basalt weighing many tons from deposits up to 37 miles away.

93 right
"Altar" no.4 at La Venta shows the customary image of the sovereign emerging from a cave represented by the jaws of a jaguar (the creature's face can be seen in the upper part of the photograph). It is possible that these representations referred to the link between the ruler and the cosmic forces of the underworld.

PALENQUE

history

Palenque is a true jewel of the Mayan world, and its white limestone monuments set in the green tropical vegetation of the state of Chiapas may be the best example of how a city of the Classic period appeared at the height of its glory. Recent studies have shown that it is probable that the city was known to the ancient Maya by the name *Lakam Ha* ("Great Water") and its kingdom as *Bak* ("Bone").

The foundation of the city – one of the westernmost in the Mayan territory – probably occurred in the 5th century AD when Bahlum Kuk ("Jaguar-Quetzal") ascended the throne in 431 AD and began a dynasty that claimed its origins lay in the ruler U-Kix-Chan whose mythical kingdom was founded in 967 BC. Bahlum Kuk's dynasty ruled the city until 604 AD when the reign ended of the Lady Kanal Ikal (583-604 AD) who had perhaps ascended the throne due to a lack of male heirs. Her son Ac Kan founded a new dynastic line but once again, for unknown reasons, in 612 AD power passed into the hands of a woman, Sak Kuk ("White Quetzal"), who was married to a foreigner of royal birth. It was her son who founded the third and most famous dynasty in the world of the Maya.

The new ruler was Pacal II ("Shield II"), known as Pacal the Great, who was the instigator of the wealth and splendor of Palenque. Pacal took to the throne in 615 AD at the age of twelve and reigned until 683 AD; during his reign and that of his son, Chan Bahlum II (684-702 AD), Palenque developed into one of the most powerful cities in the lowlands and the "capital" of the southwest. Pacal and Chan Bahlum were the forces behind an ideological and architectural program that changed the face of the city and it was under these two that most of the monuments now in existence were built.

The reign of Chan Bahlum II's brother, Kan Xul II (702-711/720 AD), marked the beginning of the end for Palenque. In 711 AD Kan Xul II (also known as Kan Hok Chitam II) was captured in battle by the ruler of Toniná

(a beautiful Mayan city close to Palenque that can also be visited) who held him prisoner until 720 AD when he was sacrificed. During Kan Xul II's imprisonment, Palenque was governed by a regent and a new king did not ascend the throne until after his death.

However, the throne had been weakened and the last monumental construction took place at the end of the 8th century shortly before Palenque was struck by the crisis of the Classic period and the city abandoned.

95 Stucco head found in Pacal's funerary crypt inside the Temple of the Inscriptions. It is not apparent if it was a portrait of the ruler or of his wife, Ahpo Hel.

94 Low relief of a sovereign found below Pacal's sarcophagus together with many other objects, including the two famous stucco heads detached from the decoration of some building.

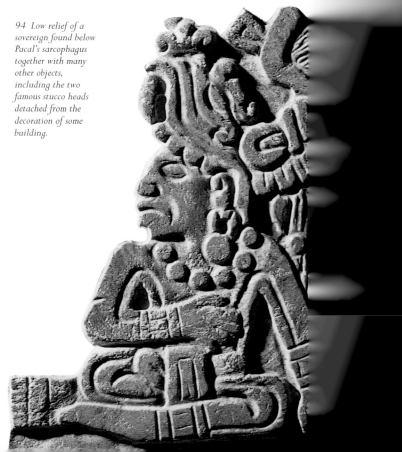

the site

96-97 Aerial view of the Palace at Palenque. The internal structure of the Palace is formed by two main courts with the other buildings arranged around them.

96 bottom right The tower that dominates the Palace was probably an astronomical observatory from which the rulers of Palenque watched the heavens. Astronomical events were often skillfully manipulated for purposes of political propaganda.

As mentioned above, many of the monuments visible today date from the reigns of Pacal and his sons. This compacted history allows the details of the ideology at the base of the royal power and manifested in the renewal of the city's architecture to be understood fairly completely.

The importance paid to architectural decoration is a characteristic that distinguishes Palenque from the other lowland Classic cities in which the "language of power" was mainly expressed through carvings on stelae and altars.

The history of Pacal and his sons is therefore to be seen in the monumental buildings and stone and stucco low reliefs that adorn the walls, pillars, roofs and crests of the buildings.

The focus of the monumental center is without doubt the Palace; this was the residence of the royal family and its rooms, corridors and courtyards were modified by each of the sovereigns that lived there. What is seen today mostly derives from the reign of Pacal and his family and its most distinctive feature is the tower that was probably used as an astronomic observatory.

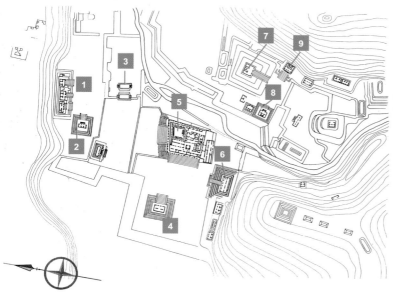

PALENQUE

1 NORTH GROUP
2 TEMPLE OF THE COUNT
3 BALL COURT
4 GREAT TEMPLE
5 THE PALACE
6 TEMPLE OF THE INSCRIPTIONS
7 TEMPLE OF THE CROSS
8 TEMPLE OF THE SUN
9 TEMPLE OF
   THE FOLIATED CROSS

97 top right The Palace at Palenque. This was the seat of the reigning dynasties of the city. Much of its current appearance dates to the reign of Pacal II the Great.

97 center right Court of House C in Palenque Palace. The balustrades of the stairway are made from large monolithic slabs

decorated with low reliefs of bound prisoners of war. These courts would have been used for private ceremonies for the royal family.

97 bottom right One of the porticoed galleries inside the Palace. Note the false vault — a typical feature of Maya architecture — and

the small T-shaped window, typical of Palenque. The walls were originally decorated with polychrome paintings.

The pillars of the portico above the entrance stairway to the Palace are decorated with stucco low reliefs of the sovereigns. The long corridors inside the Palace still contain traces of paintings and stucco reliefs, including the Oval Tablet that commemorates the coronation of Pacal who is shown seated on a throne in the form of a two-headed jaguar while his mother gives him a sort of "tiara" adorned with jade beads and the face of God K, the true symbol of royal power.

97 top left The Oval Tablet in the Palace shows the coronation of Pacal II seated to the right on a throne in the shape of a two-headed jaguar. His mother, Zak Kuk, the previous queen of the city, places a sort of tiara formed by dozens of jadeite pearls crowned with a high plume of quetzal feathers on her son's head.

House C faces one of the inner patios of the Palace; its hieroglyphic stairway commemorates a battle and the lunar eclipse of 659 AD which was watched by Pacal with the sovereign of Tikal and a noble from Yaxchilán, though it is not clear whether the noble in question was a guest or a prisoner.

The event was celebrated with the sacrifice of six prisoners of war like those depicted on the large balustrades. The frequent military clashes between Palenque and Calakmul (the traditional rival of Tikal and her allies) are frequently referred to on the same stairway and on other monuments.

97 bottom left One of the stucco low reliefs that decorate the palace pillars. These reliefs portray different members of the royal

dynasties of the city and are a typical art form of Palenque although low reliefs on stone stelae are almost completely absent.

Pacal's reign also saw the construction of the Olvidado Temple and the Temple of the Count; the name of the latter follows from the fact that it was chosen to be the residence of Count Waldeck, a curious historical figure who was one of the first to explore Palenque and lived in the temple named after him from 1834-36 AD.

The last of Pacal's constructions was the Temple of the Inscriptions which was the funerary pyramid later completed by his son, Chan Bahlum II. It was Chan Bahlum who had the pillars of the porticoed entrance decorated with stucco low reliefs of Pacal and his ancestors holding Chan Bahlum II in the form of God K to confirm his divinity.

The glyphic panels inside the temple recount the entire dynastic history of Palenque. It is divided into three

sections: the first commemorates the ends of nine twenty year calendaric cycles (*katun*) and the nine corresponding reigns up until the ceremonies that marked the *katun* during Pacal's reign.

Pacal's date of birth in the second section is related to the mythical birth date of a god from more than one million years before and to a calendaric event due to take place on October 23, 4772 AD.

The third section is the most "profane" and commemorates various events in Pacal's reign such as the welcome given to the king of Tikal, certain ceremonies and Pacal's wedding. This section was completed during the reign of Chan Bahlum since it includes the death of Pacal and the ascent to the throne of the heir.

Pacal's ideological and political strategy is made clear in the temple

inscriptions: not being able to claim his descent from a male sovereign, Pacal linked his reign to those of predecessors through particular calendaric events and associated the name of his mother to a goddess called Sak Bak ("White Gauze"), better known as "Bestial Lady" or "First Mother" as she was the mother of the divine triad that dominated the pantheon of Palenque. This was Pacal's scheme to uphold his own divinity and his claim to the throne, and obviate the customary rules of descent from a male.

The temple floor contains a trapdoor that gives access to a narrow stairway that descends into the inside of the pyramid down the nine levels that represent the nine levels of the Underworld. Pacal's burial chamber is found on the ground level, symbolically the "bottom of the world of the dead." It is filled with the large monolithic

sarcophagus that marked the beginning of the building's construction (the pyramid was then built around and over the sarcophagus). A stone chest in front of the entrance to the crypt contained the remains of five or six individuals who were sacrificed and dismembered to accompany the king to the world beyond the tomb.

The low relief figures of nine individuals on the walls of the crypt are perhaps the Nine Lords of the Night or the king's nine predecessors deliberately "confused" with these gods. The sides of the sarcophagus are decorated with the ten busts of individuals emerging from narrow cracks in the ground, each accompanied by a tree. These are Pacal's predecessors with his parents shown twice. The same figures are mentioned in the inscription that appears on the edge of the stone cover of the

99 right Pacal's
funerary crypt. Below
the covering slab it is
possible to see the
sarcophagus with the
space in which the
ruler's body lay. The
size of the monolithic
sarcophagus shows
that it was placed
there before the
pyramid was built
above it.

represent the entrance to the world of
the dead; inside a plate-censer
decorated with the face of the dead sun
contains the instruments used for
sacrifice: a shell, the spine of a sea-ray
and part of a plant.

Mayan mythology tells that the
cosmic tree (*Wakah-Kan* or "Raised
Sky") was born during the last Creation
thanks to a self-sacrifice made using this
plate.

The king's body lay inside the
sarcophagus covered with cinnabar and
ornamented with a pectoral, armbands,
a diadem and a jade funeral mask that
are now displayed in the Anthropology
Museum in Mexico City.

sarcophagus in which the dates of their
deaths and that of Pacal follow the
phrase "they closed the sarcophagus of
the Maize God (Pacal)."

The covering slab is decorated with
what is perhaps the most famous Mayan
relief: contained within a "celestial
band" of star signs, the body of the
dead king in the form of the Maize
God descends the trunk of the cosmic
tree.

A bird nesting on the top of the tree
is the manifestation of the celestial
dragon Itzamná, and halfway up the
trunk a two-headed snake represents
the conduit through which the Mayan
sovereigns entered into contact with the
heavens and their ancestors. Pacal's
body is about to enter the open jaws of
the "White Skeletal Serpent" that

His mouth was encircled by a mica
frame, his ringed fingers clutched a jade
sphere and cube, and two other spheres
lay below his feet. A jade statuette lay
on his skirt close to a jade plaque
engraved with the motif *te* ("tree")
which was an allusion to the cosmic tree
and the king's role as a pillar of the
universe that he had performed during
his life.

Two famous stucco heads taken
from statues were placed beneath the
sarcophagus to accompany Pacal; we do
not know if they represent Pacal and
his wife or whether they were portraits
of the sovereign at different stages of
his life.

98 left The Temple
of the Inscriptions
seen from the Palace.
The stairway leads to
the upper temple in
which panels of
glyphs recount
the dynastic history
of the city and
provide the modern
name of the pyramid.
On the right we just
see the pyramid
that holds the tomb
of the "Red Queen"
and, in the
background, the
Skull Temple.

98-99 The Temple
of the Inscriptions.
This is the pyramid
that contains the
funerary crypt in
which Pacal II's

sarcophagus was
buried in 683 AD.
The nine platforms of
the pyramid refer to
the nine levels the
underground world
was divided into
according to Mayan
cosmology.

99 top left
Jadeite funeral mask
placed on Pacal's face.
The ruler's funerary
goods included many
other objects made of
green stone.

99 bottom left The
drawing reproduces the
sarcophagus lid with
the figure of Pacal
climbing down the
trunk of the cosmic
tree clearly seen.

A few years ago the discovery was made of an elaborate tomb of a woman in the building that stands next to the Temple of the Inscriptions; it was probably either Pacal's wife or another woman of the same family. To the right of the temple containing this tomb stands the Temple of the Skull named after the low relief on its facade.

If the celebrations that marked the burial of Pacal were one of the defining moments of Chan Bahlum II's political life (he ascended the throne 132 days

after his father's death), the new ruler continued on the road taken by Pacal and manifested his own glory and power in the construction of a new and imposing architectural complex known today as the Cross Group. He marked the legitimisation of his reign in this building by emphasizing his descendancy from Pacal and the link between the Lady Sak Kuk and the mythical "First Mother." The tallest and northernmost building in the group, the Temple of the Cross was a "celestial pyramid" consisting of thirteen levels on which a number of large terracotta censers depicting the Sun God were found.

The small shrine inside the temple that crowns the pyramid contains a low relief showing Pacal and Chan Bahlum II respectively to the left and right of a cosmic tree (the "cross").

The heads between the figures record Chan Bahlum as heir, his ascent to the throne and a self-sacrifice. The two low reliefs on the posts of the shrine represent Chan Bahlum (left)

and God L (right); the god, who was one of the most important deities of the world of the dead, is shown smoking and dressed in a jaguar skin. Chan Bahlum, on the other hand, is depicted with all the royal insignia on the tenth day of celebration of his ascent to the throne; this day coincided with the maximum trajectory of Venus as the Evening Star and probably with the formal assumption of power by the new king. The relief is a clear claim to legitimize the new king's power and shows how Chan Bahlum had been received by his dead father (shown smaller and accompanied by God L) during the ten days of celebrations that were also connected with astral events that were part of the Mayan conception of royalty.

The glyphic panels to the sides of the central relief summarize Palenque's dynastic history from December 7, 3121

BC (the date of birth of the "First Mother"), and includes those of her divine sons from that of U-Kix-Chan, the mythical founder of the dynasty who was crowned on March 28, 967 BC, up till that of Chan Bahlum (September 20, 524 AD).

Whereas the Temple of the Cross alludes to the celestial and supreme nature of royalty, the panels in the other

two temples in the group seem to emphasize two other aspects that symbolize royal power. The Temple of the Foliated Cross stresses the link between the sovereign and fertility and therefore portrays the king's earthly aspect with the representation of Pacal and Chan Bahlum on either side of the cosmic tree in the form of a maize plant (the "foliated cross").

100 left View of the Temple of the Foliated Cross. The collapse of the front of the Temple revealed the internal gallery; the pyramidal base on which the temple stands has never been excavated. The modern name of the temple is given by a mistaken interpretation of a low relief shown the axis mundi *as a maize plant. Overall, the central low relief in the temple stresses the link between sacred regality and the forces of fertility.*

100 top right The front gallery in the Temple of the Sun. The bay containing the shrine and low relief panels is featured on the left.

100 bottom right The Temple of the Sun. Low reliefs inside allude to the solar and warlike aspects of royalty. What remains of the crest that was typical of Palenque buildings can be seen on the roof of the temple; roof decorations included stucco reliefs on the slopes of the roof and polychrome low reliefs on the crest.

Two images of Chan Bahlum look on, one to the left on the day of his coronation and the other to the right ten days later. The two glyphic panels relate various events in the life of Chan Bahlum to mythical events that took place in antiquity.

The warrior and underworld aspect of royalty is the theme of the Panel in the Temple of the Sun (which naturally stands to the west). Here, a shield decorated with the face of the Sun-Jaguar in front of two crossed spears lies between the two sovereigns. The spears rest on a throne from which two bloodied dragon heads and a jaguar head emerge.

The throne is supported by two gods from the world of the dead, and their position – like that of the figures on which the king's feet rest – resembles the position of prisoners of war in commemorative images. It is a clear reference to the myth told in the *Popol Vuh* in which the divine twins – as prototypes of Mayan sovereigns – defeat the gods of the world of the dead.

Chan Bahlum's designation as heir in the glyphic panels is connected to events that characterize him as a manifestation of the sun.

Recent studies in other buildings in the Cross Group (Buildings 19 and 20) have led to the discovery of new reliefs that show how later rulers around the mid-8th century AD referred to the ideology shown in Chan Bahlum's works. One of these sovereigns may be buried in the tomb found in Building 20 which has not yet been opened.

Although much of Palenque stretches to the south and west of the central groups (behind the modern parking lot), the standard route for visitors passes in front of the Temple of the Count, leads to the ball court and other buildings decorated with low reliefs, continues along the river Otolum passing by several residential complexes inhabited by noble families, and then comes out by the modern Site Museum where several masterpieces discovered on the site are displayed.

100-101 The Cross Group at Palenque built by Chan Bahlum after the death of his father, Pacal. The main temples in the group are the Temple of the Cross (left), the Temple of the Foliated Cross (center) and the Temple of the Sun (right).

101 top The Temple of the Count was built during the reign of Pacal II. The temple's modern name comes from the fact that it was chosen as a residence by the eccentric Count Waldeck who lived in the city's ruins from 1834-36.

101 bottom View of the North Group that bounds the north side of the Central Square at Palenque. The straw canopy to the right protects some stucco low reliefs that decorated the facade of the buildings.

WRITING

Writing and the recording of calendaric dates appeared on Mesoamerican monuments during the Middle and Late Pre-Classic periods (i.e., from 600 BC onwards) in the Zapotec and Epi-Olmec areas. The inscription "1 Earthquake" below the image of a sacrificed prisoner in Monument 3 in San José Mogote would appear to be the oldest example of writing known to us and the precursor of a tradition that continued with the *danzantes* in Monte Albán and later bloomed with the Zapotec script during the Classic period.

The progressive symbolic formalization of Olmec iconography in the area of the isthmus resulted in a complex writing system seen in monuments like the Tuxtlas Statuette and the La Mojarra Stele in which inscriptions are evidence of the use of Mixe-Zoque languages. It was in this area around the time of Christ that the first calendaric recordings were made using the Long Count. Judging by the typology of the monuments, it seems there was a close link between the use of writing and the propaganda requirements of the emerging reigning dynasties of the Pre-Classic period. It is not therefore surprising that Mesoamerican writing reached its level of greatest complexity in the Classic world of the Maya at the height of the dynastic political systems. Corroboration of the close connection between writing and political power is given by the almost total absence of

writing at Teotihuacan. As we are unable to suppose that the inhabitants of the city were not aware of it, we are obliged to conclude that "they did not need it" because of the political system they used and the different methods used to legitimize power.

Mayan writing was based on the use of signs (glyphs) that were given a pictographic, ideographic or phonetic-syllabic value. The glyphs were joined together in a form similar to a modern rebus and so complex that for decades they resisted all efforts to decipher them. Small signs linked to the main sign in a glyph (a little like a prefix or suffix) served as phonetic indicators that specified the correct reading of the principal glyph or which performed grammatical functions like indicating time, pronouns, etc. It seems that the choice between the various ways in which a single concept could be expressed (for example, ideographically only or ideographically and pictographically, etc.) and the "tone" of the glyphs used depended on the scribe and the theme in question. There is no doubt that calligraphy was central to Mayan art.

In recent decades, our progressive understanding of Mayan inscriptions has profoundly changed our perception of the culture by revealing complex interrelations between propaganda, myth and history that have allowed us to reconstruct the history of Mayan cities through names, events and precise dates; this is something that we cannot do with other Mesoamerican civilizations.

There are three or four large categories of Mayan inscriptions. The best known is the one seen in inscriptions on stelae, altars and low reliefs as well as those seen in most inscriptions painted on buildings. This type of text usually deals with historical, political or commemorative topics and is always associated with mythical or astronomic events. A second category is the one used in inscriptions on polychrome pots that were often "captions" to images of mythical episodes or court scenes. The names of the painters-scribes were also given on some of these pots (significantly, the Mayan

language did not distinguish between painting and writing) and the translation of some texts has shown that the most important artists were members of the high nobility if not actually the rulers. The third category of inscriptions is seen in the three Mayan codices (*Dresdensis*, *Peresianus* and *Tro-Cortesianus*) to which a fourth codex (*Grolier*) was added whose authenticity is still debated. The texts in these codices deal primarily with calendaric, astronomic and religious topics but still remain greatly undecoded as, having been written during the Post-Classic period, the system used differs from the better known system of the Classic era. We do know, however, that

*102-103
Reproduction of one of
the polychrome stucco
panels inside the
Temple of the Sun at
Palenque. The drawing
is by Frederick
Catherwood, the
pioneer of
Mesoamerican
archaeology
(1799-1854 AD).*

*103 bottom Detail of a
Mayan inscription on a
side of Stele A at
Copán. The complexity
of the Mayan writing
system has made it
highly difficult to
decipher but the most
important step towards
solving the enigma was
taken when it was
understood that each
glyph may have had a
phonetic value in
addition to pictographic
and ideographic
values. Classic Mayan
inscriptions are read
using various Maya
languages that are very
similar to contemporary
languages.*

the ancient codices also dealt with more
"literary" themes and epic poetry, and it
would have been from this type of
glyphic codex that the Mayan work
known as the *Popol Vuh* was originally
transcribed.

After the crisis that put an end to
the flourishing Classic Mayan cities, the
custom of writing was substantially
reduced and the Long Count was
abandoned for ever. During the Post-
Classic period, the most important
writing systems were the Mixtec and
Aztec. In both cases, proper writing
was limited to names and dates which
were accompanied by representations
that were essentially pictographic.

*102 bottom Detail of
a Mayan inscription
from Palenque Palace,
Late Classic period.
The inscription has a
single column and the
four "cartouches" are
read from top to
bottom and from left
to right. Each
cartouche consists of a
primary glyph and
several minor ones that
serve as suffixes.*

YAXCHILÁN

history

Yaxchilán in Chiapas was a prosperous Mayan city on the inside of a bend in the largest river in the forest of Petén, the Usumacinta.

Inscriptions in the city put the foundation of the city's royal dynasty at 320 AD when Yat Balam ("Penis-Jaguar") was crowned.

Yaxchilán enjoyed remarkable development during the Early Classic period and received ambassadors from cities such as Tikal, Bonampak and Piedras Negras but it was during the Late Classic era that the city became one of the most important in the Mayan world, governed by famous sovereigns and embellished by what are perhaps the most beautiful Mayan reliefs so far discovered.

Around 630 AD, a sovereign called 6 Tun Bird-Jaguar ascended the throne. It was during his reign that the obscure event referred to in an inscription in House C at Palenque occurred in which a close relative of the king was received or captured by Pacal of Palenque. The inscription mentions Shield-Jaguar II (a son of 6 Tun Bird-Jaguar) who, although still a child, evidently enjoyed great fame; during the reign of his father, this prince distinguished himself in battle when he captured a noble called Ah Ahau in 680 AD. The next year, Shield-Jaguar II succeeded his father to the throne and it is probable Ah Ahau was sacrificed to celebrate the occasion. This marked the start of a splendid reign that was to last sixty one years during which Shield-Jaguar II became one of the most important figures in Mayan politics. This is confirmed by the fact that one of his wives was no less than Evening Star, a princess from the far away and powerful city of Calakmul.

After Shield-Jaguar II's death in 742 AD, Yaxchilán's splendor continued during the reign of his son Bird-Jaguar III, despite ten years passing between his father's death and his coronation that suggests there was a struggle for succession won by the legitimate successor. Bird-Jaguar III became king in 752 AD and the event was probably celebrated with the sacrifice of Chac Cib Tok whom the new king had captured less than a year earlier. Inscriptions in the city recount the military achievements of the new king, his ceaseless building, his strategic marriage with the lady Large Skull – who was a member of one of the most powerful families in the city – and reveal his clear desire to assimilate his reign to that of his dead father. However, the same inscriptions indicate the constant need to forge an alliance with the city nobles which was probably a symptom of the weakening of royal power. The political propaganda of his son Chel Te is also indicative of a weakened position; when he came to the throne, Chel Te changed his name to Shield-Jaguar III. He was the last king mentioned in the texts of Yaxchilán, whose magnificent royal dynasty disappeared at the end of the 9th century when the city was abandoned.

*104 top
Architrave 55 at Yaxchilán. We see a sovereign seated on a throne facing a woman who is probably his wife. At Yaxchilán, low relief art was primarily practiced on the architraves inside the building entrances to be "read" from the bottom to the top.*

*104 bottom
Low relief from the entrance step at Temple 33 at Yaxchilán. It shows the ruler Bird Jaguar playing ball on October 21, 744 AD.*

105 Architrave 26 at Yaxchilán. The relief shows the sovereign Shield Jaguar receiving a warrior headdress in the form of a jaguar from his wife Lady Xoc. This architrave is the only one of the three in

Temple 23 at Yaxchilán to be seen in the Museo de Antropologia in Mexico City. The other two, among the greatest masterpieces of Maya low reliefs, are in the British Museum in London.

the site

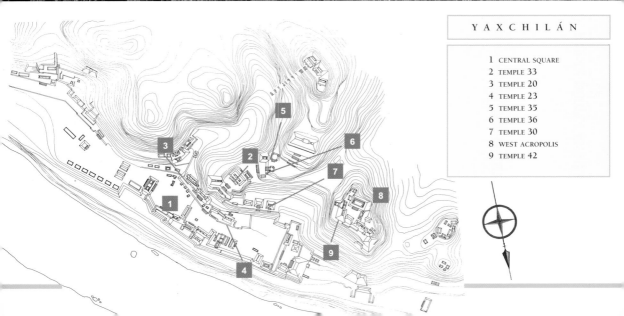

YAXCHILÁN

1 CENTRAL SQUARE
2 TEMPLE 33
3 TEMPLE 20
4 TEMPLE 23
5 TEMPLE 35
6 TEMPLE 36
7 TEMPLE 30
8 WEST ACROPOLIS
9 TEMPLE 42

One of the loveliest cities in the Mayan world, Yaxchilán can be reached by canoe down the river Usumacinta. Its monumental center is only partially excavated, so that much of the city remains covered by vegetation. The long central square is surrounded by monumental buildings and contains a ball court, stelae and altars; on the south side it is dominated by a series of architectural complexes that stand on the slopes of large hills. Many of the loveliest buildings that can be seen date from the reigns of the city's two most famous rulers whose feats are celebrated in the low reliefs carved on stelae and on the architraves of buildings.

On the top of the tallest hill, Shield-Jaguar built Temple 41 and Stele 16 that commemorates a ritual act celebrated on each summer solstice, but the most

through her tongue. The blood that flows out is collected in a bowl containing bark paper at the feet of her husband.

The following scene, carved on Architrave 25, shows the effect of the self-sacrifice: Lady Xoc is depicted kneeling in an ecstatic state in front of a serpent (the "Serpent of the Vision") that rises from the smoke produced by burning the blood-soaked paper. A face emerges from the serpent's open jaws that is probably that of Yat Balam, the founder of the dynasty. Architrave 26 shows Shield-Jaguar in war dress

107 top Building in the main square at Yaxchilán. Many of the ruins in the city have not yet been excavated and are therefore still covered by a thick blanket of vegetation.

106-107 View of temples 41, 40 and 39, the tallest in Yaxchilán. Temple 41 on the far left was built by Shield Jaguar while Temple 40 was constructed by his son Bird Jaguar in an apparent attempt to emulate the magnificence of his father's reign. Originally standing opposite Temple 40 was the famous Stele 11 with its representation of both sovereigns and a scene depicting the capture of prisoners by Bird Jaguar.

important building of his reign was Temple 23 in the central plaza. The three entrances to the temple are crowned by architraves that probably represent the peak of Mayan low relief art but they have unfortunately been removed from the site: one, (26) is now in the National Museum in Mexico City while the other two (24 and 25) are in the British Museum in London. Architrave 24 shows the sovereign holding a torch or a fan over his wife, Lady Xoc, on the occasion of the birth of his son Bird-Jaguar II (though he was in fact the son of the other wife, Evening Star).

Lady Xoc is dressed in elaborate clothes and her face marked by refined decorative scars; she is shown involved in a ritual self-sacrifice in which she passes a string tied with agave spines

receiving a helmet in the form of a jaguar's head from his wife.

One of the last buildings constructed during Shield-Jaguar's reign was Structure 44 which stands in the center of the architectural complex that overlooks the western sector of the site. It was built when the king was already eighty years old to celebrate the military achievements of his lifetime.

The ascension to the throne of Bird-Jaguar brought a huge advance architecturally and artistically. The moments before the succession are shown in the famous Stele 11 that originally stood in Temple 40 built by Bird-Jaguar next to his father's Temple 41 in an apparent attempt to emphasize the continuity between the two reigns. The stele now stands in the city plaza

107 bottom left View of the main square at Yaxchilán. These ruins are some of the most attractive in the world of the Maya; they are buried in the forest on the banks of the river Usumacinta on the border of Mexico and Guatemala.

107 bottom right View of one of the buildings which stand in the main square of the archaeological site.

and portrays Shield-Jaguar on the left side and Bird-Jaguar on the right on 26 June 741 while they both perform a ritual celebration known as the "Flapstaff rite" linked to the summer solstice. This celebration is analogous to the one celebrated by Shield-Jaguar in Temple 41. Below the images of Shield-Jaguar and Evening Star (his parents) on the other side of the stele, Bird-Jaguar is depicted receiving the act of submission from three prisoners who were probably sacrificed during celebrations of the ruler's imminent ascent to the throne.

During the years straddling his effective taking of command and in support of a construction program that had the aim of legitimizing his position as sovereign, Bird-Jaguar built Temples 10, 12, 13, 20, 21 and 22, all of which were decorated with architraves carved with scenes of the capture of prisoners, self-sacrifices made by the royal couple to celebrate the birth of an heir, and other ceremonies. Bird-Jaguar's attempt to emulate his father's works is apparent in Temple 21 which was built beside the famous Temple 23.

The architraves of the new temple are decorated with low reliefs that repeat the themes of its older counterpart: architrave 17 depicts the king seated in front of one of his wives who performs self-sacrifice; architrave 15 shows the wife during an ecstatic vision, and architrave 16 repeats the

warrior theme showing Bird-Jaguar with Chac Cib Tok, one of the prisoners sacrificed during his coronation celebrations. A stele showing Evening Star perforating her tongue was found inside the temple.

The second phase of Bird-Jaguar's political strategy is seen in a new series of buildings (Temples 33, 1, 42, 54 and 55) in which the reliefs are intended to legitimize the heir to the throne and win the support of the other noble families of the city.

The portrayal of various wives and some of their relatives seems to have been a cornerstone of the king's new propaganda program. The architraves in Temples 1 and 42 show at least three other royal wives (one of which is a princess from the city of Motul de San José) and various minor nobles.

The most important of these is Kan Toc who accompanies the sovereign in the famous scene on Architrave 8 of Temple 42 in which the two are shown

Temple 33 dominates the plaza and is the most famous. The temple's stairway is carved with scenes of the ball game in which we see Bird-Jaguar, his father and his grandfather playing using balls containing prisoners of war. The architraves of the temple depict the coronation ceremony, an anniversary of the coronation and a ritual that marked the end of a cycle; in these scenes, the king is shown in the company of his wife Large Skull, his son Chel Te and, unusually, a noble named Ah Mac Kin Mo' Ahau.

capturing two prisoners. Bird-Jaguar's son, Chel Te, is shown several times on architraves in Temples 55 and 54 with his mother and maternal uncle who was evidently the head of the queen's family and therefore one of the most influential nobles in the city.

Bird-Jaguar's attempts at alliance were not limited to the noble families in the city: monuments from nearby settlements show the sovereign's diplomatic activities, for example, as he performs a bleeding rite together with the cahal ("*governor*") of La Pasadita and

108 bottom left
Entrance gallery of a
building at Yaxchilán.
Note the use of the
false vault and a stone
bench along an inner
wall.

108-109 Building in
Yaxchilán square. The
main architectural
characteristics of the
buildings of the
"palace" type are quite
apparent; they are
horizontality, high
sloping roofs and roof
crests that are
somewhat reminiscent
of those at Palenque.

109 top left
Mutilated head of a
full relief statue
inside Temple 33 at
Yaxchilán. It is a
portrait of Bird
Jaguar who wears a
headdress made from
a fantastic central
mask surrounded by
a broad band of
quetzal feathers.

while he superintends the ascent to the
throne of a ruler in the city of Piedras
Negras.

Bird-Jaguar's innovative political
strategy did not have the desired
effects, at least, not in the long term.
The kingdom of Yaxchilán rapidly lost
its prestige during the reign of Chel Te
– Shield-Jaguar III and his successor
Skull Tah III, and then disappeared
completely in just a few years. The last
dated monument in the city was built in
808 AD.

109 top right
The internal gallery
in Temple 33 with the
bust of the statue of
Bird Jaguar. Note the
large pectoral
ornament made from
small beads of jadeite.

109 bottom right
Temple 33 was built
during the reign of
Bird Jaguar. The three
architraves of the
temple respectively
depict his ascent to the
throne, a ritual
conducted by the king
with his son Chel Te,
and a calendaric
ritual during which

the ruler is
accompanied by a
local governor. A large
step in front of the
temple has been
sculpted with images
of the king, his father
and his grandfather
playing the ball game.
An engraved stalactite
stands in front of the
temple.

BONAMPAK

history

Bonampak in the state of Chiapas was a minor center that lies about 19 miles from Yaxchilán but today has become very famous for the superb wall paintings inside one of its buildings. During the Early Classic period, Bonampak had close relations with Yaxchilán as is shown in the monuments of the more powerful city. The good relations continued during the Late Classic epoch when Bonampak reached the peak of its prestige under Chan Muan II ("Sky-Harpy Eagle II") who came to the throne in 776 AD. It was he who commissioned the famous paintings in Building 1 which was inaugurated between 790-92 AD.

110-111 Detail of the original paintings from Temple I at Bonampak showing parading musicians. The bright blue of the background was typical of Maya wall paintings.

110 bottom Stele 4 in the central square at Bonampak. In the background, the entrance stairway to the acropolis where Building 1 (the Temple of the Frescoes) was built by Chan Muan II.

111 As can be seen in this drawing, the entire surface of the walls and vaults of the three rooms in the Temple of the Frescoes is covered with a thick coat of stucco which is in turn filled with fluent paintings of great compositional balance. Unfortunately, the original frescoes are now quite badly damaged.

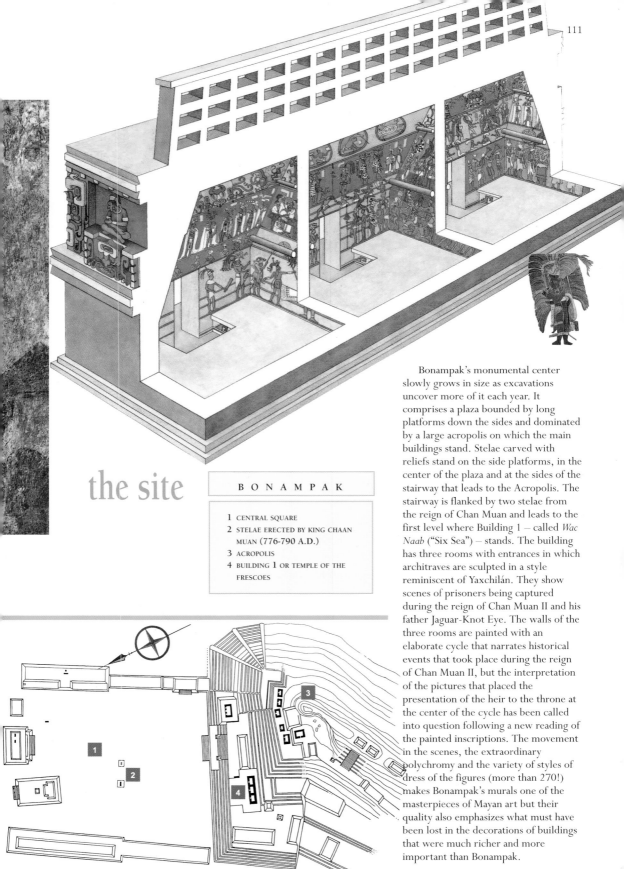

the site

BONAMPAK
1 CENTRAL SQUARE
2 STELAE ERECTED BY KING CHAAN MUAN (776-790 A.D.)
3 ACROPOLIS
4 BUILDING 1 OR TEMPLE OF THE FRESCOES

Bonampak's monumental center slowly grows in size as excavations uncover more of it each year. It comprises a plaza bounded by long platforms down the sides and dominated by a large acropolis on which the main buildings stand. Stelae carved with reliefs stand on the side platforms, in the center of the plaza and at the sides of the stairway that leads to the Acropolis. The stairway is flanked by two stelae from the reign of Chan Muan and leads to the first level where Building 1 – called *Wac Naab* ("Six Sea") – stands. The building has three rooms with entrances in which architraves are sculpted in a style reminiscent of Yaxchilán. They show scenes of prisoners being captured during the reign of Chan Muan II and his father Jaguar-Knot Eye. The walls of the three rooms are painted with an elaborate cycle that narrates historical events that took place during the reign of Chan Muan II, but the interpretation of the pictures that placed the presentation of the heir to the throne at the center of the cycle has been called into question following a new reading of the painted inscriptions. The movement in the scenes, the extraordinary polychromy and the variety of styles of dress of the figures (more than 270!) makes Bonampak's murals one of the masterpieces of Mayan art but their quality also emphasizes what must have been lost in the decorations of buildings that were much richer and more important than Bonampak.

The paintings in Room 1 are laid out in horizontal registers on the various walls. The lowest register shows a procession of musicians playing long bugles, rattles, turtle shells and a wooden drum, plus nobles with fans and three figures wearing large plumed headdresses.

Much of the register above is covered with inscriptions and shows several nobles seated. The third register is the main one and portrays the city's highest ranking nobles, the sovereign with a huge plumed headdress and a

figure standing on a platform holding the sovereign's son. Behind this figure there are two figures on a throne who are thought to be Chan Muan and his wife.

A sequence of large masks of gods decorates the highest section of the walls. As a whole, the scene seems to depict the preparation of the sovereign and other nobles for a ceremony linked to the gods of the underworld shown on the bottom register.

Room 2 is the most famous in the building. The east, south and west walls are completely covered by a large battle scene showing warriors dressed in an extraordinary variety of costumes. The sovereign Chan Muan II is portrayed holding the hair of a prisoner and several experts have hypothesized that the high ranking warrior behind the king is Shield-Jaguar III from Yaxchilán.

The northern wall shows the scene after the battle: Bonampak's royal court is gathered around the sovereign, while his mother and his wife – Green Rabbit, a princess from Yaxchilán – are shown on the right.

The prisoners of war, many of whom have had their fingernails torn out and drip blood, lie on the stairway and a decapitated head rests on one of the steps.

Some commentators believe that the figure lying below the feet of the king represents the highest point achieved in Mayan wall painting. The upper parts of the walls depict images of prisoners and other symbolic references to astral bodies like the Pleiades and the planet Orion which are probably an allusion to the "astral" context of the battle.

Room 3, unfortunately the worst for wear, is decorated with a large dance scene that probably represents the celebrations after the battle. The dancers wear large plumed headdresses and hold triangular articles similar to standards. The

middle register on the east, north and west walls is filled by a scene showing the sovereign and his nobles wearing long white cloaks while a group of enthroned women watch the scene with one of them perforating her tongue.

Large masks of gods line the top of the walls.

112 left
Reproduction of Bonampak paintings in Room 1 of the Museo de Antropología in Mexico City. Detail of the parade of musicians below the court scene on the register above.

112 right
Reproduction of Bonampak paintings
in Room 1 of the Museo de Antropología in Mexico City. Detail of the parade of musicians; note the large rattles.

112-113
Reproduction of Bonampak paintings in Room 2 of the Museo de Antropología in Mexico City. In the detail one can see the pompous headdresses of the warriors.

*113 bottom
Reproduction of
Bonampak paintings
in Room 2 of the
Museo de
Antropología in
Mexico City. Detail
from the battle scene.
Military clashes
between the various
Mayan cities were
symbolic and
astronomic events were
often used to signal
the beginning of the
conflict.*

TIKAL

 history

114 top How the
center of Tikal would
have looked during
its period of greatest
splendor, around
750 AD.

114-115 Aerial
view of Tikal. The
tops of the tallest
pyramids rise above
the huge expanse of
the tropical forest in
Petén.

The ancient name of the city of Tikal in Guatemala was probably *Mutul* ("Hair bun"). It was the most powerful Mayan city during the Classic period and at several times in its history was the capital of alliances or confederations of various city-states.

It was founded during the Late Pre-Classic period and may have been subordinate at first to the large Pre-Classic city of El Mirador, but Tikal soon became the seat of a wealthy nobility whose tombs have been discovered in the deepest layers of the Northern Acropolis. The decline of El Mirador at the end of the Pre-Classic period allowed other cities to expand and develop, among which Tikal soon played a role of prime importance. The founder of a new and longlasting royal dynasty, Yax Moch Xoc, lived during the 3rd century AD and, in 292 AD, a sovereign of the city was portrayed on Stele 29 (the first Mayan stele in the lowlands to use the Long Count); this year is conventionally used by scholars as the start of the Classic period.

During the reign of Great Jaguar Claw (Yax Moch Xoc's ninth successor)

who ascended the throne in the mid-4th century, Tikal began a policy of expansion with an attack on the nearby city of Uaxactún which it conquered in 378 AD. The leader of the Tikal forces was Smoking Frog – maybe the brother of the ruler of Tikal – who was immediately appointed sovereign of the conquered city. The fact that war carried out for the purposes of conquest had till then not been part of the Mayan world, plus the discovery of a series of archaeological and epigraphic clues, has led historians to suppose that the war between Tikal and Uaxactún was based on Teotihuacan customs and was probably the first case of the "star war" or War of Tláloc-Venus.

Certainly the influence of Teotihuacan in Tikal was much stronger during the reign of Curl Nose (379-411 AD) and his son Stormy Sky (411-457 AD) who was one of the city's most famous rulers. Under the latter's government, Tikal became one of the most powerful cities in the lowlands holding diplomatic relations with Yaxchilán and perhaps with the distant cities of Copán and Quiriguá. It seems

that for sovereigns like Stormy Sky, the linking of his power with a sort of "Teotihuacan patronage" represented an element of special prestige, rather like the model of Post-Classic Tollan.

Tikal's continual increase in power led to confrontations with other emerging cities, in particular, Calakmul in the modern state of Campeche which was an enormous city in the northern Petén known in ancient times as *Kan* ("Serpent") where archaeologists are currently unearthing extraordinary remains. The rivalry between the two powers and their allied cities resulted in clashes that threw Calakmul, Caracol, Naranjo and Tikal into confusion and seems to have ended in victory in 526 AD for Caracol over Tikal. The consequences of the defeat were disastrous for the city: the last monument known to have been built before the war (in 557 AD and portraying a sovereign called Double Bird) was followed by almost one hundred and thirty years of "silence" in terms of dated constructions in the city. This hiatus forms the conventional threshold between the Early Classic and Late Classic periods.

After the long crisis, Tikal's renaissance coincided with the reign of Ah Cacaw, the greatest sovereign in the city's history, who came to the throne in 682 AD. After renewing the monumental center to mirror his political propaganda that presented the ruler as the new Stormy Sky, Ah Cacaw moved on to re-establish Tikal's "international" prestige. On the anniversary of a war fought 260 years earlier by Stormy Sky, in 695 AD Ah Cacaw attacked Calakmul and captured its ruler Jaguar-Claw. The prisoner and other nobles from the enemy city were paraded in front of Tikal's public before

115 Funerary mask made from jadeite, Spondylus, shell and obsidian. It shows the face of a dead sovereign with a headdress in the form of a bird. The jaguar ears above the human ears allude to the dead ruler's relationship with the underworld.

being sacrificed forty days later.

After a reign of forty five years, Ah Cacaw died in 723 AD leaving the throne to his son Yax Kin ("Green Sun") who continued his father's glorious tradition and maintained Tikal at the top of the Mayan political hierarchy. His successors were, however, not so successful and we know little of their reigns until 889 AD when the city's last monument was built. The crisis that struck the Classic world had by this time reached the heart of the Mayan territories.

the site

Tikal's central square, with its slanting pyramids that rise above the top of the forest, is perhaps the most famous place in the world of the Maya. It is closed on the short sides by Temples I and II and lined by two large monumental complexes, the Central and the North Acropolises, that represent much of the city's history.

The first was the residence of the royal family, the second their burial place and the setting for their political and ideological propaganda.

Much of what can be seen in the plaza today dates from the reign of Ah Cacaw. His first great work following his ascent to the throne was Temple II, the large, three-stepped pyramid on the west side of the square. It stands 125 feet high and is distinguished by its architectural style of solidity and embedded corners that dates from the Early Classic period. The wooden architrave of the entrance is decorated with the carving of a woman, perhaps the sovereign's wife, and the stairway faces a large stele and an altar, neither of which are decorated.

The monumental section that most clearly displays the sense of Ah Cacaw's

architectural activity is the North Acropolis that had been the traditional burial place of the city's rulers since the Pre-Classic period.

The stelae aligned on the facade were produced in different epochs but placed in their current position during the Post-Classic period.

Dozens of older structures have been found inside the North Acropolis containing tombs of rulers like Great Jaguar Claw and Curl Nose. The building at the eastern end contained the tomb of Stormy Sky and we know that hundreds of years later Ah Cacaw built a large pyramidal building over it (which has today been completely disassembled by excavation work). When the building was constructed, Ah Cacaw also removed the famous Stele 31 (portraying Stormy Sky and two figures

dressed in "Teotihuacan style") from the facade of the temple and had it placed inside so that it would be buried by the new building constructed to celebrate the anniversary of the ancient king's death.

Ah Cacaw's building (the one that no longer exists) was very similar to Temple I and gave rise to the "vertical" architectural style that distinguished Tikal. From the time of its construction, no other sovereign was buried in the North Acropolis.

The significance of Ah Cacaw's work was to commemorate an ancient heroic sovereign and a period of great splendor with the monumental "sealing" of the Acropolis and the birth of a new style that would symbolize a new era of glory and the resurgence of Tikal from its darkest age.

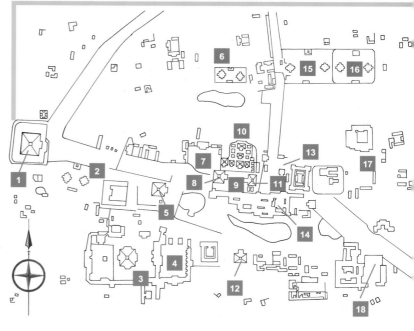

116 Temple I at Tikal. This underworld pyramid with its nine levels was built as the funerary temple of Ah Cacaw, the most important of the Late Classic rulers of the city. The pyramid features the new "vertical" architectural style introduced during this sovereign's reign.

TIKAL

1	TEMPLE IV	10	NORTH ACROPOLIS
2	COMPLEX N	11	TEMPLE I
3	SOUTH ACROPOLIS	12	TEMPLE V
4	PLAZA OF THE AEVEN TEMPLES	13	EAST SQUARE
5	TEMPLE III	14	CENTRAL ACROPOLIS
6	COMPLEX O	15	COMPLEX R
7	WEST PLAZA	16	COMPLEX Q
8	TEMPLE II	17	GROUP F
9	GREAT SQUARE	18	GROUP G

116-117 Temple II at Tikal dominates the central square of the city. This pyramid was built during the early part of Ah Cacaw's reign in the architectural style typical of the Early Classic period. The stelae and altars in the foreground rise in front of the North Acropolis.

117 bottom left Polychrome cylindrical pot found in the tomb of the sovereign Hasaw Ka'an K'awil (Governor A), Late Classic period. The sovereign (who was a scribe and painter) is shown on a throne receiving the homage of a kneeling dignitary.

117 bottom center Polychrome pot with lid dating from the Early Classic period found in a noble's tomb at Tikal. The main image shows a god with attributes that associate him with the rain god of central Mexico though the style is pure Maya.

117 bottom right The roof crests of Temples I and II face one another in this view from the top of Temple IV. The crests were once decorated with polychrome low reliefs. The image of Ah Cacaw seated on his throne was painted on the crest of Temple I.

The climax of Ah Cacaw's building program was of course the construction of a new and majestic funerary temple for himself, Temple I. The new style was applied to the large "underworld" pyramid of nine levels crowned by a high crest originally painted red, white, green and blue showing the enthroned sovereign. The wooden architrave portrays Ah Cacaw seated below a large guardian serpent while another architrave inside the temple shows the king dominated by an enormous jaguar.

His tomb, now displayed in the site museum, was found in a crypt at the base of the pyramid with the king's body covered by one hundred and eighty jade beads in the form of bracelets, anklets, earrings, diadems, a superb portrait-vase and, in particular, a necklace made from large jade balls that made a total of seven kilos of precious green stone. A sort of stone "table" was covered by matting with tassels made from jade beads and shell ornaments on which the body lay. All around were large polychrome plates and dozens of engraved bones, one of which shows the sovereign

travelling by canoe towards the world of the dead.

To the south of Temple I lies a small ball court and the area to the south of the square is occupied by the Central Acropolis, which is a complex of residential buildings that the city rulers lived in for centuries. They are portrayed in decorations like the one of Ah Cacaw next to his prisoner, the sovereign of Calakmul.

The Central Acropolis also faces onto the East Plaza behind Temple I where a four-sided complex may be the remains of the city market. Nearby there is Tikal's largest ball court. Méndez Avenue runs from the East Plaza to Group G and the Temple of the Inscriptions.

Group G is a large complex with painted walls where the city elite lived and the Temple of the Inscriptions is a pyramid crowned by a tall crest inscribed with the date 766 AD.

118 bottom View of Temple II from the North Acropolis. Some experts believe that the tomb of Ah Cacaw's wife — portrayed on one of the temple's architraves — may be buried below the building.

PLAN OF NORTH ACROPOLI

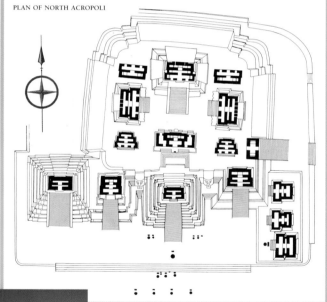

118-119 View of
the central square in
Tikal. The North
Acropolis is on the
left and Temple I on
the right. All Tikal's

rulers were buried in
the North Acropolis
until Ah Cacaw
changed this tradition
by being buried in a
chamber below Temple I.

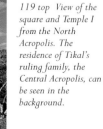

119 top View of the
square and Temple I
from the North
Acropolis. The
residence of Tikal's
ruling family, the
Central Acropolis, can
be seen in the
background.

119 bottom
View of Temple I, seen
from the top of the
Central Acropolis.
On the left the
buildings of the
North Acropolis can
be seen in thje
background.

Returning to the East Plaza, the large Temple V stands behind the Central Acropolis; it is the second tallest pyramid in the city and was built around 700 AD, probably as a funerary temple for an unknown sovereign. Further west, past the South Acropolis and the Plaza of the Seven Temples (that incorporates a triple ball court) lies the Mundo Perdido, a complex mostly built during the Early Classic period and dominated by a large pyramid from the Pre-Classic era. Excavation of the Mundo Perdido has thrown light on the earliest history of the city and allowed us to understand the extent of the influence of Teotihuacan on Tikal during the Early Classic period.

To the north of the Mundo Perdido stands Temple III, the last funerary pyramid to be built in the city, probably in honour of king Chitam around 810 AD. Inside there is a wooden architrave with a fine representation of an obese man dressed in a jaguar skin in the company of two attendants who hold stone "insignia" known as "eccentrics."

As one continues behind Temple III along Tozzer Avenue, one passes a large palatial complex known as the Bat Palace before reaching the Twin Pyramid complex built to celebrate the end of a twenty year calendaric cycle. Although twin pyramid complexes had existed in other areas of the Mayan territories since the Early Classic period, this was the first built in Tikal. It dates from 711 AD, i.e., from the reign of Ah Cacaw.

The sovereign is in fact portrayed on Stele 16 with a large plumed headdress, and Altar 5 shows two individuals who seem to be performing a funeral ceremony near a pile of human bones.

Further west lies the massive bulk of Temple IV, the highest pyramid in Tikal and built, like Temple VI, during the reign of Yax Kin, the son of Ah

121 top left Pyramid in the Mundo Perdido complex. Many finds from the Pre-Classic and Early Classic periods have been found in this part of the city.

121 top right The main pyramid in the Mundo Perdido section of Tikal seen from the top of Temple IV. The structure is known as

5C-54. It was built during the Pre-Classic period and is decorated with grotesque masks to the sides of its four stairways.

Cacaw. One of the extraordinary wooden architraves of the temple (the originals are in Basle) shows Yax Kin with an enormous serpentine headdress overlooked by a large two-headed feathered serpent, and the other depicts the king in front of a gigantic solar god. A wonderful view of the entire city can be had from the top of this temple.

Some experts believe that Yax Kin's tomb lies below Temple IV or Temple VI but a very fine tomb found in a small building in the Central Plaza has features that suggest it belongs to the

121 center The twin pyramids of Complex Q. The central square contains various stelae and altars. The entire complex was built in 771 AD to celebrate the end of a twenty year calendar cycle; this year corresponded to the data

9.17.0.0.0. in the Long Count. This custom had been established by Ah Cacaw sixty years before.

121 bottom Structure with a tall crest that rises above the Mundo Perdido and the square of the Seven Temples.

120-121 A pyramid from Tikal's Mundo Perdido. The mass of Temple IV — the highest pyramid in the city — rises out of the vegetation in the background.

120 bottom Structures in the Central Acropolis. The residences of several sovereigns and works of art commemorating military successes have been identified in this complex.

sovereign, above all because in many ways it resembles the tomb of Yax Kin's father, Ah Cacaw.

Maudslay Avenue heads north of Temple IV towards a large palatial building known as Group H and two other Twin Pyramid complexes constructed during Chitam's reign (ca. 768-810 AD) who was probably trying to emulate the deeds of Ah Cacaw.

The rest of the ancient city is spread around the buildings described above over an area of six square miles. To have an idea of how much there is to be discovered at Tikal, consider that it has been calculated that below those structures that are visible today, there are another ten thousand more ancient ones still buried!

UAXACTÚN

history

The small center of Uaxactún (ancient name *Sian Kan*, "Born in Heaven") lies about 25 miles to the north of Tikal. It was one of the main centers in the lowlands during the Pre-Classic period and it was prosperous and independent until Smoking Frog, Tikal's military commander, conquered the city in 378 AD and became its new sovereign. For a number of years after the conquest, however, Uaxactún maintained a position of prestige and Stele 5 in Uaxactún indicates that Curl Nose (who ascended to Tikal's throne in 379 AD) "showed the sceptre in the land of Smoking Frog," a formula that seems to invert the hierarchic order of the two sites.

Some scholars suggest that Smoking Frog was Curl Nose's uncle and that therefore his power was increased by his blood relationship with the king of Tikal

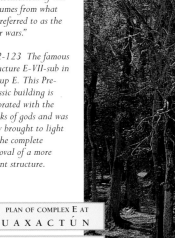

122 top right Stele 5 at Uaxactún depicts the military leader, Smoking Frog, who conquered the city on January 16, 378 AD with the troops of Tikal. Smoking Frog is shown in profile with a club made from obsidian blades in one hand and a spear sling in the other; a quetzal with a long tail is shown on his headdress. This is one of the oldest known representations of war costumes from what are referred to as the "star wars."

122-123 The famous Structure E-VII-sub in Group E. This Pre-Classic building is decorated with the masks of gods and was only brought to light by the complete removal of a more recent structure.

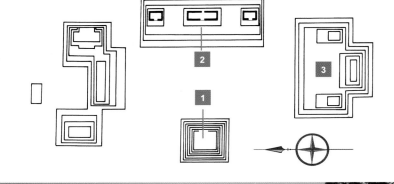

PLAN OF COMPLEX E AT
UAXACTÚN

1 STRUCTURE E VII-SUB
2 EAST COMPLEX
3 GROUP A-5

123 top left Palace 5 in Group A at Uaxactún. These buildings were built during the Late Classic *period during which Uaxactún had practically become a satellite of the nearby city of Tikal.*

122 bottom Although of less importance, Structure E-10 in Group E bears similarities to structures at Tikal, the city to which Uaxactún was long subjugated.

and by the reputation he had won in the battle for the city.

However, by the end of the reigns of Curl Nose and his successor Stormy Sky, Tikal returned to take the leading role and from then on Uaxactún was no more than a simple satellite of its large neighbor.

Uaxactún seems to have been abandoned during the first part of the Post-Classic era.

the site

Uaxactún's main monuments lie in different temple and residential groups. Excavation of some of them — Complexes A, B and E between 1926-37 — was a major event in the history of Mesoamerican archaeology since the oldest buildings then known in the Mayan world were discovered. The name Uaxactún ("Eight Stone") was conventionally assigned to the site on the basis of the discovery of a series of

123 *bottom left*
Inside of a structure at
Uaxactún. Note the
false vault, the plaster
that still covers the
walls, and the wooden
crosspieces.

six very ancient monuments that date from the eighth *baktun* in the Mayan calendar, i.e., between 328-416 AD.

One of the first groups to be excavated was Complex E which centered on a central east-facing pyramid that stands opposite a platform on which three smaller buildings are arranged so that, when seen from the pyramid, they were aligned for observation of the dawn of the solstices and equinoxes. In front of these buildings stood some of the ancient stelae already mentioned. The central pyramid was in very poor condition and was completely removed to allow Structure E-VII-sub below to be examined. This was a Pre-Classic construction adorned with sixteen stucco masks – four on each side – of Venus as the Morning Star, Venus as the Evening Star, the rising Sun and the setting Sun.

This iconography is typical of many Pre-Classic buildings, for example, those in Cerros in Belize and in the Mundo Perdido in Tikal.

Groups A and B are residential complexes from the Early Classic period that contain ceremonial structures. A superb wall painting, now no longer in existence, was found in Group B that showed court scenes.

In recent years, a new research project has concentrated on Complex H where an important complex from the Late Pre-Classic era has been found below the constructions from the Late Classic period. One of these sub-structures (H-sub-3) is decorated with stucco masks of the Sacred Mountain (*witz*) that would have indicated the symbolic function of the structure. The nearby structure H-sub-10 was decorated with *ahau* ("lord") masks and matting motifs (*pop*, one of the primary symbols of Maya power) which alternated around enthroned kings surrounded by volutes.

Uaxactún's oldest structures reveal the formation of the political ideology of the Maya in which the sacredness of power was linked to identification of the sovereign with Venus and the Sun, stars which, like the twins in the *Popul Vuh*, fought the forces of the underworld in the heart of the Sacred Mountain before emerging into the sky that lay over the world of the living.

123 *top right* Palace
5 *in Group A was*
probably the seat of
the local governing
elite during the
Classic period.

123 *bottom right*
View of Structure 16
in Group A; note how
the building has been
only partially
restored.

COPÁN

history

124 Altar G1 was built by Yax Pac in 800 AD in Copán's central square. The altar depicts the two-headed celestial dragon with its open jaws in a representation of the

supreme deity Itzamná in animal form. The head on the left is in skeletal form as a symbol of duality. The ball in the middle of the inscription is probably an image of the sun.

125 Detail of Stele A, dated 731 AD, that depicts the sovereign, 18 Rabbit. This stele is famous because its inscription mentions Copán, Tikal, Calakmul and

Palenque in association with the four points of the compass as though these cities were considered the "capitals" of the Maya world.

The archaeological ruins and the monuments of Copán in Honduras are the remains of over two thousand years of continuous occupation and of an extraordinary development in architecture and sculpture during the Classic period. During that era, the city became the capital of a vast political system that spread its influence over many Mayan cities and ethnic groups in the south from its location in the extreme southeast of the Mayan world (its indigenous name, *Xuk*, meant "corner").

The first signs of habitation in the Copan Valley date from 1000 BC, but the start of the city's golden period began in the third decade of the 4th century AD with the foundation by Yax Kuk Mo' ("Green Quetzal Parrot") of the dynasty that was to govern the city until its abandonment.

The policy of expansion undertaken by the state of Copán seems to have

begun during the reign of Butz Chan ("Smoke-Serpent" or "Smoke-Sky," 578-628 AD) and been continued under Smoke-Imix-God K (628-695 AD) who extended its boundaries to incorporate the nearby Quiriguá.

'18 Rabbit' (whose real name was Waxaklahun-Ubah-K'awil, "Eighteen images of K'awil") was the thirteenth successor to Yax Kuk Mo' and came to the throne in 695 AD. It was he who turned Copán into one of the most powerful cities in the Mayan world. In 738 AD after forty three years of rule, 18 Rabbit was captured by Cauac-Sky, the king of Quiriguá, whom had been placed on the vassal throne by 18 Rabbit himself. On May 3 of the same year, 18 Rabbit was sacrificed and thirty nine days later, on the day of Venus's maximum trajectory as the Morning Star, a new sovereign, Smoke-Monkey, was crowned king of Copán and began a reign lasting eleven years (738-749

AD). His successor, Smoke-Shell (749-763 AD) married a princess from Palenque and succeeded in raising Copán to the heights of the Mayan political hierarchy. When his son Yax Pac or Yax Pasah ("New Dawn") succeeded, Copán was still a powerful kingdom. The fifty seven years of Yax Pac's reign (763-820 AD) were marked by the construction of many of the monuments to be seen today in Copán, but his death seems to have marked the collapse of the city's political system and the monument that celebrated the ascent to the throne of his successor, U-Cit-Tok, who became king on February 10, 822 AD, remained uncompleted. Although the ceremony marking the new king's ascension was held on the day the Morning Star began its journey into the world of the dead and Mars and Jupiter were in conjunction, the stars were not providential and Copán fell into oblivion.

126 top Square A in the Las Sepolturas complex. This is an important residential complex where the elite lived on the periphery of the monumental center of Copán.

the site

Copán's monumental center consists of an Acropolis that overlooks a large Monumental Plaza. The Acropolis is dominated by Structures 11 and 16 and is organized around two large patios, the West Patio and the East Patio. In modern times, all the eastern section has been washed away by the Copán river but, in doing so, it has enabled archaeologists to enter the mass of buildings above through miles of tunnels.

We consequently know that construction of the Acropolis began around 400 AD and that a substantial

126 bottom left Stele P at Copán. This stele from the end of the 6th century AD portrays the governor Butz' Chan. It was later moved from its original location to in front of Structure 16 on the city acropolis.

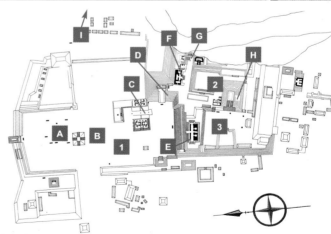

COPÁN

1 GREAT PLAZA	D HIEROGLYPHIC STARWAY
2 EAST PATIO OF THE ACROPOLIS	AND TEMPLE 26
3 WEST PATIO OF THE ACROPOLIS	E STRUCTURE 11
A STELAE ERECTED BY KING 18 RABBIT	F STRUCTURE 22
B STRUCTURE 4	G STRUCTURE 21
C BALL COURT	H STRUCTURE 16
	I LAS SEPOLTURAS

126 center right Detail of Altar Q, probably a throne that was carved for Yax Pac to endorse his membership of the dynastic line of the city. The sides of the altar are carved with the sixteen sovereigns of the dynasty founded by Yax Kuk Mo'. From right to left in the photograph there are portraits of the third, fourth and fifth governors of Copán.

126-127 View of the Great Plaza with the Ball Court in the foreground and Structure 4 to the right in the middle ground. The many stelae on the huge expanse can also be clearly seen.

127 top Tomb inside Square A in the Las Sepolturas complex. On the left we see the stone slabs that closed the entrance.

increase in building activity occurred during the reign of the founder of the dynasty, Yax Kuk Mo'.

Archaeologists have discovered the ruler's residence (built in the Teotihuacan style of *talud* and *tablero* architecture) containing his tomb below the Acropolis.

Here the body of the sovereign was discovered lying among grave goods made of jade, the spines of sea-rays, jaguar teeth, shells and high quality pots, many of which were in Teotihuacan style.

The ruler's son and successor, K'inich Ah Pop ("Solar Eye-Lord of the matting") constructed a magnificent funerary temple (the Yehnal Structure) above his father's tomb with walls adorned with stucco low reliefs of the Sun God that show no influence from Teotihuacan.

Above this building, the magnificent Margarita structure was erected with a stairway lined with large reliefs giving the name of the founder of the dynasty, but these too were soon built over with other platforms. All these modifications were made, however, without blocking the entrance to the tomb of Yax Kuk Mo' in which, many years later, his wife was also buried near to a warrior in arms.

The continual overbuilding of structures and royal tombs continued for centuries until the large architectural complex known today as the Acropolis was created.

The most impressive structure found inside is the Rosalila Structure built in 571 AD during the reign of Jaguar Moon with extraordinary polychrome moulded facades. The current appearance of the Acropolis is greatly due to the building activity of Yax Pac who was responsible for the current versions of Temples 11 and 16. He had the entire dynastic history of the city carved on the famous Altar Q that was placed in front of Temple 16. Stele P showing the sovereign Butz Chan can be seen on the left of the altar.

127 bottom Square C in the Las Sepolturas complex. On the left we see structure 9N-82, the residence of an important family of scribes in the city. The facade of the building is decorated with sculptures of the guardian deities of scribes and inside there is a finely carved stone bench.

A series of large important buildings faces onto the East Patio. Structure 22 was built by 18 Rabbit, perhaps as his personal residence. The four corners feature *witz* monsters (monsters of the "Sacred Mountains") and the inner portal is crowned by a frieze depicting the Celestial Monster surrounded by spurts of sacrificial blood and supported by two figures called Pahuatun (a type of "Atlas").

Evidently the palace was a sort of cosmogram and its portal represented the jaws of the Sacred Mountain that only the sovereign was allowed to enter. Close by, Yax Pac built Structure 18 which was officially opened on August 12, 801 AD. The turbulence that occurred during the last years of his reign is apparent in the iconography on the pillars in which the king and his brother are portrayed in war dress. Inside, there are large friezes in the form of plumes and a bench decorated with masks of gods. Below the building there is a burial chamber where Yax Pac was probably buried but it was plundered during antiquity.

Structure 11 may have been Yax Pac's residence and was a clear attempt to imitate Structure 22 built by 18 Rabbit.

The lowest level symbolizes the waters of the Underworld and the portal the jaws of the Sacred Monster; there are also two large *pahuatun* (since fallen) that supported the Cosmic Monster at the corners of the building. The rear of the base, i.e., the side that faces the West Patio, is built like a false ball court with stone scorers; the inscriptions on the steps and the shell decorations identify it as a court that opens onto the waters of the Underworld and it is possible that prisoners – symbolically associated with balls used in the game and destined to end, metaphorically and literally, in the world of the gods of death – were thrown from the steps of Structure 11.

128 top Sculpture on the facade of Structure 11 (known as the Temple of the Inscriptions) which is one of the most important structures on the Acropolis. The sculptural complex of the facade depicts it as a sort of symbolic ball court that opens onto the waters of the Underworld.

128 bottom Facade of the inner chamber in Temple 22 built by 18 Rabbit at Copán. The elaborately carved decoration forms a sort of cosmogram. In the foreground we see a Bacab (god that supports the heavenly vault) from behind and crouching on a skull that represents the underworld. The two Bacab hold up a serpentine celestial monster that passes over the entrance.

128-129 Sculpture located on the Jaguar Steps in the East Patio of the Acropolis. The pupils with the internal "hook" and the decoration on the god's forehead identify him as the sun god kin.

129 bottom left View of Structure 11 from the West Patio of the Acropolis.

129 bottom right Temple 18 that faces the East Patio on the Acropolis. Low reliefs with images of Yax Pac and his brother in battle dress are carved on the pillars of the structures. A burial chamber below the temple — unfortunately raided in ancient times — probably contained the remains of the sovereign.

Descending the steps of Structure 11 towards the plaza, one reaches Temple 26 that was built over another of 18 Rabbit's buildings by Smoke-Shell in 756. Smoke-Shell himself is portrayed in Stelae M and N that stand next to the temple.

The large Hieroglyphic Stairway is engraved with the longest head in pre-Columbian America and the entire dynastic history of the city. Several sculptural portraits of sovereigns line the stairway at intervals of twelve steps.

The Ball Court, whose current appearance was finalized during the reign of 18 Rabbit, lies to the north of the Hieroglyphic Stairway. The side linings of the court are decorated with sculptures of parrot heads as the bird was one of the most common animal manifestations of the sun god who, in turn, alluded to the astral symbolism of the game. Three rectangular stone scorers stand on the ground of the ball court. Large mosaics on the two temples at the sides of the court depict parrots with open beaks, their wings spread and claws in view. Stele 2 on the structure to the north of the ball court is decorated with images of Smoke-Imix-God K, and Altar L, the last and uncompleted monument in Copán, shows the sovereign U-Cit-Tok with his predecessor.

130 bottom left The altar of Stele M in the foreground at Copán depicts the monster Cauac. In the center of the photograph, Stele M portrays the sovereign Smoke Shell. Behind the stele there is the Hieroglyphic Stairway which bears the longest known Mayan inscription on stone; it narrates the dynastic history of the city.

131 top
Detail of the inscription
on Stele 2. The stele
portrays the sovereign
Smoke Imix God K on
the day after his ascent
to the throne (652 AD).
As can be seen, the style
of the inscription is
particularly complex
and affected and, as
such, suitable for a
commemorative
monument as important
as the portrait of the
ruler.

131 bottom The main
ball court in Copán,
situated in the Great
Plaza. The sculptures
in the form of parrots
heads can be seen
along the facings but
their purpose is not
understood.

130 bottom right
Central scorer in
another ball court at
Copán. The sovereign
18 Rabbit is shown
on the left dressed for
the game in front of
the God 0, an
underworld god
distinguished by
having a hand in
place of his jaw. A
large inscribed ball
lies between the two.

130-131 Splendid
sculptural mosaic of a
scarlet macaw that
adorns one of the
buildings at the side of
the ball court in Copán
square. This sculpture
has been created from
parts of different but
identical sculptures
that lined the court.
Note the spread wings
and talons in the
foreground.

From the ball court, one comes to the Monumental Plaza where there stands what some experts consider the Maya thought of as a "forest of kings." The plaza is filled with the sculptures of sovereigns in the form of "cosmic trees." Stele E on the west side dates from the early years of the 6th century and is decorated with a portrait of Waterlily-Jaguar, while Stele I in the southeast corner shows Smoke-Imix-God K. All the other stelae (A, B, C, D, F, H and 4) were placed in the plaza between 711-736 AD and depict 18 Rabbit as various gods that he incarnated by means of ecstatic rituals. The superb Stele J; it stands at the end of the East Plaza and bears an inscription carved in the form of matting, the symbol of royal power.

Facing the stelae, a number of altars show the Earthly Crocodile, also known as the Cauac Monster. The portraits of 18 Rabbit are certainly some of the masterpieces of Copán's sculptural works and typical examples of the "Baroque" character of the city's art. The zoomorphic altars of Celestial Serpents (G1, G2 and G3) were placed in the Monumental Plaza by Yax Pac in an attempt to associate his reign with that of his illustrious predecessor.

Of the many buildings that stand around the monumental center, Structure 9N-82 is embellished with sculptures and inscriptions that inform us that the building was the residence of an important family of scribes in the city.

132 Detail of Stele H, one of the most famous portraits of 18 Rabbit and certainly a fine example of the "Baroque" style of the art of Copán. The sovereign is depicted as the God of Maize at the moment he danced during the creation of the world.

*133 top left
View of Copán square with Stele H in the foreground. Some experts believe the shape of stelae made them symbolic "stone trees" and therefore representations of the cosmic tree. This interpretation has led to the square being described as the "forest of kings."*

*133 bottom left
Altar of Stele D with representations of a skeletal jaguar from the Underworld that was probably linked to the journey the sovereign made during the ecstatic state he achieved shown on the corresponding stele.*

*133 top right
Stele D is also a portrait of 18 Rabbit in the central square at Copán. The ruler is shown having achieved ecstasy during a ritual of self-sacrifice; this state is revealed by the Perforator God dancing on the king's head.*

*133 bottom right
Stele A. 18 Rabbit is shown holding a ceremonial bar with the double head of a snake. This was a symbol of the sovereign's authority and ability to communicate with beings from other cosmic regions.*

QUIRIGUÁ

history

The ancient Guatemalan city of Quiriguá (indigenous name *Tzuk*, "Division") was founded in the lower Motagua valley at the start of the Early Classic period, perhaps by colonists from the central lowlands. Its location was strategic from the point of view of acquiring supplies of obsidian and jadeite. Interpretation of several monuments suggests that a local dynasty was already in place at the end of the 5th century AD but that from this time on Quiriguá was subordinate to the nearby city of Copán. Under the protection of Copán's sovereign, 18 Rabbit, the ruler of Quiriguá, Sky-Cauac, took the throne in 725 AD and quickly showed his desire to shake off the yoke of his more powerful neighbor by taking the title *k'ul ahaw*, "divine lord," which was reserved for supreme sovereigns. Sky-Cauac's political strategy culminated in the famous war of 738 AD in which he managed to capture and sacrifice 18 Rabbit himself. During the sixty years of his reign, Sky-Cauac followed a building program that transformed Quiriguá into a smaller version of Copán.

Sky-Cauac adopted the same propaganda policy that 18 Rabbit had used by erecting impressive portrait-stelae in the city's binomial acropolis-plaza layout that was another derivation from Copán. Some of the stelae bore inscriptions describing Sky-Cauac as the "fourteenth governor" and by this it is possible he was not referring to the local dynasty but to the fact that he had succeeded 18 Rabbit, the thirteenth king of Copán. Another allusion to the larger city was Sky-Cauac's adoption of a bat's head (*zotz*) among his royal titles which was the symbol of Copán.

Sky-Cauac was succeeded by Xul-Sky (784-800 AD) and Jade Sky (800-?) under whose rule Quiriguá enjoyed its most prosperous period, indicated by the intense construction that took place on the Acropolis. We do not know what happened at the end of his reign but, following a short period in which Quiriguá seems to have been controlled by groups from the Caribbean coast, the city was abandoned at some time between 900-1000 AD.

134 left
One of the many stelae in the Monumental Plaza; this too contributes to making Quiriguà a smaller "copy" of nearby Copán.

134 top right
Standing a formidable 35 feet high since it was erected in 771 AD, Stele E is the largest Mayan monument of this sort. The king Sky-Cauac was portrayed facing forward, standing on a mask of the Earthly Crocodile or, according to another interpretation, a jaguar.

QUIRIGUÁ

1 MONUMENTAL PLAZA
2 BALL COURT
3 TEMPLES SQUARE
4 EAST GROUP

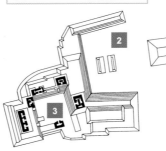

the site

As mentioned, the monumental center of Quiriguá was similar to the one in Copán. The large acropolis embraces an intermediate plaza where the ball court lies and which leads into a Monumental Plaza ornamented with stelae and altars.

To the south and east of the Acropolis there stand two residential

134-135 Monument P, the masterpiece of the local artists, is a baffling mass entirely carved with high reliefs. The sovereign is portrayed on the front facade (in the picture) as he exits from the open jaws of the Earthly Crocodile.

135 top right The figure of the sovereign is also shown emerging from the jaws of the Earthly Crocodile on Monument B. Monuments of this type are peculiar to Quiriguá; they are referred to as "zoomorphic" but their function is unknown.

135 bottom right The famous "Tortoise" of Quiriguá is one of the most mysterious and fascinating Mayan

sculptures. The monolithic shell rests on five blocks a little in the style of paws and a head.

perhaps the masterpieces of the sculpture of Quiriguá. They are in the form of the Cauac Monster – or Earthly Crocodile – from whose jaws the figure of a sovereign emerges; a splendid altar in front of each is decorated with the figure of a god next to an inscription.

The sculptures in the Monumental Plaza are equally famous: these include a number of zoomorphic altars but are

complexes similar to those that once used to lie around the city.

The east arm of the Acropolis was probably used to host the cult of the local ruling dynasty and the tomb of (probably) its founder has been found below one of its buildings.

Two large structures (1B-1 and 1B-5) built by Jade Sky stand on the north and south sides of the patio of the central body of the Acropolis. On the east side of the patio, Altars Q and R face Structure 1B-6 and, on the west

side, there are two structures below which a buried ball court was discovered. The small Structure 1B-2 in the southwest corner of the patio was probably Sky-Cauac's residence and preserved by his successors for cult reasons.

Low reliefs of the Sun God can be seen on the exterior of the west side of the Acropolis.

Two large pairs of monuments (O and P) in the small plaza facing the Acropolis next to the ball court are

mostly stelae, the tallest in the Mayan world, representing "stone trees," seven of which (A, C, D, E, F, H, J) portray Sky-Cauac. The sides of stelae D and E are decorated with the loveliest Mayan glyphic inscriptions yet found.

The sculptures in the plaza show that though the artists in Quiriguá were heavily influenced by Copán, they were able to develop their own vigorous style that was no less refined than that of their neighbor.

ITINERARY V

THE MAYA IN THE YUCATÁN

136-137 Detail of the base of the columns in the form of feathered serpents that line the entrance to the Temple of the Warriors at Chichén Itzá. During the Post-Classic period,

the cult of the Feathered Serpent that was tied to new forms of political power was as widespread in the Yucatán as it was elsewhere in Mesoamerica.

The huge limestone expanse of the Yucatán peninsula was occupied by the Maya during the earliest stages of their prehistory. Across this immense area — today divided into the Mexican states of Campeche, Yucatán and Quintana Roo, and the republic of Belize — the Yucatecan Maya developed several cultural traditions that were clearly distinguished artistically despite the strong ties, not just linguistic, that bound the various peoples.

The long pre-Hispanic history of the Yucatán is well represented by sites like Edzná, Acanceh, Dzibichaltún, Ek' Balam, Cobá, Kohunlich and Dzibanché, the stylistic differences between individual sub-regions and remarkable monuments of which are evidence of the succession of occupations that took place during much of the pre-Hispanic era.

From the Pre-Classic period, many Yucatecan sites stood out for their exceptional cultural development and, during the Early Classic era, much of the peninsula seems to have kept close ties with the central lowlands. The northern limits of the lowlands were marked by the area of influence of the enormous metropolis of Calakmul in the south of the state of Campeche. Links with the area of the Petén are particularly evident in southeastern sites like Kohunlich and the splendid monuments of Cobá, an attractive site in the northwest of the peninsula still greatly covered by vegetation.

The cultural peak of the Yucatán was reached during the Late and Terminal Classic periods when several cultural traditions produced some of the most superb architectural constructions in the Mayan world. The best examples of these late developments are the architectural styles of Río Bec and Chenes located in the regions of the same names in the south and northwest of the peninsula. Contemporary with these two, but longer lasting, was the great Puuc tradition that evolved in centers like Uxmal, Kabah, Sayil and Labná. It dominated the north of the peninsula during the Terminal Classic period and created a link with the succeeding Post-Classic traditions. The

uninterrupted sequence of Yucatecan traditions up till the end of the Post-Classic period is perhaps the best indication that the crisis of the Classic period did not have uniform effects throughout the Mayan world and, in their artistic developments, it is possible to identify the repercussions of the great ethnical and political changes that characterized the transition from the Classic to Post-Classic eras in all of Mesoamerica.

During the Terminal Classic and Post-Classic periods, the Yucatán was the destination of new groups of Maya who brought with them a strongly "Mexicanized" culture that marked the successive Yucatecan developments. These groups — the best known being the Itzá and the Xiú — are usually referred to as Putún Maya or Chontal Maya and came originally from the border area between Tabasco and Campeche. They were the main instigators of the flow of cultural influences that united central Mexico with the Mayan world from the end of the Classic period onwards.

It was the Itzá who were responsible for the development of Chichén Itzá that, having originated as a Puuc center and grown to share regional supremacy with Uxmal during the Terminal Classic period, became the capital of a regional state that dominated the political landscape of Yucatán from 900 to 1250 AD. It evolved into a splendid new Tollan of the southeast and the home of the cult of the Feathered Serpent.

Clashes with nearby Mayapán, occupied by the Cocom dynasty of the Itzá, led to the collapse of Chichén Itzá at the end of the Early Post-Classic and to the birth of a new multi-ethnic kingdom headed by Mayapán which was built as a smaller version of Chichén Itzá. According to historical sources, Mayapán was at the head of a league of three cities and a multi-ethnic political system in which the Cocom co-existed with other groups such as the Xiú, Chel, Tzeh, Canul, Cupul, Luti, Pech and Cochuah. The struggle between the Xiú and the Cocom Itzá resulted in the destruction of

the city around 1450. The lords of the different dynasties migrated to various regions in the Yucatán founding small political entities known as *cuuchcabal* or "provinces." The political landscape in the Yucatán remained in this divided state until the arrival of the Spanish when the Yucatán was divided into eighteen *cuuchcabalob*, each governed by a lord referred to as *halach uinic* who lived in his own small capital. One of the more prosperous regions during this last pre-Hispanic phase was the Caribbean area, where small coastal centers like Tulum controlled the sea routes that united the Yucatán with the Gulf of Mexico and the

ports in Honduras and Nicaragua. These small seigniories were the first indigenous Mesoamerican political entities to come into contact with the Spaniards who later undertook the difficult task of conquering the region between 1527 and 1546.

After the fall of Chichén Itzá, a group of Itzá emigrated to the forest of the Petén where they founded Tayasal on the shores of Lake Petén Itzá. This was to be the last bulwark of indigenous independence. After meeting Cortés in 1524, they resisted all attempts at conquest until 1697, the date that marks the complete subjection of Mesoamerica to the Spanish crown.

THE CHENES SITES

The Chenes region lies north of the Río Bec area and south of the Puuc hills; like much of the Yucatán, there is very little surface water and cenotes (natural wells) are the source of drinking water. The name Chenes is derived from this environmental feature and means something like "near the well."

There are more than thirty Chenes sites (the most important are Hochob, El Tabasqueño, Dzibilnocac and Santa Rosa Xtampac) and they are in many ways similar to those in Río Bec, especially with regard to the square

stone architectural decorations formed without the use of stucco, and the zoomorphic facades with entrances in the form of open jaws. A typical feature of Chenes style is the palace-pyramid in which a single floor palace is crowned by pyramid-shaped temples. Unlike the Río Bec temples, the Chenes versions have real stairways and rooms at the top.

The main Chenes site is probably Hochob built on a rocky elevation and laid out around three open spaces. What seems to be the principal plaza is dominated by Building I which has a central chamber flanked by two smaller

chambers at a lower level in accordance with a model that was common to both Río Bec and Chenes. The facades of the three rooms are covered by "mosaic" decorations of masks of gods whose open jaws are also the entrances.

The posts and architrave of the central doorway represent the jaw of the Earth Monster, the creature's large eyes and pupils in the form of hooks appear above, and the tongue and teeth appear in front of the threshold. The crest of the building is composed of two rows, one above the other, of highly stylised human figures.

138-139 Detail of a frieze in the Temple of the Warriors in Chichén Itzá. The Toltec figures of eagles and rampant jaguars show the influence that the political ideologies that originated in central Mexico had in the Post-Classic Yucatán.

THE RIO BEC AND CHENES STYLES

During the course of the Late Classic period (600-900 AD), two regions of the Yucatán were the settings for the development of two of the most unusual Mayan architectural styles: Río Bec and Chenes. In the Río Bec region near the southern border between Campeche and Quintana Roo, there are constructions characterized by tower-like "false pyramids" marked by a strong emphasis on verticality. Although the fronts of

these "towers" were built with a flight of steps, it was purely ornamental in that the tiny size of the steps meant they could not be used. The towers and lower sections of the buildings were adorned with large masks of gods and, in many cases, the entrances were designed to represent the open jaws of the Earth Monster. This last feature was also seen in the Chenes region in the north of Campeche where superb portals in animal form gave access to temples and palaces.

Unfortunately, the absence of inscriptions in the Río Bec and Chenes areas has limited our knowledge of the

history of these regions, but it is clear that the development of these styles – the remote origin of which may be found in the architecture of Calakmul at the north tip of the Petén – is evidence of the prosperity of the Yucatecan region during the Late Classic period. The partial chronological overlap of the Río Bec, Chenes and Puuc styles is a clear indication that the crisis that struck other areas of the Mayan world during the Classic period not only did not affect the Yucatecan regions, but may have exerted a beneficial effect on them as they were to develop into the new "heart" of the Mayan world.

140 top Considered a masterpiece of Chenes style architecture, the spectacular façade of Temple II in Hochob has been faithfully reconstructed in the garden of the Anthropology Museum in Mexico City. The representation of the portal as the open jaws of the Earth Monster is quite apparent.

140 bottom The same type of construction is seen at Chicanná, the main pyramid of which is shown here. Much of this archaeological site is still be explored, like its neighbor Dzibilnocac.

140-141
A demanding project of
rebuilding the entrance
of Structure 2 at
Chicanná using the
original materials has
made it possible to
understand its original
design. To enter the
building, one has to
pass over the creature's
extended tongue and
between its stone teeth.

141 bottom Detail of
one of the large masks
of the god Chac who
can easily be
recognized by his long
nose. This carving on
the corner of
Building XXI is one of
the most common
ornamental motifs in
the Yucatecan area.

Xpuhil, Becán, Hormiguero, Río Bec and Chicanná are the best known of the more than sixty sites in the region known as Río Bec.

Xpuhil is the location of the famous Building I, a structure with three entrances and three towers, two at the sides and an unusual one in the center.

Each of the towers is over 82 feet in height and topped by an architectural crest in the form of a fantastic mask with open jaws that surround a false entrance. The false stairways on the towers are also embellished with large masks.

row of entrances that grow smaller towards the sides of the building. Two tall side towers in Río Bec style rise above the row of rooms. A pyramid over 98 feet in height, Structure IX, stands in the center of the site.

The sites of Hormiguero and Chicanná contain buildings with decorations on the facades that are similar to those in the Chenes sites and exemplify the similarity between the two areas.

The monumental center of Becán is surrounded by earthworks nearly 2 miles in length and contains a number of buildings grouped in architectural complexes arranged around two main plazas. Although the site has a history that dates back at least to 600 BC, most of the construction took place in the 7th and 8th centuries AD, including the superb example of Río Bec style in the complex at the southeast end of the monumental center. Building I is a sort of palace with the lower level characterized by a long

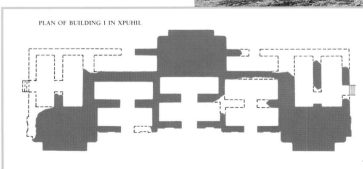

PLAN OF BUILDING I IN XPUHIL

142 top View of the Southeast Plaza at Becán, one of the largest Mayan cities in the Rio Bec area. The circular structure in the foreground is somewhat anomalous and of dubious interpretation.

142 bottom The most famous and unusual monument at Xpuil is unquestionably Building I, dominated by three towers topped with "false temples."

143 top View of the impressive remains of Building I at Becán; the structure is characterized by two lateral "towers" typical of the vertical style of Rio Bec that originally looked like slender pyramids on four levels.

142-143 Another view of Building I at Xpuil in which it is possible to see the steepness of the three towers. The "stairways" that led to the three "false temples" are quite impracticable.

143 bottom Structure II also faces onto the plaza of the Southeast Complex in Becán. Originally the building was probably a residence of the local elite.

DZIBICHALTÚN

history

144 top
Internal gallery in the
Palace. Note the
remains of the red
painted plaster on the
pillars that once
covered the entire
building.

144 bottom
Fragment of Stele 19.
Note the face of a ruler
wearing a large
headdress who holds a
sceptre-mannequin with
one hand. The sceptre
is decorated with the

image of God K who
can be recognized by
his long "nose" and
snake-shaped leg. The
sceptre was a
traditional symbol of
royalty during the
Classic Maya period.

Dzibichaltún is one of the more important sites in the Yucatán. Its period of greatest splendor was during the Late Classic period but occupation of the zone began in the Pre-Classic era when the north of the peninsula was enjoying a phase of great development. After a time of abandonment during the Late Classic period, Dzibichaltún reached its peak around 800 AD when the great majority of buildings visible today were constructed. This was also the phase when the stelae on the site were carved, one of which is inscribed with a date that corresponds to the year 849 AD. During the Late Post-Classic period, Dzibichaltún was almost completely abandoned until another, short-lived "renaissance" began around 1200 AD, but it was abandoned once more before the Spanish conquest.

the site

Dzibichaltún is a huge settlement of roughly eight thousand structures spread over an area measuring 7 square miles. Its monumental center comprises a hundred or so stone constructions laid out around four main squares.

The South Plaza and the Central Plaza form the heart of the site. A large building in the South Plaza has a central stairway topped by twin temples while, in a corner of the Central Plaza, the *cenote* Xlacah can be seen which would not only have provided drinking water but probably also have been one of the most important ritual sites in the city.

The south side of the Central Plaza is closed by a long, recently excavated building known as the Palace that has more than one hundred rooms; a Spanish chapel in the center of the plaza was built in 1590. Two buildings have recently been excavated on the east and west sides of the plaza, and also a pyramid on the northeast side in which an offering of thirty one pieces of green stone were found.

144-145
View of Structure 44 known as the Palace. This large building faces onto the main square and was probably the seat of the political and religious ruling class in Dzibichaltún.

DZIBILCHALTÚN

1 TEMPLE OF THE SEVEN DOLLS
2 PLATFORM OF THE SEVEN DOLLS
3 SACBE'
4 CENTRAL PLAZA
5 CENOTE XLACAH
6 SOUTH PLAZA
7 PALACE

*145 top left
Structure 38 at
Dzibichaltún. As can
be seen from the ruins
of the stairway, this
building went
underwent various
phases of rebuilding
work during its long
occupation.*

*145 top right
The cenote Xlacah in
the central square at
Dzibichaltún. These
natural karstic wells
were an important
source of water but
were also believed to
form the entrance to
the aquatic world of
the underworld gods.
This is why the
remains of ritual
offerings are sometimes
found at the bottom of
the cenotes.*

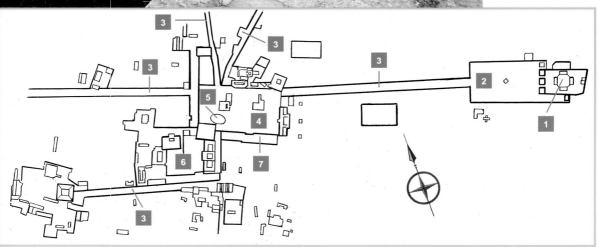

147 top Sacbé 1 at
Dzibichaltún seen
from the Seven Dolls
Group. Sacbeob
(literally "white
roads") are a typical
feature of Yucatán
sites; they are earthen
roads that joined the
various areas of a
single site or different
sites. It is probable
that they also had a
ceremonial or political
function, for example,
as material approval
of alliances between
Mayan cities.

Various roads (sacbeob) join the central zone to the rest of the site and to the other two main architectural groups: one to the southeast and the other to the east. The latter, known as the Group of the Seven Dolls, has a rectangular plaza with a central stele and an altar with four steps. The east side of this plaza is closed by three low structures behind which rises the city's best known structure, the Temple of the Seven Dolls. The temple stands on a four-sided platform, has four flights of steps and embedded corners, and was built around 700 AD. The facades are embellished with four masks. Inside there is a perimetral corridor, and a central room over which a sort of tower stands. The temple was completely incorporated inside a larger structure at the end of the Classic period but, during the Late Post-Classic, it was excavated to be used once more and an altar built in the central chamber. Seven statuettes that gave the name to the temple were found in a hollow in front of the painted and inscribed altar.

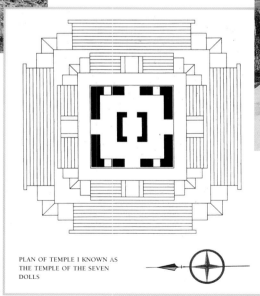

PLAN OF TEMPLE I KNOWN AS
THE TEMPLE OF THE SEVEN
DOLLS

*146 bottom left
The outer corridor in
the Temple of the
Seven Dolls. The
central chamber
contains the Post-
Classic altar near
which the seven
terracotta figures that
gave the building its
modern name were
found.*

*146 bottom right
Anthropomorphic
sculpture with a
representation of a
sovereign holding up a
"control bar," i.e., a
symbol of royal
authority.*

*147 bottom
Structure 12 is a
platform with four
stairways and an
aniconic stele on top.
The Temple of the Seven
Dolls stands in the
background.*

*146-147 The Temple
of the Seven Dolls is
the most famous
building in Dzibichaltún.
Constructed around 700
AD, it was later built
over but then
uncovered during the
Post-Classic period.*

EDZNÁ

history

The city of Edzná was inhabited from the Middle Pre-Classic (600 BC) to the Post-Classic (1450 AD) periods and during the course of its long existence was one of the most important centers in the Yucatán. In the Late Pre-Classic era, a complicated water system was built consisting of thirteen main channels, thirty one secondary channels and eighty four deposits of water. During the Late Classic period, Edzná's commercial relations with the central lowlands – to which it sold cotton, salt and sea products – are demonstrated by the strong stylistic similarities to the area seen in its stelae decorated with low reliefs. During the last phase of the Classic period, Edzná was influenced by the new cultural developments in the Puuc area and the city continued inhabited until the middle of the 15th century. The name the site is known by today appears to be derived from the word Itzná, "The House of the Itzá" and dates from the Post-Classic era.

the site

Edzná's monumental center consists of a central plaza bounded to the north by the Platform of Knives, to the west by a building called Nohoch-Ná, to the south by the South Temple and ball court, and to the east by what is referred to as the Acropolis. The Acropolis is a platform measuring 525 x 492 feet in the center of which a patio is ringed by three buildings. The famous Five-Story Building stands on the east side; it is a sort of Late Classic pyramid-palace with a large central flight of steps that was an architectural feature typical of the Puuc world. The four lower levels, similar to the steps of a pyramid, are in fact filled with a series of rooms while the highest level is the location of a temple crowned by a crest. Only recently excavated completely, the building measures roughly 197 x 197 feet at the base and stands about 98 feet high.

A pyramid dating from the Early Classic period has been identified below the Five-Story Building; it has architectural features, for example,

148 bottom
The North Temple in the Great Acropolis at Edzná. This structure seems to date from between 850-1100 AD when the city was occupied by the Chontal Maya.

148-149
The Five-Story Building. This is a pyramid-cum-palace in the Great Acropolis and the formal seat of political power in this important Yucatán center. The buildings has a combination of Classic Yucatán and innovative Puuc architectural features.

EDZNÁ

1 GREAT ACROPOLIS
2 SMALL ACROPOLIS
3 CENTRAL PLAZA
4 PLATFORM OF KNIVES
5 NOHOCH-NA'
6 SOUTH TEMPLE
7 BALL COURT
8 FIVE-STORY BUILDING

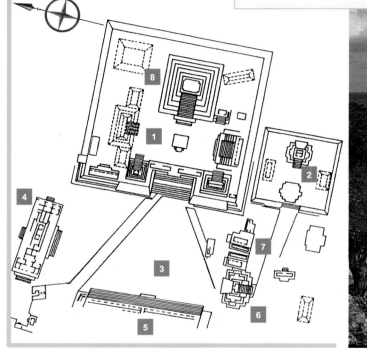

149 top The structure at the top of the Five-Story Building. The large architectural crest that crowns the temple is a traditional feature of Classic Maya architecture from the lowlands.

149 center right Glyph carved on the stairway of the Five-Story Building. The glyph represents the Sun God in his aspect as a sovereign.

149 bottom left The Great Acropolis seen from Nonoch-Ná, the large building that closes the west side of the main square in Edzná.

149 bottom right Large stucco mask that adorns the facade of Structure 414 also known as the Temple of the Masks. This is a representation of Kin, the Sun God, whose distinguishing characteristics are an aquiline nose and a squint. Note the two large round earrings.

embedded corners, that are typical of the Petén. More stylistic features typical of the Petén and also Cobá can be seen in the thirty stelae at Edzná which are dated to Baktun 8 (41-435 AD) and to 810 AD.

South of the Great Acropolis stands the Small Acropolis formed by four buildings. One of these is the Temple of the Stairway with Reliefs on which the flight of steps is embellished with fragments of stelae and low reliefs. The remains of many Classic era stelae have been found in front of the Small Acropolis where they were placed in the Early Post-Classic period. To the west of the Small Acropolis stands the Temple of Masks (Structure 414) decorated with Petén style stucco masks of Kinich Ahau, the Sun God, whose distinctive feature is a squint.

Other architectural complexes lie around the city's central plaza covering a surface area of roughly 7 square miles.

EK BALAM

history

Ek Balam ("Black Jaguar" or "Jaguar Star") was an important center in the Yucatec peninsula that was occupied without break from the Late Pre-Classic period to the Spanish conquest. During the Early Classic period (400-600 AD), Ek Balam began a rapid growth that led to a period of great splendor between 700 and 1000 AD. At first, the city had close relations with Cobá and, through Cobá, with the Mayan sites in the Petén, but at the end of the Classic period it strengthened its contacts with Chichén Itzá and other Puuc sites.

Around 1200 AD, Ek Balam began a slow decline for unknown reasons although it remained one of the largest cities in the Yucatán until the 16th century.

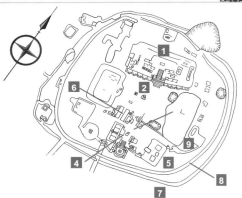

EK BALAM

1 ACROPOLIS
2 NORTH PLAZA
3 SOUTH PLAZA
4 TWIN PYRAMIDS
5 OVAL PALACE
6 BALL COURT
7 FIRST DEFENSIVE WALL
8 SECOND DEFENSIVE WALL
9 THIRD DEFENSIVE WALL

the site

The imposing monuments of Ek Balam show a remarkable fusion of architectural styles typical of Petén, Puuc, the east coast of the Yucatán and the Río Bec region.

The central section of the site is organized around two plazas. The main one (North Plaza) is overlooked by three large structures; the only one so far to have been excavated is the majestic Acropolis that is the second largest building in the Yucatán (it measures 541 x 6213 feet and is 115 feet tall). A large stucco frieze, one of the loveliest in the Mayan world, can be seen on the Acropolis; it depicts a governor, probably

Ukit Kan Lek (Ukit IV) emerging from the jaws of a monster. On either side of the governor there are two images of Bacab, the gods that held up the heavenly vault.

The south plaza is looked down upon by twin pyramids and the "Oval Palace," which was probably the residence of the city nobility. The only two stelae found in the city stand on the small Platform of the Stelae. Stele 1 shows two figures, the upper one of which (thereby represented as an ancestor of the other) is the ruler Ukit Kan Lek; the same stele is also decorated with the glyph emblem of the city.

The ball court lies between the two plazas. It was the site of offerings and there is a frieze (now covered) that portrays a governor seated on a throne with his face covered by a mask of the god Chac and holding a bird in his hand.

The central part of the site is surrounded by two of the three walls that enclose the entire settlement. Each of the five gates in the walls opens onto a *sacbé* (white road) that runs in the direction of the four points of the compass (there are two that run south) and joins Ek Balam to other nearby sites.

UXMAL AND PUUC SITES

history

The main Puuc centers became established around 700 AD in the northwest region of the Yucatán near the low hills of Ticul but it is still not clear if the new ethnic groups contributed to the foundation and development of these cities. The new groups are generically identified as Chontal Maya and reached the peninsula from the southwest. According to some historical sources, the Itzá reached Chichén Itzá around 672-692 AD and the Xiú reached Uxmal in 770 AD; other sources, however, indicate both groups arrived at later dates and only became involved in Yucatán history after the Puuc era. Although it is difficult to correlate the historical and archaeological data, it is certain that towards the 8th century, sites such as Chichén Itzá, Uxmal, Kabah and Sayil had become to flourish, probably as "capitals" of small political entities. At the end of the 9th and the start of the 10th centuries, Uxmal and Chichén Itzá succeeded in creating two large regional states that divided dominion of the north of the peninsula. During this stage, Uxmal was the most important political center in the Yucatán and its pre-eminence, according to some sources, was linked to a close alliance with Kabah and Nojpat. This was also the time that Uxmal's most celebrated ruler, Lord Chaac, governed the city to whom many of the monuments that can be seen today owe their existence. During the 10th century – perhaps following the end of Chaac's rule – Uxmal suffered a decline that was countered by the rise of Chichén Itzá, the city that was to become the new large center of power in the Yucatán over the following centuries.

The architecture of the Puuc centers was principally characterized by elaborate mosaic friezes that decorated the walls of the buildings. The friezes were geometric – with matting (the symbol of power) or Greek key patterns – or figurative, for example, the famous large masks with long noses that became distinctive elements of Puuc architecture, though they have also been found at Río Bec and Chenes. Although they are often identified with the god Chac, it is probable that they also represent different deities such as the monster Wits (Mountain), Itzamná in his manifestations as Earth Monster and Celestial Dragon, and God K. Their long noses (often thought to be a sort of trunk) were in fact extensions of the face of a serpent. In some cases the facades of the buildings are also decorated with full relief sculptures of the sovereigns themselves. Another typical element of Puuc and other Yucatán sites is the presence of sacbeob ("White Roads") which were earthen embankments that joined the various sites, probably as material celebrations of political alliances and means for courts and diplomatic missions to travel on.

153 Detail of a corner of the East Building in the Nunnery Quadrangle at Uxmal. The mask with its snake-like "trunk" probably represents the rain god Chac.

152 top
This limestone slab carved with a low relief was placed on the rear facade of the Palace of Masks in Kabah. The slab shows a sovereign with a prisoner in the presence of a god.

152 bottom
One of the statues found on the east facade of the Codz Pop at Kabah. The statue depicts a richly dressed sovereign wearing a headdress and necklace against a background of quetzal feathers.

UXMAL

The monumental center of Uxmal comprises four main architectural complexes.

The largest building is undoubtedly the Pyramid of the Magician that stands about 131 feet high with unusual rounded corners. Its eastern side is characterized by a small building whose portal is decorated with an enormous mask and the fact that it rests on one of the four palaces that form the recently restored Birds Quadrangle, thought by some to have been the residence of Lord Chaac. To the east of this quadrangle lies the famous Nunnery Quadrangle built by Lord Chaac between 900-910 AD. Its four

buildings are adorned with friezes whose symbology alludes to the myths of creation and their link with the ideology of royalty. The main building stands on the north side and is decorated with a series of large grotesque masks while a stone column in the center of the court symbolizes the cosmic tree.

After passing a games court decorated with images of the Feathered Serpent and sculptural rings to the south of this first architectural group, one arrives at the largest monumental section where the east square is dominated by the large Governor's Palace.

154 top View of the south sector at Uxmal. The Governor's Palace stands on the left and the House of Turtles in the center. In the background we see the huge mass of the Great Pyramid and the House of the Pigeons, and to the right there lies the ball court.

154-155 The Pyramid of the Magician at Uxmal seen from the west side that faces the Birds Quadrangle. The rounded shape of this pyramid is unusual in Mesoamerican architecture.

UXMAL

1 NORTH GROUP
2 PLATFORM OF THE STELAE
3 NUNNERY QUADRANGLE
4 PYRAMID OF THE MAGICIAN
5 CEMETERY GROUP
6 BALL COURT

7 HOUSE OF THE TURTLES
8 PALACE OF THE GOVERNOR
9 HOUSE OF THE PIGEONS
10 GREAT PYRAMID
11 SOUTH GROUP
12 PYRAMID OF THE OLD WOMAN

155 top left The
Pyramid of the
Magician and the
Birds Quadrangle seen
from the Nunnery
Quadrangle. The series
of columns and
gratings on the left are
typical of Puuc
architecture.

155 bottom left
What is referred to as
the "Queen of Uxmal."
This architectural
sculpture seems to
represent a divine
being whose head
emerges from the open
jaws of a serpent.

155 right Portal on
the west side of the
Pyramid of the
Magician. The
decoration is formed by
mosaic masks typical of
Puuc style.

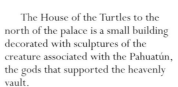

The three-part facade of the palace (where a sculpture representing the Lord Chac can be seen) faces the point on the horizon where Venus rises when at the southernmost tip of her journey; the star passes exactly behind the throne in the form of a two-headed jaguar in front of the palace where, in all probability, the lord sat during the event to emphasize his association with Venus. It is also probable that the Governor's Palace (below which there is a previous palace in Chenes style) was the Popul na ("House of the Mat") where the governing council of the ruler and the heads of the most important families met.

The House of the Turtles to the north of the palace is a small building decorated with sculptures of the creature associated with the Pahuatún, the gods that supported the heavenly vault.

The body of the South Pyramid connects the area of the palace to the Birds Quadrangle, a vast complex of patios and rooms whose buildings are topped by roof combs like a dovecote that have given the name to the complex. Other architectural complexes known as the Cemetery and the North Group lie to the north of the Birds Quadrangle.

156 top right
Detail of the decoration on the West Building in the Nunnery Quadrangle. Note the sculptural representation of the Feathered Serpent, the "guardian deity" of the Post-Classic administrations in the Yucatán.

156 center
The architectural masses of the Nunnery

Quadrangle and the Pyramid of the Magician rise above the vegetation of the Yucatán peninsula.

156 bottom East Building in the Nunnery Quadrangle. Note how the play of light and shade accentuates the decorations of this Puuc style building.

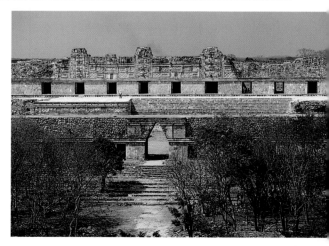

156-157
The Nunnery
Quadrangle is one of
the largest
architectural complexes
in the city. It was built
by Lord Chac between
900-910 AD.

157 top left Detail of
the decoration in the
East Building in the
Nunnery Quadrangle.
The sculpture portrays
a god covered by a

mask made from jade
beads framed by an
elaborate headdress of
plumes.

157 top right Detail
of the decoration on the
East Building in the
Nunnery Quadrangle.
The small human
figure is placed against
a background of
symbols that allude to
the division of the
universe in four parts.

157 bottom The
south access to the
Nunnery Quadrangle.
The facade of the
North Building is
characterized by
columns decorated
with mosaic masks.

158 top One of the rings in Uxmal ball court. These "baskets" only began to appear in the ball courts at the end of the Classic period. Note that the ring has a glyphic inscription.

158 bottom Central sculpture on the facade of the Governor's Palace in Uxmal. The seated figure wearing an enormous headdress is Lord Chac, the most important of Uxmal's rulers.

158-159 The two-headed throne that faces the Governor's Palace in Uxmal. The sculpture is placed so that on the day that Venus is at its southernmost point, the planet rises exactly behind the enthroned sovereign.

159 top The throne in the shape of a two-headed jaguar faces the Governor's Palace. The association between the jaguar and the sovereign had a long tradition in the Mayan world; the similarity between this throne and the one that Pacal sat on in the Oval Palace Tablet in Palenque is remarkable.

159 bottom View of Uxmal with the Governor's Palace in the foreground. It is probable that this building was the Popol Na (Council House) which was the seat of the city government.

160-161 *The House of Pigeons at Uxmal. The modern name of the building is given by the perforated roof crests.*

160 bottom Detail of one of the turtles that decorate the House of Turtles. In Mayan mythology this animal was traditionally associated with the deities that held up the celestial vault.

161 top The House of Turtles at Uxmal. The name is given by the sculptures on the upper moulding. Like the other buildings in Uxmal, it dates from the Terminal Classic period.

161 bottom
The Great Pyramid that joins the Governor's Palace with the House of Pigeons. The photograph shows that much of the building has yet to be excavated.

KABAH

The monumental center of Kabah is literally crossed by the road Route 261. Buildings to the west of the road include the large pyramidal structure called the Great Temple, the House of the Witches, the West Quadrangle and a large arch that marks the point of arrival of the *sacbé* (white road) that connected Kabah to Uxmal 11 miles away. Seen to the north of the West Quadrangle are the remains of the Temple of the Keys and the Temple of the Architraves;

unfortunately, the architraves of the latter were removed by the site's discover, John Stephens, and taken to New York where they were destroyed in a fire.

Kabah's more important buildings stand to the east of the road, including the Temple of the Columns, the Pyramid of the Masks and the Palace. Although not as grandiose as the example at Sayil, the Palace is an excellent example of Puuc buildings with every entrance marked by a central column. The most celebrated of the Kabah buildings is certainly the *Codz Pop* which stands out for the complexity of its decoration.

It is a ten-room palace that was probably the seat of the city administration; the facade is completely covered with more than 250 grotesque masks of gods, each of which is composed of 30 different parts that have been carved and assembled. The remains of seven statues were placed on the rear facade but only two remain *in situ*. They depict a richly dressed figure with a face decorated with ornamental scars, probably a ruler of the city (generically known as the King of Kabah) who is also

shown on the jamb of Room 21 in the same building.

The discovery of the sculptures on the west side of the building has led to a different interpretation of the temple's iconography. New studies suggest that the masks represent Itzam Cab Ain, the monster in the form of an alligator who was the terrestrial personification of Itzamná, the supreme Mayan god. The west side of the building seems to be the nocturnal and underworld side as opposed to the celestial side to the east.

It is the celestial aspect of Itzamná that formed the legitimate basis of the King of Kabah's power, the statues of whom stand on a feathered serpent, the symbol of royal lineage.

The new interpretation of the *Codz Pop* and other Puuc buildings has therefore altered the rather stereotyped image of a world obsessed with the rain god to one based on artistic and ideological models that better tally with what we know of the rest of the world of the Maya.

162 top Detail of the masks on the west facade of the Codz Pop. *In contrast to what was generally believed, a recent interpretation of the masks suggests they do not represent the rain god Chac but Itzam Cab, the alligator that was the terrestrial aspect of the supreme god Itzamná.*

162 center Internal gallery of the Codz Pop. See how the long "nose" of the mask below the threshold of the inner bay acts as a step.

162 bottom Kabah arch built using the corbeled vault or "false arch" technique. This is where the

11 miles sacbé starts that joins the city to Uxmal, probably as the material sign of an alliance between the two cities.

162-163 The west facade of the Codz Pop *at Kabah, covered by more than 250 sculptural masks.*

163 top left East facade of the Codz Pop. *Note the unique two full relief statues on the facade. Both represent the ruler of the city known by the generic name, the King of Kabah.*

163 top right The Palace at Kabah faces the central square. Two monolithic columns on the left are typically Puuc in style.

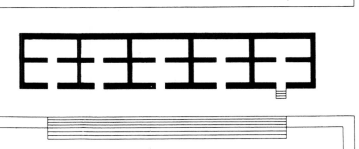

PLAN OF CODZ POP OR PYRAMID OF THE MASKS,
THE MAIN BUILDING IN KABAH

SAYIL

The monumental center of Sayil is dominated by its large, multi-story palace with a facade embellished by a chain of columns and the masks of gods.

This building, clearly the residence of the ruling family, is without doubt the loveliest in the entire Puuc region. A *sacbé* starts directly from the square below the Palace and runs south to a games court where there is a two-story building that was probably used by the nobles and functionaries of Sayil to run the administration of the city.

There is also a platform where stelae and their altars would have stood. Sayil and Uxmal were two of the few Puuc cities to maintain the ancient tradition of low reliefs with portraits of

the periphery has shown that Sayil spread over an area of about 2 square miles which was mostly covered by residential platforms linked to water tanks; the existence of water tanks suggests that the density of population was high.

The residential areas were flanked by gardens that studies have shown contained prickly pears, chili and corn plants and fruit and flowering trees. The limits of the city – that appears to have been a real garden-city – were marked by four small pyramidal structures to the north, east, south and west.

These recent studies have also shown that Sayil was occupied by Maya Yucatechi and not by Maya Chontal as was previously thought.

governors and prisoners. About half-way down the *sacbé* there stands the building known as El Mirador, to the south of which an area believed to have been the city market has recently been identified.

The most recent archaeological research carried out at Sayil has centered on the identification of the smaller buildings and the production of a detailed map of the site. Exploration of

164 top Corner mask on the Palace at Sayil. From left to right we see the long serpentine "nose," the eyes and the elaborate ear ornament.

164 bottom Facade of the Palace at Sayil with elements typical of Puuc architecture: monolithic columns, sequences of "false columns" and masks of gods.

164-165 The Palace at Sayil is perhaps the best example of this type of Puuc building. Note the similarity to the Five -Story Building at Edzná.

165 top right Detail of the decoration in the form of a serpent on the Palace. Look carefully at the

animal's face; it is clear the long "nose" of the Maya gods is actually a sort of serpentine "lip."

165 bottom Mosaic mask on the Palace. The long "nose" of the god seems an attribute of sacredness shared with many other Maya gods.

PLAN OF THE PALACE,
MAIN BUILDING IN SAYIL

166-167 View of part of Labná from the top of the pyramid known as El Mirador.

166 bottom left View of Labná Palace which is joined to the rest of the monumental center by a sacbé on the right.

166 bottom right Detail of the decoration on a building at Labná.

167 left The main pyramid at Labná known as El Mirador. The temple on the summit is crowned by a large architectural crest that was originally decorated with sculptural elements as noted by John L. Stephens in 1840.

167 top right Labná arch with geometric decorations. This is certainly the best example of this distinctive feature of Puuc architecture.

LABNÁ

Labná is a very good example of a Puuc site of average size. Its monumental center includes a fine two-story building similar to the one in Sayil.

Among the sculptures on its facade is a human face that emerges from the open jaws of a serpent on a corner of the east wing. Very similar to the "Queen of Uxmal" when seen close up, this sculpture may have represented Kukulkan.

A *sacbé* leaves from in front of the building and passes by a large pyramid temple known as El Mirador crowned by a high crest.

We know that until the 19th century the temple was decorated by sculptures

of human figures and skulls which today no longer exist. The *sacbé* continues as far as two complexes joined by an arch, one of the loveliest monuments in the Puuc world.

The two faces of the arch are decorated in different manners: the east side has a band of spiral and triangular elements, while the west side depicts two huts with straw roofs entered via a niche that probably contained sculptural elements that today are missing. The arch was illustrated in a famous drawing by Frederick Catherwood and has become one of the symbols of Mayan architecture. Paradoxically, archaeological knowledge of the site is almost zero as no intensive research has been carried out. Various structures around the monumental center still await study.

CHICHÉN ITZÁ

history

At an early stage of its history, Chichén Itzá ("On the Edge of the Well of the Itzá") was a thriving Puuc city from which several monuments still exist. The city's peak, however, was reached in 950 AD when the Itzá transformed it into the most splendid of the Mesoamerican Tollans and into one of the most important centers for worship of Kukulkan (the Yucatecan Maya translation of Quetzalcóatl, the Feathered Serpent). Kukulkan is portrayed on many of the monuments and often cited by sources as the sovereign of the city. The new city monuments were built in an obviously "Toltec" style (even if the division of the two styles is anything but clean) and some of them are actual copies of the monuments in the contemporary Toltec capital, Tula, in the state of Hidalgo. This derivation has given rise to a large number of conflicting hypotheses on the relations that linked the two cities (see the box "Toltec or Zuyuan?").

What is certain is that Chichén Itzá became the capital of a very powerful multi-ethnic regional state whose rulers forged alliances with other Itzá dynasties in centers like Izamal, Mayapán and, perhaps, Edzná, yet it was the rivalry between these other centers brought an end to the rule of Chichén Itzá. According to the traditional "romantic" version of the facts, the governor of Izamal kidnapped the wife of the lord of Chichén Itzá and, in the war that followed, Hunac Ceel, the Cocom Itzá lord of Mayapán, defeated and sacked the capital in 1221 with the help of Mexican mercenaries. We do not know how much of this story is true, but it is a fact that the monumental center of Chichén Itzá shows signs of pillage and abandonment around 1200-1250 AD. This would have occurred at the same time as Mayapán rose to assume the role of new regional capital; its monuments are seemingly copies of those at Chichén Itzá but of inferior quality.

*168 top right
Corner mask in the
Nuns' Annex.*

*168 bottom left
The Red House at
Chichén Itzá. The
Puuc style of this
structure is evident in
the building's upper
frieze.*

the site

The archaeological site of Chichén Itzá is spread over 12 square miles, and its monumental center is divided into various architectural complexes.

The oldest monuments date from the Puuc era: the complex known as The Nunnery (made up of the Nunnery itself, the Church and an Annex), the Akab' Dzib, the Red House group and the terrace on which El Caracol stands. Of these, the Nunnery is the most significant and its buildings are

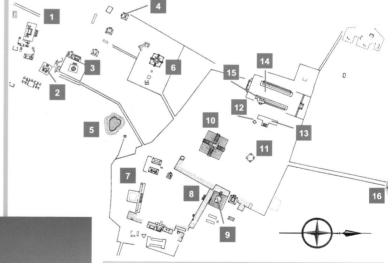

CHICHÉN ITZÁ

1	THE NUNNERY	9	TEMPLE OF THE WARRIORS
2	TEMPLE OF THE TABLES	10	THE CASTILLO
3	EL CARACOL	11	PLATFORM OF VENUS
4	THE RED HOUSE	12	PLATFORM OF THE EAGLES
5	CENOTE	13	TZOMPANTLI
6	TOMB OF THE HIGH PRIEST	14	GREAT BALL COURT
7	THE MARKET	15	TEMPLE OF THE JAGUARS
8	PATIO OF A THOUSAND COLUMNS	16	SACRED CENOTE

embellished with large "long-nose" masks and intricate decorations typical of Puuc style.

El Caracol is a sort of tower that was used as an astronomic observatory and its upper section was probably remodelled at the start of the Post-Classic period.

To the north of the Puuc zone stands the second complex that centers around the pyramid known as the Ossuary or Tomb of the High Priest. The building was decorated with sculptural panels of birds of prey with the head of God K and the famous man-bird-serpent that also appears in the Temple of the Warriors; there are

also balustrades depicting a Feathered Serpent intertwined with a Cloud Serpent (in Náhuatl, Mixcóatl). The pyramid is topped by columns in the form of the Feathered Serpent and, at its base, there is a cave that was probably a symbolic entrance to the world of the dead.

The large masks in Puuc style and the myriad of fragments of Post-Classic censers found near the temple are indicative of the building's long history. The same group includes a Platform of Venus very similar to the one in the central plaza with the only difference being that the serpents on the upper frieze are Cloud Serpents rather than Feathered Serpents.

168-169
The Nunnery is one of the sectors in Chichén Itzá that was built in pure Puuc style. The Nunnery Annex can be seen on the left and, on the right, the back of the Church.

169 bottom left View of El Caracol, a structure from the Puuc era remodelled at the beginning of the Post-Classic period.

169 bottom right El Caracol. It is thought that this building was an astronomic observatory but its specific function has not yet been fully understood.

Heading north, one enters the large Central Plaza surrounded by a *talud* wall 20 feet high that contains the city's most famous monuments. The large nine level pyramid called El Castillo stands in the center crowned by a temple whose entrance is lined by columns in the form of Feathered Serpents. Similar figures representing the god to whom the pyramid was dedicated decorate the balustrades of the four stairways. The interplay of light and shade gives the impression that the large serpents are sliding down the pyramid on the spring and autumn equinoxes. An earlier version of the same pyramid can be visited below El Castillo; it contains two sculptures, a throne in the form of a red jaguar with incrustations of green stone and a mosaic disc on its back, and a Chac Mool which is the famous sculpture of a reclining man who supports an offerings plate on his stomach.

PLAN AND SECTION OF EL CASTILLO IN WHICH THE EARLIER STRUCTURE CAN BE SEEN

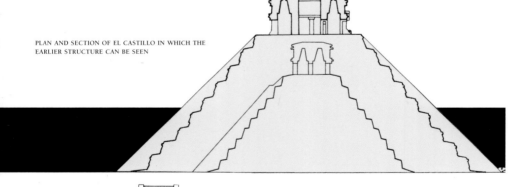

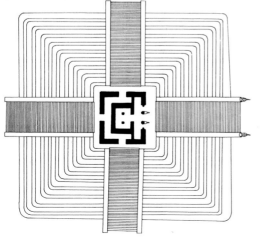

170 top
The earlier version of the pyramid has been found below El Castillo. Two statues were found in the temple on top of the earlier structure: one of Chac Mool and a

throne in the shape of a jaguar painted red. The spots of the animal's hide were represented by green stone and a wooden disc with a turquoise mosaic was placed on its back.

170-171 El Castillo, was dedicated to the cult of Kukulkan, the Mayan equivalent of the Feathered Serpent. The god is represented on the columns of the temple at the top of the pyramid and on the balustrades of the four stairways.

171 bottom left
The Akab Dzib, one of
the buildings in purest
Puuc style at Chichén
Itzá.

171 bottom right
The Ossuary or Tomb
of the Great Priest, a
small pyramid built
over a natural hollow.
The balustrades of the

stairway are
decorated with images
of entwined Feathered
Serpents and Serpents
of Clouds though
with a single head.

The sculpture of a
rattlesnake that
comes from the
temple decoration
can be seen next to
the tree.

172 top One of the
Atlases that support
the table altar in the
Temple of the
Warriors. Note the
resemblance to
analogous sculptures
found at Tula.

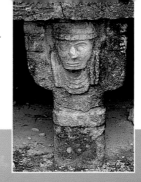

The Temple of the Warriors on the east side of the plaza seems to be a copy of Temple B in Tula and much more refined than the original. The outer walls of the upper temple are decorated with Puuc style masks and images of the man-bird-serpent that may represent Tlahuizcalpantecuhtli or Venus as the Morning Star.

Behind the Chac Mool on the top of the stairway, an entrance lined by superb serpentine columns leads into the temple proper where sculptural benches and columns are decorated with low reliefs of warriors. An earlier Chac Mool Temple lies below the Temple of the Warriors with mural paintings and polychrome benches depicting members of the city elite seated on jaguar skin cushions and armed warriors on jaguar thrones. The Temple of the Tables to the north of the Chac Mool Temple is very similar with columns still covered with their original polychromy.

The arcade that stands in front of the

Temple of the Warriors contains low reliefs similar to those in the temple; it joins up with the large colonnades that surround the Patio of a Thousand Columns on the south side of which lie one of the monumental center's three ball courts and a building known as the Market.

172-173 The Temple
of the Warriors at
Chichén Itzá. This
temple seems in part
a copy of Temple B at
Tula and is the result
of a mix of Puuc and
"Toltec" architectures.

172 bottom The pillars
in front of the Temple of
the Warriors are decorated
with low reliefs showing
soldiers at arms and
Tlahuizcalpantecuhtli,
Venus as the Morning
Star.

173 top
El Castillo seen from
the top of the Temple
of the Warriors. A
sculpture of Chac
Mool stands in front
of the entrance to the
temple.

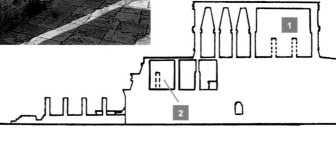

SECTION OF THE TEMPLE OF WARRIORS

1 TEMPLE OF WARRIORS
2 TEMPLE OF CHAC MOOL

173 center left Part
of the Patio of a
Thousand Columns,
the large porticoed
court that stretches to
the south of the
Temple of the
Warriors. The
colonnaded rooms and
open areas — northern
in origin — are typical
of monumental centers
from the Early Post-
Classic period.

173 center right
Table altar inside the
Temple of the
Warriors. The table is
supported by small
sculptures in the form
of Atlases.

173 bottom
The center of the
complex known as
The Market, to the
south of the Patio of
a Thousand Columns.

174 top left
Sculpture in the form
of a snake's head that
decorates the top of
the balustrade of the
stairway on the Temple
of the Warriors. A
small anthropomorphic
standard holder can be
seen above it.

174 top right
Sculpture on the
facade of the Temple
of the Warriors. It
shows a human face
appearing from the
jaws of a fantastic
animal with the
body of a bird of
prey and the head

of a serpent.
It probably represents
Tlahuizcalpantecuhtl,
Venus as the
Morning Star,
a deity associated
with the Feathered
Serpent to whom
Temple B at Tula was
dedicated.

174 center
Detail of a frieze on
the Temple of the
Warriors with
depictions of either a
jaguar or a puma and

a warrior armed with
a spear. The warrior
wears a nose ornament
and has circles around
his eyes like the Rain
God of central Mexico.

174 bottom
The Temple of the
Warriors. A more
ancient structure
known as the Temple
of Chac Mool has
been identified below
this building.

175 The Chac Mool
at the entrance to the
Temple of the
Warriors. Two columns
in the form of
feathered serpents with
open jaws stand
behind the sculpture.
The "capitals" on the
columns are feathered
rattlesnakes.

176 top Detail of one of the masks of the god Chac that adorn the facade of the Nunnery.

A number of smaller platforms stands in the central plaza. The Platform of Venus has balustrades and upper mouldings decorated with feathered serpents and low relief panels of the man-bird-serpent that was identified with the morning aspect of the planet.

The reliefs on the nearby Platform of the Eagles are decorated with birds of prey and jaguars eating human hearts, which is an iconographic motif also seen in Tula. Next to this platform lies the *tzompantli*: this structure used to support the wooden rack on which the skulls of sacrificed individuals were hung; its base, unsurprisingly, is decorated with low reliefs of human skulls.

176 center right Platform of the Jaguars and the Eagles. Low reliefs on the side of the platform depict birds of prey and wild cats eating human hearts. The upper frame is decorated with images

of warriors dressed in central Mexican "fashion." It is probable that the platform was used to sacrifice prisoners of war.

176 center left The Platform of Venus. The sides are filled with low

reliefs of the man-bird-serpent that was identified as Venus as the Morning Star. Feathered serpents can be seen on the upper cornice and symbols of the planet Venus on the corners.

*176 bottom Detail of the sculptural decoration of the tzompantli. This platform is completely covered with the images of skulls and had a wooden rack on which the skulls of sacrificed prisoners were displayed.
The tzompantli is* one of the many elements that originated in north Mexico to be seen in Chichén Itzá.

176-177 The heads of wild cats decorate the balustrades of the Platform of the Jaguars and the Eagles.

*177 bottom Low relief panel of the Platform of the Jaguars and the Eagles with the image of a jaguar devouring a human heart.
On the right it is possible to make out the head of an eagle doing likewise.*

178 top View of the
ball court. The
presence of battle-
scenes in the annex
Temple of the Jaguars
(right) suggests that
the games represented
ritual battles.

178 top View of the
ball court. The
presence of battle-
scenes in the annex
Temple of the Jaguars
(right) suggests that
the games represented
ritual battles.

178-179 The ball
court at Chichén Itzá
is in the standard I
shape and one of the
largest and most
impressive in
Mesoamerica.

The west side of the plaza is closed
by the famous ball court and its related
structures.

Facing the plaza is the Lower Temple
of the Jaguars that contains low reliefs
and a sculpture-cum-throne in the form
of a jaguar.

The Upper Temple of the Jaguars
faces onto the ball court and contains a
wall painting of a battle.

The facings that dress the large ball
court are covered with relief panels of
two groups of players converging on a
central scene that shows the decapitation
of a player. On the left a figure holds up
the decapitated head and a knife, while
on the right – in addition to the central
ball containing a skull – we see the body
of the beheaded man with spurts of
blood gushing from the neck in the form
of serpents.

The *sacbé* that leads to the Sacred
Cenote starts from the north side of the
central plaza. The *cenote* is the natural
well that was thought to be the entrance
to the underground world of the aquatic
gods and was therefore considered to be
one of the most sacred places in
Mesoamerica.

Inside the *cenote* (from which the
name Chichén Itzá was derived)
precious offerings imported from places
as far away as Colombia were found
with the remains of sacrificed
individuals.

Taken as a whole, the architecture of
Chichén Itzá is the best example of the
extraordinary mixture of styles that
characterized the Mayan Post-Classic
period and an indication of the new
ideological and political models that had
arrived from central Mexico.

179 center
The upper Temple of the Jaguars with columns in the form of Feathered Serpents. A mural painting of a battle runs throughout the inside of this temple that faces onto the ball court.

179 bottom left Low relief of the ball court with a decapitated player; blood spurts from his neck in the form of snakes. Part of the ball can be seen at the bottom left and, behind, a player who holds the cut head and a sacrificial knife. On the right a player wears the customary games dress that includes a belt, a "palm" (that sticks out of the belt) and an "axe" (in his hand).

178 bottom The lower Temple of the Jaguars is decorated with low reliefs and faces the main square. A throne in the form of a jaguar stands at the temple entrance.

179 top left Detail of the low reliefs of the ball game in which the ball contains a skull. The association between the rubber ball and the human head appears in several works of art as well as in myths like the Popul Vuh.

179 top right One of the two rings in the middle of the ball court at Chichén Itzá. It is decorated with two intertwined feathered serpents. Sources from the colonial era report that if a player in the Aztec game succeeded in getting the ball through the narrow hole in the ring, his team won the match.

179 bottom right The sacred cenote at Chichén Itzá. This is a karstic well into which offerings and human sacrifices were thrown in honour of the aquatic gods of the Underworld. The name Chichén Itzá means "On the edge of the well of the Itzá." The different origins of the offerings found in the well indicate that the fame of this natural shrine extended well beyond the territory controlled by Chichén Itzá.

MAYA-TOLTECS OR ZUYUANS?

180 Atlas from Chichén Itzá. This figure is one of the many of Toltec origin found in the Post-Classic iconography at Chichén Itzá. The fact that many of these images are military in nature long suggested that Chichén Itzá was conquered by the Toltecs but today it is thought that the two cities shared the same political ideology.

The similarity between Chichén Itzá and Tula is immediately apparent. The Temple of the Warriors in Chichén Itzá is almost an exact copy of Temple B in Tula, the Patio of a Thousand Columns resembles the Burned Palace, and elements like the *chac mool*, the columns in the form of feathered serpents, the images of "atlases," the sculptural benches and *tzomplantli* appear in both cities. As it was in central-northern Mexico that these architectural elements originated, Chichén Itzá was considered the city of Tlapallan to which Ce Actal Topiltzin Quetzalcóatl emigrated after his flight from Tula and where the Toltecs who went with him built a magnificent copy of their city of origin. The many images of war suggested that Chichén Itzá had required a military campaign of conquest during which the Toltecs had subjected the local Maya (who had built the Puuc section of the city) and made Chichén Itzá into the capital of a new Maya-Toltec kingdom.

Recently, however, the situation has become more complex and it seems that this interpretation is too simplistic. The chronology of the two cities does not seem to confirm their sequence and close analysis of the monuments has shown that many of the Puuc and "Toltec" buildings were in fact contemporary. Chichén Itzá appears to be more Tula's "sister" than her "daughter," which threatens the traditional interpretation of Chichén Itzá's role.

Recently, the Mexican scholars Alfredo López Austin and Leonardo López Luján have put forward a new approach. They suggest that at the end of the Classic period, a new political and ideological system founded on the Feathered Serpent came into being in Mesoamerica which endured until the Spanish conquest. This system, called *zuyuano* (from Zuyuá, one of the many names the mythical city of Tollan was known by) was based on the co-existence of several traditional ethnical and political units under a single political system; the system would have governed multi-ethnic communities under a sovereign who presided over "councils" consisting of lords of the individual ethnic blocks. In parallel, the traditional guardian deities of these ethnic groups would have been subordinated to the supra-ethnic and territorial protection of the Feathered Serpent.

Particular forms of political aggregation and warlike activities corresponded to this new political and ideological system: the first were essentially in the forms of confederations of cities (like the Mayapán League or Triple Alliance) that took on jurisdictive responsibilities and went far beyond simple military or blood relation alliances that were typical of the Maya civilization during the Classic period; from the point of view of war, the Zuyuan organizations developed into proper militarist regimes for which military conquest – very rare in previous epochs – became a common and widespread activity with the aim, not simply of the subjection and public humiliation of the defeated sovereigns, but their assimilation into the new power system.

It is hypothesized that the Zuyuan system came into being during the Epiclassic era in sites like Teotenango, Xochicalco and Cacaxtla in which parts of the culture of Teotihuacan were taken up and developed. It seems that many Zuyuan elements were derived from Teotihuacan and that this city was probably the first great earthly Tollan. The new form of power was then spread through much of Mesoamerica by the Toltecs and associated peoples like the Chontal Maya. In this interpretation, Tula would not have been the capital of a large Mesoamerican empire but the center that diffused Zuyuan ideology that dominated the Post-Classic political landscape.

The capitals of the Zuyuan political systems like Tula, Cholula, Chichén Itzá, Mayapán, México-Tenochtitlan and many others therefore became the terrestrial replicas of the mythical Tollan where the Feathered Serpent reigned. This would explain why many of their rulers are mentioned in the sources with the name of Quetzalcóatl or their local translations such as Kukulkan, Gucumatz, Nacxit, etc. The reputation of the Zuyuan system also spread into the Mixteca (the area of the Mixtec people) and to the highlands of Guatemala where sources refer to confederations of expansionistic capitals and to sovereigns that went to Tollan to receive the insignia of power.

The Zuyuan political system would thus have been imported to Chichén Itzá by Chontal immigrants that would have learned of it through their close contact with central Mexico. A multi-ethnic

government would then have been set up that is perhaps recognisable in the iconography of the city: there are, for example, no images of individual sovereigns but of groups of members of the elite, apparently of equal rank, and the inscriptions often refer to them as "brothers" (*yitah*), the meaning of which was probably along the lines of "colleagues" within a single governmental structure. In regard to the government of Chichén Itzá, Diego de Landa explains, "… where they say that three brother lords reigned who were very religious and arrived there from the west […]." A similar system of government called *multepal* (from *mul*, "together," and *tepal*, "govern") spread to Mayapán and other Yucatecan cities at the time of the Spanish conquest. It is probable that the title of Kukulkan was given to a sort of 'first among equals' who would have held supreme authority in the government council.

During the centuries before the arrival of the Spanish, a new model of political organization was appearing alongside that of the Zuyuan model and seemed destined to replace it: the two powerful expansionistic states of the Aztecs and the Tarascans were basing their political ideology on the supremacy of the guardian deity of their own ethnic groups over those of other peoples: Huitzilopochtli had already led the Mexica armies in their wars of conquest and perhaps Curicaueri would have done the same thing for the Tarascan armies if the Spaniards had not put an end to everything and imposed their own power and ideology.

181 top Toltec Atlas wearing a standard butterfly pectoral like that of the large Atlases in Temple B at Tula. These images of warriors are one of the commonest iconographic elements from the Early Post-Classic period. The art at this time clearly reflected the new "Zuyuana" ideology used to legitimize the emerging and expansionist multi-ethnic political systems.

181 bottom Mosaic disc with images of serpents, called tezcacuitlapilli. Discs of this type have been found at Tula and Chichén Itzá and are often represented on the back of the belts of Post-Classic warriors, for example, on the sculptures of Atlases in the two "twin" cities.

Tulum

history

During the rule of the Cocom Itzá of Mayapán, the east coast of the Yucatán experienced a period of remarkable development primarily based on trade that had been well rooted during the Classic period when coastal sites probably served as ports for the city of Cobá. Around 1441 AD, a revolt by the Xiú of Mayapán headed by Ah Xupán destroyed Cobá and the Cocom people and led to the setting up of small centers headed by various Chontal Maya dynasties, for example, the Cheles at Tecoh, the few surviving Cocom at Tibolón, the Tutual Xiú at Maní, etc. A powerful kingdom arose in ancient Chetumal on the south coast that may perhaps not have been the site of the modern city of the same name, but the archaeological site of Santa Rita Corozal.

The remains of the Post-Classic

182 top
El Castillo was the main temple structure in the city and a typical example of highland Maya architecture from the Late Post-Classic period.

182 bottom The entrance to the temple on El Castillo. As can be seen, the tradition of snake-shaped columns found at Tula and Chichén Itzá was continued at Tulum. It is probable that El Castillo was dedicated to the cult of Kukulkan, the Feathered Serpent.

coastal development can be seen today at sites like San Gervasio (on the island of Cozumel), Akumal, Xelhá, Tancah and Tulum. This last site was probably the city of Zamá ("Dawn") mentioned in historical sources; it is the largest of the group and the beauty of its ruins is heightened by its superb natural setting. Looking over the Caribbean Sea, Tulum was founded around 1200 AD and remained occupied until the arrival of the Spanish. It was at Tulum that the expedition of Juan de Grijalva was sighted and described in 1518 AD.

182-183 Tulum was one of the most important sites from the Late Post-Classic period in the Yucatán. The archaeological site consists of a number of structures surrounded by a defensive wall.

183 top Stucco sculpture on the facade of El Castillo. In addition to representations of the Descending God, the facade of the temple is also decorated with images of unidentified gods like the one in the photograph.

183 center View of the stairway to El Castillo at Tulum. The small buildings next to it are in typical parallelepiped shape with projecting mouldings on the upper section.

183 bottom The Descending God seen in pottery and decorative friezes of the temples at Tulum has been identified as Xuk Ek, "Star Wasp," a god associated with Venus.

184

*184 top
The more important
residential structures at
Tulum had colonnaded
porticoes in front.*

*184 bottom One of
the buildings in the*

*complex at Tulum is
the long "Palace" with
a colonnaded atrium.
An image of the
"descending god" —
often seen on buildings
in this site — is shown
on the main facade.*

*184-185 Tulum faces
out over the
Caribbean Sea in a
position that allowed
the city to control
much of the coastal
trading links that
connected the Gulf of*

*Mexico with the
coasts of Central
America. The city
was probably
identified with the
ancient Zamá
mentioned in the
sources.*

the site

The ruins of Tulum are enclosed by a "turreted" wall ("*tulum*") on the south, west and north sides while the eastern part of the city looks out over the magnificent waters of the Caribbean towards the horizon where the sun rises and which gave the city its name: Zamá ("Dawn").

The monumental complex is dominated by the Castillo, a two level platform with a building on top. The entrance to the building is lined with columns in the form of serpents and has various stucco sculptures of gods: the central one is the Descending God who can probably be identified with Xuk Ek, i.e., Venus as the Evening Star.

The same god is shown on the front of the Temple of the Descending God and the Temple of the Frescoes. The central register of three in wall paintings in the first of the two temples depicts two scenes in which a goddess makes an offering to a god; between the two figures there are two intertwined serpents and a third god at the edge of the scene.

The upper and lower registers respectively show the celestial and underground worlds.

The Temple of the Frescoes has large masks of the god Itzamná on the corners and contains similar paintings in which various gods, ears of corn and beans can be recognized.

Like those in the Temple of the Descending God, these paintings were executed in black and white and their style is similar to that seen in the Paris Codex, one of the few Mayan codices to have been discovered.

185 top left Portico at the perimeter of the Temple of the Frescoes. The style of the paintings on the wall on the left is similar to that of the Maya codices that are known to us, in particular, the Madrid Codex.

185 top right Temple 16 or Temple of the Frescoes. The corners on the upper cornice of the temple are decorated with stucco masks of the supreme god Itzamná.

185 center Detail of the wall paintings of the Temple of the Frescoes. Note the goddess who holds up a small image of God K, a symbol of royalty.

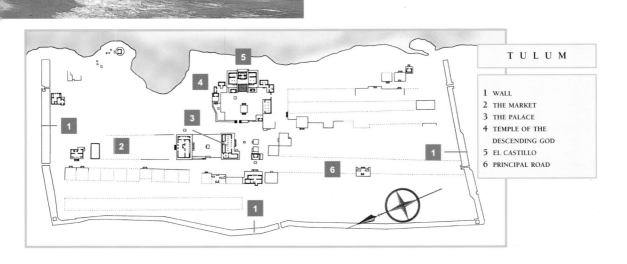

TULUM

1 WALL
2 THE MARKET
3 THE PALACE
4 TEMPLE OF THE
  DESCENDING GOD
5 EL CASTILLO
6 PRINCIPAL ROAD

GLOSSARY

(THE LANGUAGE TO WHICH THE WORD BELONGS OR FROM WHICH IT IS DERIVED IS GIVEN IN BRACKETS)

ACOLHUA (Náhuatl): "They who have Canoes," Nahua people who settled in central Mexico during the Post-Classic Period. Their most famous capital was Texcoco, an ally of Mexico-Tenochtitlan.

AH PUCH (Maya): "the Flayed One," also called *Kisin*, "The Fetid," the Maya god of death, shown in skeletal form and also known as God A.

AZTECS: conventional name applied to the people originally known as Mexica. Derived from the Náhuatl name *aztecatl* which was applied by the Mexica to the people whose dominion they lived under in their original homeland of Aztlan.

CACAXTLI (Náhuatl): "bundle," name used to indicate the characteristic bundle or backpack carried by merchants.

CALLI (Náhuatl): "house," also the name of a day in the ritual calendar.

CALMÉCAC (Náhuatl): school for the sons of the Mexica nobility.

CALPULLI (Náhuatl): a group of relatives that formed the basic unit of Aztec society.

CALPULTÉOTL (Náhuatl): guardian deity of a *calpulli*.

CENOTE: natural karstic shaft formed following the collapse of the vault in an underground gallery. *Cenotes* often provide the only source of fresh water in much of the Yucatán and they often became places of worship to gods of the underworld.

CENTZON HUITZNAHUA (Náhuatl): "The Four Hundred Brothers," the brothers defeated by Huitzilopochtli on Coatepec. The number four hundred is synonymous with "innumerable" and the Innumerable Brothers symbolized the stars of the night sky.

CHAC (Maya): Maya god of rain with a long snake-like nose; also known as God B.

CHAC MOOL (Maya): name of particular Post-Classic sculptures of a man lying and holding an offerings plate on his stomach. The name means "Red Claw" and is modern, purely conventional and has nothing to do with the scupture.

CHALCHIUHTLICUE (Náhuatl): "She who has a Jewelled Skirt," Aztec goddess of terrestrial waters, probably the "descendant" of the Teotihuacan Great Goddess.

CHICHIMECS (Náhuatl): the Aztecs referred to the northern "barbarian" peoples collectively as *chichimécatl*, including the groups of hunter-gatherers and farmers. The region occupied by "Chicimecs" included the southwest of the USA.

CINTÉOTL (Náhuatl): Aztec god of maize, from *cintli*, "maize."

CIPACTLI (Náhuatl): Aztec god who represents the Earth Monster in the form of an alligator. The name also represents the first day of the ritual calendar.

COATLICUE (Náhuatl): "She who wears a Skirt of Snakes," Aztec goddess, mother of Huitzilopochtli.

COCIJO (Zapotec): Zapotec god of the rain.

COPAL: from the Náhuatl word *copalli*, resin milked from the *Bursera jorullensis* tree and burned as incense in many Mesoamerican religious ceremonies.

COYOLXAUHQUI (Náhuatl): "Pendants on Cheeks," Aztec lunar goddess killed and dismembered by her brother Huitzilopochtli.

CUCHCABAL (Maya): Yucatec political entity typical of the Post-Classic period and the early colonial era; can be translated approximately as "province."

EHÉCATL (Náhuatl): Aztec god of the wind with a beak shaped mask. A manifestation of Quetzalcóatl.

EXCAN TLATOLOYAN (Náhuatl): "The Tribunal with Three Seats," name of the Triple Alliance that united the Mexica of Mexico-Tenochtitlan, the Acolhua of Texcoco and the Tepanechi of Tlacopan.

HAAB (Maya): name of the solar year.

HUITZILOPOCHTLI: "The Hummingbird of the South," Aztec tribal god with solar and warrior connotations at the apex of the Mesoamerican pantheon.

HUNAB KU (Maya): dual creator god at the apex of the Maya pantheon.

HUNAPU (Maya): name of one of the twins in the *Popol Vuh*. Represents the planet Venus like his traditional antecedent *Hun Ahau* ("One Lord").

ITZAM CAB AIN (Maya): Maya Earth Monster in the form of an iguana or alligator that corresponds to the Aztec Cipactli; its Classic version is known as Cauac Monster.

K'AWIL (Maya): god also called Bolon Dz'acab ("Nine Generations") associated with maize, blood and royal sperm; was a sort of patron god of the Maya sovereigns and depicted on the handles of sceptres held by royalty. Distinguished by a long nose and legs in the shape of snakes; from this and from his association with rain comes his other name of *Hun Racan* ("One legged thunderbolt") from which the word "hurricane" is derived; also known as God K.

KINICH AHAU (Maya): "Lord of the Solar Eye," Maya god of the sun; also known as God G.

KUKULKAN (Maya): Yucatec Maya translation of Quetzalcóatl, the "Feathered Serpent."

MACEHUALTIN (Náhuatl): the common (i.e. non-aristocratic) mass of Aztec people.

MAYA: generic name (more correctly *mayance*) used to describe the dozens of related languages (ancient and modern) that comprise the Maya linguistic family. The two main Maya languages of the lowlands during the Classic period were Chol Maya and Yucatec Maya.

MEXICA (Náhuatl): original name of the Aztecs; it is derived from the name of a patron god, Mexi.

MICTLAN (Náhuatl): "World of the Dead," Aztec name for the underworld of the dead.

MICTLANTECUHTLI (Náhuatl): "Lord of the World of the Dead," Aztec god who ruled the world of the dead; he was represented as a skeleton.

MIXE-ZOQUE: linguistic family that today includes the Mixe, Zoque and Popoluca languages; it was widespread across the area of the Isthmus of Tehuantepec.

MIXTECS: people who spoke Otomangue and settled mainly in the north of the state of Oaxaca. The name is a Náhuatl word that means "Peoples of the Clouds."

NAHUA: group of peoples settled in central Mexico who spoke languages in the Uto-Aztec family.

NAHUATL: language spoken by several Nahua groups including the Aztecs.

OLMEC-XICALANCA: people who occupied part of the Gulf coast from the Epiclassic period. Scholars have derived the name Olmec from the first term (derivation from the Náhuatl word *Uhlmécatl*, "Rubber People") which they have applied to the famous Pre-Classic culture that has nothing to do with the above ethnic group.

OLMECS: conventional name of the most famous Pre-Classic culture in Mesoamerica who were probably formed by groups that spoke Mixe-Zoque.

OTOMANGUE: linguistic family common in Mesoamerica and modern Mexico; the family of languages includes Zapotec and Mixtec.

OMETÉOTL (Náhuatl): "Two Lord," the Aztec god of duality.

OTOMI: people from central-northern Mexico who spoke Otomangue.

PAHUATUN (Maya): gods in the form of old men who held up the four corners of the Universe.

PIPILTIN (Náhuatl): the nobles of the Aztec population.

PITAO COZOBI (Zapotec): Zapotec god of maize.

QUETZALCOATL (Náhuatl): "Feathered Serpent," one of the most important gods in the Mesoamerican pantheon. He was associated with Venus, the creation of man, maize and the weather. The name also refers to the cultural hero who was his earthly representative.

SACBÉ (Maya): "White Road," roads built on raised earth platforms that united settlements in the Yucatán.

TABLERO: element of Teotihuacan architecture consisting of a vertical panel with a four-sided moulding that decorated much of the bodies of pyramids in Teotihuacan. Supported by the *talud*.

TAJIN (Totonac): Totonac god of rain and thunder.

TALUD: element of Teotihuacan architecture consisting of a sloping wall, often crowned by the *tablero*.

TECUHTLI (Náhuatl): "Lord," generic name of the chief or lord. During the Aztec imperial era, Techutli was a functionary appointed by the emperor to superintend the administration of the *calpulli*.

TELPOCHCALLI (Náhuatl): school reserved for the children of non-noble Aztec families.

TEMAZCAL (Náhuatl): steam bath characteristic of many Mesoamerican sites in which one could take a sort of sauna by throwing water on heated stones. The activity was both hygienic and ritual.

TENOCHTITLAN (Náhuatl): "The Place where prickly pears abound on the Stone," name of the Aztec capital.

TEOCALLI (Náhuatl): "House of the God," generic name of a temple. The *Huey Teocalli* ("Large House of the God") was the Great Temple of Tenochtitlan.

TÉOTL (Náhuatl): "God."

TEPANECS: Nahua people who settled in central Mexico during the Post Classic period. Two of their major cities were Azcapotzalco and

Tlacopan: the first subjected the Aztecs on the arrival of the latter in the Valley of Mexico, the second was part of the Triple Alliance.

TEZCATLIPOCA (Náhuatl): "Smoking Mirror," Aztec god linked to the world of darkness, magic and destructive forces and often the adversary of Quetzalcóatl. In his anthropomorphic form, he is represented with a smoking mirror instead of a stone; in animal form, he is a jaguar.

TLAHUIZCALPANTECUHTLI (Náhuatl): "Lord of the House of the Dawn," the manifestation of Quetzalcóatl in his form of Venus as the Morning Star.

TLALOC (Náhuatl): Aztec god of rain, heir of the analogous Teotihuacan god.

TLATLACOLIZTLI (Náhuatl): a sort of slavery for debts in the Aztec world.

TLATOANI (Náhuatl): "Orator," name of the Aztec ruler and of the rulers of other Nahua cities in central Mexico.

TONALAMATL (Náhuatl): prophetic almanac. Composed of *tonalli*, a term that includes the meanings of "heat," "irradiation" and "day" (and which referred to one of the three souls of man), and of *amatl*, "bark paper."

Therefore, translated freely as "Book of the Influences of the Days."

TONALPOHUALLI (Náhuatl): "Count of the Days," name of the ceremonial calendar consisting of 260 days.

TONATIUH (Náhuatl): Aztec god of the Sun.

TZOLKIN (Maya): "Count of the Days," conventional name used for the Maya ceremonial calendar as the original Maya name for it is unknown.

TZOMPANTLI (Náhuatl): rack on which the skulls of human sacrificial victims were fixed.

UHLE (Náhuatl): resin extracted from the rubber tree; used for ritual purposes and for making balls used in the ball-game.

WITS (Maya): "Mountain," the name of the Sacred Mountain inside which the entrance to the underworld lay. In Maya iconography, the Sacred Mountain is often shown in anthropomorphic form (Wits Monster).

XBALANQUE (Maya): name of one of the twins in the *Popol Vuh*; like his ancestor Yax Balam ("Green Jaguar") he was a symbol of the Sun.

XIBALBA (Maya): "Place of Fear," Maya name for the World of the Dead.

XIPE TOTEC (Náhuatl): "the Flayed One," Aztec god of regeneration and spring. He is shown wearing the skin of a sacrificed human and this how his priests were dressed during sacred ceremonies.

XIUHMOLPILLI (Náhuatl): "Bundle of the Days," bundle of 52 canes that symbolized the Mesoamerican "century" and was burned on the occasion of the New Fire ceremony. It was often represented in Aztec sculpture.

XIUHPOHUALLI: "Count of the Years," Náhuatl name of the calendar consisting of 365 days.

XIUHTECUHTLI: "Lord of the Year" or "Precious Lord," Aztec god of fire and protector of the center of the universe. He is often confused with *Huehuetéotl*, "Old God," who was also a Lord of Fire and Lord of the center of the universe.

YUM KAAX (Maya): Maya god of maize, also known as God E.

ZACATAPAYOLLI (Náhuatl): "Ball of Straw" in which the bloodied spines were placed that were used during self-sacrifice.

ZAPOTECS: a people settled in Oaxaca that spoke Otomangue.

BASIC BIBLIOGRAPHY

AA.VV., *La pittura murale mesoamericana*, Corpus Precolombiano, Jaca Book, Milan 1999.

Adams Richard E.W., *Prehistoric Mesoamerica. Revised Edition*, Oklahoma University Press, Norman 1991.

Bernal Ignacio and Mireille Simoni-Abbat, *Le Mexique des origines aux Aztèques*, Gallimard, Paris 1986.

Blanton Richard, Kowalewski Stephen, Feinman Gary and Finstein Laura, *Ancient Mesoamerica. A Comparison of Change in Three Regions*, Cambridge University Press, Cambridge 1993.

Broda Johanna, Carrasco Davíd, Eduardo Matos Moctezuma (eds.), *The Great Temple of Tenochtitlan. Center and Periphery in the Aztec World*, University of California Press, Berkeley-Los Angeles-London 1987.

Bustos Gerardo and Ana Luisa Izquierdo (eds.), *Los Mayas. Su tiempo antiguo*, Universidad Nacional Autónoma de México-Instituto de Investigaciones Filológicas, Mexico 1996, pp. 221-258.

Carrasco Davíd, *Quetzalcóatl and the Irony of Empire. Myths and Prophecies in the Aztec Tradition*, University of Chicago Press, Chicago 1982.

Carrasco Davíd, *Religions of Mesoamerica. Cosmovision and Ceremonial Centers*, Waveland Press, inc., Illinois 1990.

Caso Alfonso, *El pueblo del Sol*, Fondo de Cultura Económica, Mexico 1953.

Clark John E. (ed.), *Los Olmecas en Mesoamérica*, Citibank, Mexico 1994.

Davies Nigel, *The Aztecs. A History*, Macmillan, London 1973.

Flannery Kent and Marcus Joyce, *Zapotec Civilization. How Urban Society Evolved in Mexico's Oaxaca Valley*, Thames and Hudson, London-New York 1994.

Freidel David, Schele Linda and Parker Joy, *Maya Cosmos: Three Thousand Years on the Shaman's Path*, William Morrow and Company, New York 1993.

Gendrop Paul and Heyden Doris, *Architettura mesoamericana*, Electa, Milan 1980.

Gonzalez Licón Ernesto, *Zapotechi e Mixtechi*, Corpus Precolombiano, Jaca Book, Milan 1991.

Hammond Norman, *Ancient Maya Civilization*, Rutgers, The State University of New Jersey, 1988.

Hill Boone Elizabeth (ed.), *The Aztec Templo Mayor*, Dumbarton Oaks, Washington D.C. 1987.

Kubler George, *Art and Architecture of Ancient America*, Penguin Books, New York 1984.

León Portilla Miguel, *Literaturas indígenas de México*, MAPFRE-Fondo de Cultura Económica, 1992.

López Austin Alfredo, *Hombre-dios. Religión y política en el mundo náhuatl*, Universidad Nacional Autónoma de México, 2a edición, Mexico 1989.

López Austin Alfredo, *Breve historia de la tradición religiosa mesoamericana*, UNAM-IIA, Mexico 1999.

López Austin Alfredo e López Luján Leonardo, *El pasado indígena*, Colegio de México-Fondo de Cultura Económica, Mexico 1997.

López Austin Alfredo e López Luján Leonardo, *Mito y realidad de Zuyuá*, Colegio de México-Fondo de Cultura Económica, Mexico 1999.

López Luján Leonardo, Mastache Guadalupe e Robert Cobean, *Xochicalco e Tula. Gli altopiani delle guerre*, Corpus Precolombiano, Jaca Book, Milan.

Manzanilla Linda e López Luján Leonardo (eds.), *Historia Antigua de México*, 3 voll., INAH, UNAM, Porrúa, Mexico 1994.

Marcus Joyce, *Mesoamerican Writing Systems. Propaganda, Myth, and History in Four Ancient Civilizations*, Princeton University Press, Princeton 1992.

Marquina Ignacio, *Arquitectura Prehispánica*, Instituto nacional de Antropología e Historia, Mexico 1951.

Matos Moctezuma Eduardo, *The Great Temple of the Aztecs*, Thames and Hudson, London-New York 1988.

Matos Moctezuma Eduardo, *Gli Aztechi*, Corpus Precolombiano, Jaca Book, Milan 1989.

Matos Moctezuma Eduardo, *Teotihuacan*, Corpus Precolombiano, Jaca Book, Milan 1990.

Miller Mary Ellen and Schele Linda, *The Blood of Kings: Dynasty and Ritual in Maya Art*, Kimbell Art Museum, Fort Worth 1986.

Miller Mary Ellen and Taube Karl Andreas, *The Gods and Symbols of Ancient Mexico and the Maya*, Thames & Hudson, London 1993.

Nalda Enrique, Benavides Antonio, De la Garza Mercedes, Staines Leticia ed Matos Moctezuma Eduardo, *Gli ultimi regni maya*, Corpus Precolombiano, Jaca Book, Milan1998.

Olmedo Bertina, De la Garza Mercedes, De la Fuente Beatriz and Maricela Ayala, *I Maya classici*, Corpus Precolombiano, Jaca Book. Milan 1997.

Piña Chan Román, *Gli Olmechi*, Corpus Precolombiano, Jaca Book, Milan 1989.

Reents-Budet Dorie, *Painting the Maya Universe: Royal Ceramics of the Classic Period*, Duke University Press, Durham & London 1994.

Riefler Bricker Victoria, *The Indian Christ, the Indian King. The Historical Substrate of Maya Myth and Ritual*, University of Texas Press, Austin 1981. Spanish translation, *El Cristo indígena, el rey nativo*, Fondo de Cultura Económica, Mexico 1989.

Sabloff Jeremy, (vol. ed.), *Supplement to the Handbook of Middle American Indians*, vol. 1: Archaeology, Riefler Bricker Victoria, (gen. ed.), University of Texas Press, Austin 1981.

Sanders William and Price Barbara, *Mesoamerica. The Evolution of a Civilization* , Random House, New York 1968.

Schele Linda and Freidel David, *A Forest of Kings: The Untold Story of the Ancient Maya*, William Morrow and Company, New York 1990.

Schele Linda and Mathews Peter, *The Code of Kings. The Language of Seven Sacred Maya Temples and Tombs*, Simon & Schuster, New York 1998.

Schmidt Peter, De la Garza Mercedes and Nalda Enrique (eds.), *I Maya*, Bompiani 1998.

Sharer Robert J., *The Ancient Maya*, Stanford University Press, Stanford 1994. Spanish translation, *La civilización maya*, Fondo de Cultura Económica, Mexico 1998, 3a ed.

Tedlock Dennis (ed.), *Popol Vuh*, 1996.

Thompson J. and Eric S., *The Rise and Fall of Maya Civilization*, University of Oklahoma Press, 1954. Spanish translation, *Grandeza y decadencia de los mayas*, Fondo de Cultura Económica, Mexico 1985, 3a ed.

Uriarte María Teresa (ed.), *El juego de pelota en Mesoamérica. Raíces y supervivencia*, Siglo veintiuno editores, Mexico 1992.

Wauchope Robert (gen. ed.), *Handbook of Middle American Indians*, 15 voll., University of Texas Press, Austin 1965-1975.

Weaver Muriel Porter, *The Aztecs, Maya and their Predecessors. Archaeology of Mesoamerica*, Academic Press, New York 1993.

INDEX

c = caption
bold = chapter

A

Ac Kan, 94
Acanceh, 137
Acolhua, 13
Acolhuacan, 13
Ah Ahau, 104
Ah Cacaw, 115, 116, 117c, 118, 118c, 119, 120, 121, 121c
Ah Mac Kin Mo' Ahau, 108
Ah Xupán, 182
Ahpo Hel, 94c
Akumel, 182
Atetelco, 38c, 39
Avenue of the Dead, 30, 32, 34, 35c, 36
Axayácatl, 26
Azcapotzalco, 13
Aztecs, 6, 13, 19c, 20, 22, 23, 24, 27, 27c, 28, 35c, 41, 45, 54c, 55, 74
Aztlan, 13

B

Bacab, 151
Bahlum Kuk, 94
Balsas, river, 57
Basle, 121
Becán, 5, 142, 143c
Belize, 8, 137
Bird Jaguar II, 107
Bird Jaguar III, 104

Bird Jaguar, 104c, 107c, 108, 109, 109c
Bologna, University Library of, 24c
Bonampak, 5, 19c, 90, 104, 110-113
Bourbon Codex, 73c
British Museum, 104, 107
Butz Chan, 124, 126c, 127

C

Cacaxtla, 4, 11, 19, 54, 57, 64-67, 181
Calakmul, 18, 90, 97, 104, 114, 115, 118, 124, 137, 140
California, Gulf of, 41c
Campeche, 19c, 62, 114, 137, 140
Cantona, 57, 72
Canul, 137
Caracol, 10, 18, 115, 168
Caribbean Sea, 182, 184c
Caso, Adolfo, 77c
Catherwood, Frederick, 103c, 167
Cauac, 130c, 133, 135, 135c
Cauac-Sky, 124, 134, 134c, 135
Cempoala, 26, 57, 69
Central America, 184c
Central Highlands, 28, 57, 58
Central Mexico, 10, 11, 12, 13, 14, 18, 19, 28, 29c, 49c, 63, 74, 76, 90, 117c, 137, 139c, 178c, 181
Centzon Huitznahua, 49, 50
Cerro Dainzú, 82
Cerro de la Campana, 86
Cerro de Las Mesas, 55, 57
Cerro de Las Minas, 74
Cerro Gordo, 34, 36
Cerro Xochicalco, 59
Chac Cib Tok, 104, 108

Chac, 23c, 55c, 82, 141c, 151, 152, 152c, 154, 156, 157c, 176c
Chac-Xib-Chac, 23c
Chalcatongo, 74
Chalchiutlicue, 38
Chan Bahlum, 14c, 101, 101c
Chan Muan II, 19c, 110, 110c, 111, 112
Chan Muan, 111
Charles V, 73
Chel Te, 104, 108, 109, 109c
Chel, 137
Cheles, 182
Chenes Puuc, 90
Chenes, 138, 140, 140c, 142
Chetumal, 182
Chiapas, 5c, 8, 9, 10c, 14c, 72, 73c, 90, 94, 104, 110
Chicanná, 5, 140, 141c, 142
Chichén Itzá, 5, 13, 20c, 42, 42c, 45, 54c, 72, 137, 138, 139c, 150, 152, 168-179, 181, 182c
Chicimecs, 13
Chinkultic, 73c
Chitam, 121
Cholula, 4, 10, 26, 57, 62-63, 64, 68, 181
Chontal, see Maya Chontal, 1, 137, 148
Cipactli, 32, 33c
Coatepec, 49, 52
Coatlicue, 48c, 50
Cobá, 90, 137, 149, 150, 182
Cocijo, 82
Cocom Itzá, 182
Cocom, 137, 168, 182
Colombia, 178
Copán, 5, 10, 11, 19, 90, 90c, 103c, 114, 124-133, 134, 135

Copán, Valley of, 124
Cortés, Hérnan, 26, 27, 27c, 28, 46, 138
Cospi Codex, 24c
Costa Rica, 8
Couenan, 62
Count Waldeck, 98, 101
Coyoacan, 26
Coyolxauhqui, 49, 50, 50c, 51c, 55
Coyotlatelco, 28
Cozumel, island of, 182
Cuauhtémoc, 26, 52c
Cuba, 26
Cuicuilco, 9, 28, 30
Cuitláhuac, 26
Culhuacan, 45
Cupul, 137
Curl-Snout, 114, 116, 122

D

Dainzu, 82-83
de Aguilar, Jerónimo, 26
de Alvarado, Pedro, 26, 27c
de Grijalva, Juan, 26, 182
de Landa, Diego, 181
de Sahagún, Bernardino, 72
Díaz del Castillo, Bernal, 46
Diquiyú, 74
Doña Marina, 26, 27c
Double Bird, 115
Dresden Codex, 25c
Dúran, Diego, 14c, 19c, 27c
Dzibanché, 137
Dzibichaltún, 137, 144-147
Dzibilnocac, 138, 140c

E

Earthly Crocodile, see Cauac
Earthquake, 25
Edzná, 5, 137, 148-149, 164c, 168
Ehécatl, 44, 47c
Eighteen Rabbit, 124, 124c, 128, 128c, 130, 131c, 133, 133c, 134
Ek' Balam, 137, 150-151
El Mirador, 9, 114, 164, 166, 167
El Tabasqueño, 138
El Tajin, 4, 11, 57, 68-73
El Tesoro, hill of, 41
El Zapotal, 68c
Epi-Olmecs, 90
Etla, Valley of, 82
Etlatongo, 74
Europe, 6
Evening Star, 107, 108

F

Far East, 69c
Florentine Codex, 16c, 17c

G

Great Jaguar Claw, 114, 116
Green Rabbit, 112

Grolier Codex, 25c
Guanajuato, 41
Guatemala, 6, 8, 9, 10, 41, 73c, 90, 107c, 114, 134, 192
Guatemala, highlands of, 9, 12
Guatemala, plateau of, 181
Gucumatz, 181
Guerrero, 8, 55, 58
Guerrero, Gonzalo, 26
Gulf Coast, 8, 9, 10, 11, 57, 58, 60, 62

H

Hasaw Ka'an K'awil, 117c
Hernández de Cordoba, Francisco, 26
Hidalgo, 11, 28, 45, 168
Historia de las Indias de Nueva España e Islas de Tierra Firme, 14c, 27c
Historia Tolteca-Chichimeca, 62
Hochob, 138, 139, 140c
Honduras, 124
Honduras, 6, 8, 138
Hormiguero, 142
Huamelulpan, 74
Huehuetéotl, 53c
Huijatzoo, 74, 86
Huitzilopochtli, 23, 46, 47c, 49, 50, 50c, 52c, 181
Hun Ahau, 25
Hunac Ceel, 168
Hunapu, 25

I

Ilhuicamina, 13
Itzá, 12, 137, 138
Itzam Cab Ain, 162
Itzamná, 152
Itzcóatl, 13
Ixtlacihuatl, volcano, 64c
Izamal, 168
Izapa, 9, 90
Iztapalapan, 26

J

Jade Sky, 134, 135
Jaguar Claw, 115
Jaguar Knot-Eye, 111
Jaguar Moon, 127
Jaina, island of, 19c
Jalieza, 74
Jalisco, 41

K

Kabah, 5, 137, 152, 152c, 162-163
Kabah, King of, 162, 163c
Kaminaljuyú, 9, 10, 90
Kan Hok Chitam II, 94
Kan Tok, 108
Kan Xul II, 94
Kanal Ikal, 94
Kin, 23c, 129c, 149c
K'inich Ah Pop, 127

Kinich Ahau, 149
Kohunlich, 137
Kukulkan, 12, 167, 168, 170, 181, 182c

L

La Esperanza, 73c
La Pasadita, 108
La Venta, 5, 8, 90, 92-93
La Ventilla, 39
Labná, 137, 166c, 167
Lady Large Skull, 104, 108
Lady Xoc, 23c, 104c, 107
Laguna de los Cerros, 8, 92
Lake Petén, 138
Lambyteco, 74, 82-83
Large Skull, see Lady Large Skull
London, 104c, 107
López Austin, Alfredo, 180
López Luján, Leonardo, 180
Luti, 137

M

Macuilxóchitl, 82
Madrid Codex, 25c, 185c
Maní, 182
Matacapan, 10, 57, 68
Maya Chontal, 11, 137, 148c, 152, 164, 181
Maya Putún, 137
Maya Quiché, 25
Maya Yucatechi, 151, 164
Maya, 6, 20, 20c, 21, 22, 24, 26, 62, 90, 137-139, 180-181
Mayapán League, 181
Mayapán, 5, 13, 13c, 55c, 137, 168, 181, 182
Menchú, Rigoberta, 55
Mesoamerica, 6-13, 18, 24, 26, 27, 28, 30, 35, 42, 44, 45, 45c, 47c, 51, 54, 62, 64, 65c, 72, 73c, 74, 77c, 90, 92, 137, 138, 178, 181
Mexica, 13, 46,
Mexico City, 12, 28, 46, 50, 54c
Mexico City, National Museum of Cultural Anthropology, 36, 50, 54-56, 92, 99, 104c, 107, 112c, 113c, 140c
Mexico, 6, 8, 10, 11, 12, 13, 14, 18, 19, 26, 27, 27c, 28, 47, 54, 57, 63, 107c
Mexico, Gulf of, 64, 68, 72,184c
Mexico, Valley of 8, 9, 13, 28, 30, 57
México-Tenochtitlan, 13, 19, 26, 28, 46-49, 181
Miacatlán, 58
Michoacán, 58
Mictlantecuhtli, 51c, 53
Mitla, 4, 74, 83, 84-85,
Mixe, 90
Mixe-Zoque, 6, 24
Mixteca Alta, 12
Mixteca, 58, 181
Mixtecs, 6, 64, 74, 74c, 77c, 84
Monte Albán, 4, 9, 10, 11, 12, 13c, 18, 54, 74, 74c, 76-81, 82, 83, 84, 85, 102
Monte Negro, 74
Morelos, 11, 57

Morelos, Valley of, 57, 58
Motagua, Valley of, 134
Motecuhzoma II, 26
Motecuhzoma, 13
Motul de San José, 108

N

Nacxit, 181
Nahua, 6, 13, 30, 44
Naranjo, 115
New York, 162
Nezahualcóyotl, 25
Nezahualpilli, 25
Nicaragua, 8, 41, 138
Nochixtlán, Valley of, 74
Nojpat, 152
Northern Mexico, 6, 12, 55, 73
Nuestra Señora de los Remedios, sanctuary of, 63

O

Oaxaca, 8, 10, 13c, 74, 83, 83c
Oaxaca, Valley of, 8, 9, 10, 11, 12, 13, 74, 76, 82
Ocoñaña, 82
Olmeca, 62
Olmeca-Xicalanca, 62, 64, 65, 66
Olmecs, 90, 92, 92c
Otomí, 30, 57, 64

P

Pacal II, 94, 97c, 99c, 101c
Pacal, 6, 94c, 96, 97, 97c, 98, 99, 99c, 100, 101c, 104, 158c
Pacific Ocean, 43c
Palenque, 5, 5c, 6c, 10c, 11, 14c, 23c, 90, 94-103, 104, 109c, 124, 124c, 158c
Paris Codex, 25c, 184
Pech, 137
Peru, 6
Petén, 9, 10, 114, 114c, 138, 140, 148, 149, 150, 151
Piedras Negras, 104, 109
Pitao Cozobi, 80
Popoluca, 90
Puebla, 10, 57
Puebla, Valley of, 41, 57, 62
Puebla-Mixteca, region of, 24c
Puebla-Taxcala, region of, 64c
Puebla-Tlaxcala, Valley of, 57, 58, 62, 74
Pueblos, 55
Putún, 11
Puuc, 138, 140, 148, 149, 151, 152-153, 162
Pyramid of the Moon, 9, 28, 30, 33c, 34c, 35, 36, 36c
Pyramid of the Sun, 9, 30, 33c, 34, 34c, 35, 35c, 36c

Q

Querétaro, 41
Quetzalcóatl, 22, 28, 42, 43, 44-45, 62, 66, 69, 71c, 180, 181
Quiché, 90

Quiebelagayo, 82
Quintana Roo, 137, 140
Quiriguá, 5, 114, 124, 134-135

R

Río Bec, 90, 138, 140-143, 151
Río Copán, 126
Rivera, Diego, 47

S

Sak Bak, 98
Sak Kuk, 94, 100
Salvador, 8
San Gervasio, 182
San José Mogote, 9, 18, 74, 76, 82, 102
San Juan, river, 32, 34
San Lorenzo, 8, 90, 92
Santa Rita Corozal, 182
Santa Rosa Xtampac, 138
Santiago Tlatelolco, church of, 52c
Sayil, 5, 137, 152, 164-166, 167
Seven Parrot, 25
Shield Jaguar II, 104
Shield Jaguar III, 109, 112
Shield Jaguar, 23c, 104c, 107, 108
Sierra di Tamaulipas, 8
Six Tun Bird Jaguar, 104
Skull Tah III, 109
Smoke Monkey, 124
Smoke Shell, 124, 130
Smoke-Imix-God K, 124, 130, 131c, 133
Smoking Frog, 114, 122, 122c
Sosonusco, 13
Spain, 138
Spanish, 26, 27, 27c, 46, 63, 69, 84, 138, 181, 182
Stephens, John L., 162, 166c
Stormy Sky, 114, 115, 116, 122
Suchilquitongo, 86

T

Tabasco, 26, 92, 93, 137
Tacuba, 26
Tajin Chico, 69
Tajin, 69, 82
Tancah, 182
Tayasal, 138
Tecoh, 182
Tehuacán, Valley of, 8
Tenayuca, 13
Tenochca, 46
Tenochtitlan, 4, 27c, 46, 47c, 52c, 53c, 69
Teotenango, 11, 57, 181
Teotihuacan, 4, 5c, 9, 10, 11, 14, 15, 18, 21, 28, 29c, 30-39, 41, 45, 54c, 57, 58, 62, 63, 64, 66, 68, 74, 76, 102, 181
Teotihuacans, 6, 102
Tepanecs, 13, 46
Tepantitla, 38, 38c, 72
Terre Alte, 10, 90
Terre Basse, 9, 10, 11, 90, 94, 114, 122, 134, 148
Teteoínnan, 49
Tetitla, 39

Texcoco, 13, 25, 26
Texcoco, lake, 13, 26, 46
Tezcatlipoca, 17, 22, 43, 44, 62, 66
Tibolón, 182
Ticul, hills of, 152
Tikal, 10, 11, 18, 19, 23c, 72, 90, 90c, 97, 98, 104, 114-121, 122, 122c, 192c
Tilantongo, 74
Tlacolula, Valley of, 82, 83
Tlacopan, 13
Tlahuizcalpantecuhtli, 44, 170, 174c
Tláloc, 18, 19, 23, 23c, 32, 35, 38, 47, 47c, 51, 52, 52c, 53, 53c, 60c, 63, 66, 82
Tlaloques, 93
Tlaltecuhtli, 55
Tlapacoya, 28, 54
Tlapallan, 44, 45, 180
Tlatelolco, 51c, 53c
Tlatelolco, battle of, 26
Tlatelolco, stones of, 27
Tlatilco, 28, 54
Tlaxcala, 11, 13, 19, 19c, 26, 57
Tlaxcala, Valley of, 57, 64
Tollan, 28, 44-45, 47, 62, 137, 168, 180, 181
Tolteca-Chichimeca, 57, 62, 63
Toltecs, 6, 44, 45, 168, 180-181
Toluca, 11, 57
Tonacatépetl, 49
Toniná, 94
Totonachi, 6, 30, 57, 68, 69
Tres Zapotes, 8, 9
Triple Alliance, see Mayapán League
Tula Chico, 11, 12, 28, 41
Tula Grande, 12, 28, 41
Tula, 4, 28, 41-43, 45, 51, 62, 168, 170, 176, 180, 181, 182c
Tulum, 5, 13, 138, 181, 182-192
Tutul Xiú, 182
Tututepec, 74
Tuzupan, 57, 69
Tzeh, 137
Tzeltal, 90
Tzotzil, 90

U

Uaxactún, 5, 18, 114, 122-123
U-Cit-Tok, 124, 130
Ukit Kan Lek (Ukit IV), 151
U-Kix-Chan, 94, 100
United States, 41, 55
Usumacinta, 90, 104, 107, 107c
Uxmal, 5, 137, 149, 151c, 152-161, 162, 164

V

Vasquez Ramirez, Pedro, 54
Veracruz, 9, 10, 13, 26, 57, 68, 68c, 92
Villahermosa, La Venta Park, 92

W

Waterlily-Jaguar, 133
Waxaklahun-Ubah-K'awil, 124
Western Mexico, 6, 55
Wits Monster, 152

X

Xbalanque, 25
Xibalba, 25
Xicalanca, 62
Xicalcoliuhqui, 69
Xitle, volcano, 9, 28
Xiú, 137, 152, 182
Xiuhcóatl, 49
Xiuhtecuhtli, 53
Xochicalco, 4, 11, 54, 57, 57c, 58-61, 181
Xochitécatl, 54, 64
Xocotlán, 74
Xpuhil, 5, 142, 143c

Xuk Ek, 182c, 184
Xul-Sky, 134

Y

Yagul, 74, 82-83, 84
Yanhuitlán, 74
Yax Balam, 25, 104, 107
Yax Kin, 115, 120, 121
Yax Kuk Mo', 124, 127, 127c
Yax Moch Xoc, 114
Yax Pac, 124, 124c, 127c, 129c
Yaxchilán, 5, 11, 23c, 90, 97, 104-109, 110, 111, 112

Yucatán, 9, 11, 12, 13c, 26, 45, 90, 137-139, 144, 148, 150, 151, 152, 182
Yucuita, 74
Yucuñudahui, 74

Z

Zaachila, 12, 74, 84
Zacatecas, 41, 184c
Zapotecs, 6, 10, 74, 74c, 84
Zipacná, 25
Zohapilco, 28
Zoque, 90
Zuyuá, 180
Zuyuani, 45, 168, 180-181

PHOTOGRAPHIC CREDITS

TRANSLATED BY
C.T.M. MILAN

192 The long flight of steps typical of Mayan temples leads to the top of the Pyramid of the Lost World at Tikal in Guatemala. The city was one of the most important settlements of the Ruta Maya.

Cover
The Chac Mool at the entrance to the Temple of the Warriors at Chichén Itzá.
© Massimo Borchi/ Archivio White Star

Back cover
top left Battle scene from wall paintings at Bonampak.
© Antonio Attini/ Archivio White Star

top right View of the south sector at Uxmal.
© Massimo Borchi/ Archivio White Star

center Reconstruction of the sacred enclosed area of Tenochtitlan.
Dawing by Archivio White Star